NEW HORIZONS IN CRIMINOLOGY

INDIGENOUS CRIMINOLOGY

Chris Cunneen and Juan Tauri

D1612579

P

First published in Great Britain in 2017 by

Policy Press
University of Bristol
1-9 Old Park Hill
Bristol
BS2 8BB
UK
t: +44 (0)117 954 5940
pp-info@bristol.ac.uk
www.policypress.co.uk

North America office:
Policy Press
c/o The University of Chicago Press
1427 East 60th Street
Chicago, IL 60637, USA
t: +1 773 702 7700
f: +1 773-702-9756
sales@press.uchicago.edu
www.press.uchicago.edu

© Policy Press 2017

British Library Cataloguing in Publication Data
A catalogue record for this book is available from the British Library

Library of Congress Cataloging-in-Publication Data
A catalog record for this book has been requested

ISBN 978-1-4473-2176-7 paperback
ISBN 978-1-4473-2179-8 ePub
ISBN 978-1-4473-2180-4 Mobi

The right of Chris Cunneen and Juan Tauri to be identified as authors of this work has been
asserted by them in accordance with the Copyright, Designs and Patents Act 1988.

The statements and opinions contained within this publication are solely those of the authors
and not of the University of Bristol or Policy Press. The University of Bristol and Policy
Press disclaim responsibility for any injury to persons or property resulting from any material
published in this publication.

Policy Press works to counter discrimination on grounds of gender, race,
disability, age and sexuality.

Cover design by Policy Press
Front cover image: www.alamy.com
Printed and bound in Great Britain by CMP, Poole
Policy Press uses environmentally responsible print partners

Contents

About the authors

Chris Cunneen is Professor of Criminology in the Faculties of Law, and Arts and Social Sciences, University of NSW, Sydney, Australia. He has an international reputation as a leading criminologist specialising in juvenile justice, restorative justice, policing, prison issues, human rights, and Indigenous people and the law. Chris has participated in a number of Australian Royal Commissions and Inquiries and with the federal Australian Human Rights Commission. He also holds a conjoint position with the Cairns Institute at James Cook University, Australia. He is a Fellow of the Academy of Social Sciences in Australia. His recent books include (with Brown et al) *Justice Reinvestment. Winding Back Imprisonment*, Palgrave MacMillan, 2016, and (with Baldry, et al) *Penal Culture and Hyperincarceration*, Ashgate, 2013.

Juan Tauri is a member of the Ngati Porou iwi (First Nation) of Aotearoa New Zealand, and a lecturer of criminology in the Faculty of Social Science, University of Wollongong, Wollongong, Australia. Juan is an established researcher and scholar on Indigenous justice issues, with a focus on Indigenous critique of crime control in settler-colonial jurisdictions, and state responses to Indigenous over-representation. He has recently completed research on white privilege and racism in academic criminology, and is currently undertaking research on race, ethnicity and restorative justice.

Acknowledgements

The authors have been engaged in critical scholarship, advocacy and activism for Indigenous peoples over many decades. This book is the result of those endeavours. Not surprisingly many intellectual debts have arisen along the way. As a non-indigenous researcher, Chris Cunneen would like to especially acknowledge the support and knowledge he has gained from working with Indigenous communities and organisations, particularly Aboriginal Legal Services and various Aboriginal and Torres Strait Islander Social Justice Commissioners. Juan Tauri would like to acknowledge the Indigenous academics and activists Moana Jackson and Biko Agozino whose work has provided theoretical and methodological nourishment for his work over the past twenty years.

We acknowledge the work done by Simone Rowe who provided research for various sections of this book.

We dedicate this book to our two youngest children both of whom were born during the time the manuscript was being written: to Ruben and Coco.

NEW HORIZONS IN CRIMINOLOGY

Series editor: Professor Andrew Millie, Department of Law and Criminology, Edge Hill University, UK

Preface

Policy Press's New Horizons in Criminology book series provides concise authoritative texts that reflect cutting-edge thought and theoretical developments in criminology and have an international scope. These short, accessible texts are written so that the non-specialist academic, student or practitioner can understand them, by explaining principles and developments clearly before going deeper into the subject. Written by leading authors in their fields, the series will become essential reading for all academics and students (and practitioners) interested in where criminology is heading.

When I first proposed a series on 'New Horizons', one criminologist suggested that criminology does not need any more criminologies. The subject of criminology has expanded so much over recent years that perhaps it should have time to draw breath – growing from 'a smallish cottage industry' (Loader and Sparks, 2012, p 4) to the extent that most universities now offer criminology and/or criminal justice at undergraduate or postgraduate levels. Yet, my reply was that without exploring new areas of enquiry, the subject could stagnate. If criminologists had not been willing to explore new horizons, there would not have been the expansion from conventional crime and justice issues into important research on, for example, state crimes, social harms, green issues or cultural identity, as reflected in 'new' criminologies such as green criminology and cultural criminology. For any discipline to remain vibrant it needs to explore new areas and, where relevant, to draw on other disciplines and investigate innovative methodologies. This does not mean that the past is cast aside. Instead, by exploring new horizons, light might be reflected back onto criminology's traditional core. The criminological imagination (see Young, 2011) continues to expand, with new approaches being adopted by criminologists, and criminological approaches being relevant to new areas of study. This book series aims to reveal to a wider audience these cutting-edge developments.

I am delighted that one of the first books in the series is on the important topic of Indigenous criminology and that this book is authored by Chris Cunneen and Juan Tauri, two of the leading authors in this area of study. Indigenous peoples are over-represented within the criminal justice systems of settler colonial states such as Canada, the US, Aotearoa New Zealand and Australia, yet are also under-represented within discussions of criminology, except perhaps within certain aspects of restorative justice. Chris Cunneen and Juan Tauri's work is both accessible and challenging. This book contributes to a decolonising of criminology, by defying the status quo and arguing for the prioritisation of Indigenous voices. It ought to be essential reading for criminologists (and many others) from countries with colonising or settler histories.

References

Loader, I. and Sparks, R. (2012) 'Situating criminology: On the production and consumption of knowledge about crime and justice', in M. Maguire, R. Morgan and R. Reiner (eds) *The Oxford Handbook of Criminology*, 5th edn, Oxford: Oxford University Press.

Young, J. (2011) *The Criminological Imagination*, Cambridge: Polity Press.

ONE

Introduction

After centuries of colonisation, the contemporary position of Indigenous peoples in the wealthy settler colonial states of Australia, Aotearoa New Zealand, Canada and the US is one of profound social, economic and political marginalisation. High rates of victimisation, high levels of over-representation in criminal justice systems, racial discrimination and hate crime are all features of Indigenous peoples' experience of settler colonialism. The significant over-representation of Indigenous peoples is generally acknowledged by policy makers and criminologists. However, dominant explanations, policies and interventions tend to rely on a narrow set of assumptions about individual offending, and on theoretical and conceptual frameworks that pathologise Indigenous peoples and problematise their cultural beliefs and practices.

For this reason, *Indigenous criminology* sets out to provide the basis for a new explanatory model for understanding Indigenous peoples' contact with the criminal justice systems; one that is firmly based in the historical and contemporary conditions of colonialism and settler colonialism. In attempting to do so, we seek to build on the work in other disciplines that has argued for the importance of Indigenous methodologies and the prioritisation of Indigenous voices in understanding contemporary problems, such as deaths in custody, high imprisonment rates, police brutality and bias, and the high levels of violence in some Indigenous communities. The book will address theoretical and conceptual underpinnings to the development of an Indigenous criminology, by drawing on comparative Indigenous material from North America, Australia and Aotearoa New Zealand in relation to the gendered nature of settler colonial crime control; the policing and sentencing of Indigenes; the construction and use of Indigenous (criminological) knowledge; and the globalisation of crime control. We see a number of core conceptual elements to developing an Indigenous criminology. These include the recognition of the fundamental importance of Indigenous knowledges and the use of engaging methodologies, the long-term and ongoing impact of colonialism, the Indigenous right to self-determination, and the importance of Indigenous agency. Finally, we argue for a critical understanding of the connections between criminology (and the wider academy) and the structures of knowledge, discourse, politics and practices that define settler colonialism.

Before discussing our conceptual framework in more detail, we begin by detailing who we are referring to when we speak of Indigenous peoples in settler colonial contexts, their social and economic position within those societies, and an overview of Indigenous engagement with criminal justice systems.

Indigenous peoples in settler colonial societies

Who are the Indigenous peoples in settler colonial states? Indigenous peoples include primarily American Indians, Alaska Natives, Native Hawaiians in the US, but also smaller groups from Pacific Islands such as the Chamorro from Guam, as well as the native Taino people of Puerto Rico. In Australia, Indigenous peoples include Aboriginal and Torres Strait Islander peoples, and in Aotearoa New Zealand, the Māori. In Canada, Indigenous peoples include North American Indian (or First Nations), Métis (of mixed Aboriginal and non-Aboriginal background) and Inuit peoples (who originally lived in the north of Canada). What these people have in common as Indigenous peoples is that they were the original inhabitants of the nation states we now know as the United States, Canada, New Zealand and Australia. While their languages, cultures, religious beliefs and systems of political organisation varied, and continue to vary, they have in common the experience of European colonisation, and subsequent marginalisation. While the question of 'difference' within and between Indigenous populations and communities is not covered in this book in detail, we recognise the importance of this issue when undertaking meaningful social inquiry into the Indigenous context. As Frideres (2008, p 314) argues, across the social sciences (and we contend that this includes criminology) there is a lack of:

> a basic understanding of Aboriginal identity; the contextual basis for contemporary Aboriginal identity and the conditions that have created the new emergent identity Aboriginal people.... This includes an understanding of generational differences, differences among various sub-groups of Aboriginal people (e.g., Indian, Inuit, Métis), the differences in Aboriginal identity that are exhibited in people who live in urban and rural settings, and the differences in identity of Aboriginal males and females.

How one identifies and 'lives' as an Indigenous person, can vary significantly *within* an Indigenous population, not to mention between Indigenous peoples residing in different continents (Harris et al, 2013). For this reason, how Indigenous criminology 'looks', how it constructs methodologies and ethics frameworks, the questions it asks, and the policies and interventions it develops, will reflect the formulation and expression of Indigenous identity within a particular jurisdiction.

We provide a brief sketch of the demographic and socioeconomic profile of Indigenous people living in settler colonial states.

Indigenous peoples in the US

According to the 2010 Census there were 5.2 million people in the United States who identified as American Indian and Alaska Natives, which comprised 1.7% of the total US population (Norris et al, 2012, p 3). The majority (78%) of American Indian and Alaska Natives lived outside reservations, trust lands and designated Alaska Native village areas (Norris et al, 2012, p 12). A further 1.2 million people identified as Native Hawaiian and Other Pacific Islander, or 0.4% of the total US population. The largest of this group were Native Hawaiians, followed by Chamorro peoples and Samoans (Hixson et al, 2012, pp 3-4, 15). There are 566 federally recognised American Indian and Alaska Native tribes and villages (Indian Law and Order Commission, 2013). Federally recognised tribes possess inherent rights of tribal sovereignty and self-government, and are entitled to receive certain federal benefits, services and protections because of their special relationship with the United States.[1]

Indigenous people in Canada

In the 2011 National Household Survey, 1.4 million people identified as Aboriginal, which represented 4.3% of the total Canadian population. First Nations people represented 60.8% of the total Aboriginal population, followed by Métis (32.3%) and Inuit (4.2%).[2]

---

[1] For a further discussion on the problem of which Indigenous peoples in the US are officially recognised by the federal government and those who are not recognised, see International Indian Treaty Council (2007 pp 6, 28-33, 39-40).

[2] The remaining 2.7% identified as of either multiple Aboriginal backgrounds, or 'other' Aboriginal background (Statistics Canada, 2011, p 4).

Of the First Nations people, three quarters are Registered Indians and approximately half live on an Indian reserve or settlement (Statistics Canada, 2011, pp 4, 11). Registered (or Status) Indians are people who are registered with the federal government as Indians, under the *Indian Act*. They have certain rights and benefits not available to Non-Status Indians. There are 614 federally recognised Indian First Nations in Canada (Lithopoulos, 2007, p 3).

Indigenous people in Aotearoa New Zealand

According to the 2013 Census, 598,605 people identified as Māori. Māori represented 14.9% of the total Aotearoa New Zealand population, or one in seven people. Nearly one quarter of Māori lived in the Auckland area of the North Island. The largest Māori *iwi* (tribe) is Ngāpuhi, with 125,601 people, followed by Ngāti Porou, with 71,049 people (Statistics New Zealand, 2013, p 1). Like all the Indigenous peoples discussed in this book, the age structure of the Māori population is heavily skewed towards young people, compared to the non-Indigenous population. Some 33% of Māori are aged under 15 years (Statistics New Zealand, 2013, p 1).

Indigenous people in Australia

Based on the 2011 Census, it is estimated that there are 669,881 Aboriginal and/or Torres Strait Islander people in Australia. Ninety per cent of Indigenous people identified as being Aboriginal, 6% as Torres Strait Islander, and 4% were of both Aboriginal and Torres Strait Islander background. Indigenous people comprise 3% of the total Australian population (ABS, 2013, pp 2-3). More than half (59%) of the Aboriginal and Torres Strait Islander population lived in the states of New South Wales and Queensland (ABS, 2013, pp 2-3). Some 21.4% of the total Indigenous population lived in remote or very remote regions of Australia, compared to 1.7% of the non-Indigenous population (ABS, 2013, p 4). Some 38% of Aboriginal and Torres Strait Islander are aged under 15 years, compared to 19% of the non-Indigenous population (ATSISJC, 2008, p 286).

Socioeconomic marginalisation

A common feature of Indigenous peoples in settler colonial societies is their significant socioeconomic marginalisation. The depth of this marginalisation varies within the settler colonial states depending, for instance, on whether Indigenous people are living in remote or urban areas, or on or off reservation. Regardless of geography, poverty is a significant issue for all Indigenous peoples in settler colonial contexts. For example, Perry (2013) reports that Māori typically have poverty rates around double that of the European ethnic group, regardless of the measure used, while the rate for American Indians and Alaskan Natives was 27% compared to 12% for both whites and Asian peoples (Macartney et al, 2013).

Key social indicators that demonstrate the oppressive levels of Indigenous social marginalisation include education and health. For example, a 2012 New Zealand government report showed that school retention rates (to age 17) for Māori students at 50.6% compared to 75.4% for non-Māori, while Statistics Canada (2013) reported that 28.9% of Canadian First Nation people aged 25 to 64 had no certificate, diploma or degree compared to 12.1% for non-First Nation people in the same age group. In Australia, Aboriginal and Torres Strait Islander young people have significantly lower post-school participation in education and training than do non-Indigenous young people (32% compared to 75%) (SCRGSP, 2014, p7.17). In relation to health outcomes, Marriot and Sim (2014) report that life expectancy for Māori men in 2010-12 was 72.8 years and 76.5 years for Māori women, compared to 80.2 and 83.7 years for non-Māori men and women respectively. For American Indian and Alaska Native people, overall life expectancy is 5.3 years less for men and women than for the general population (Devi, 2011), and in Canada it is estimated that by 2017 the life expectancy for the total Canadian population will be 79 years for men and 83 years for women, while the projections for Métis and First Nations populations are 73-74 years for men and 78-80 years for women. In Australia, life expectancy is 10.6 years lower for Indigenous men compared to non-Indigenous men, and over 9.5 years lower for Indigenous women compared to non-Indigenous women (SCRGSP, 2014, p 2).

Despite the earlier discussion, it is important to emphasise that we do not see Indigenous people as simply a disadvantaged minority within settler colonial states. As we argue in this book, there are several fundamental flaws to this view. In the first instance, the current socioeconomic position of Indigenous peoples is the outcome of the process of colonialism. The impoverishment and immiseration (the forcible imposition and maintenance of structural conditions of extreme poverty) of Indigenous people did not simply 'fall from the sky'. It was actively created and maintained through processes of dispossession, and policies of disenfranchisement and social and economic exclusion.

The criminalisation of Indigenous peoples, manifest in their significant over-representation in all facets of the criminal justice system, is one of the most important ways in which their exclusion and marginalisation are reproduced in settler colonialism.

Indigenous criminalisation and victimisation

The high level of criminalisation and victimisation of Indigenous people is relatively well known (even if inconsistently documented in some settler colonial states). The following is a brief overview of the data on Indigenous over-representation in criminal justice systems in North America, Australia and Aotearoa New Zealand. It provides the contextual background to the arguments developed in this book.

In Canada, in 2012/13, Aboriginal offenders represented 20.5% of the total federal prison population, compared to about 3% of the Canadian adult population (Correctional Services of Canada, 2014). The proportion was up from previous years – 18% in 2011 (Correctional Services of Canada, 2012). Between 2003/04 and 2012/13 the number of incarcerated Aboriginal people in the federal system had increased by 47% (46% for Aboriginal men and 77% for Aboriginal women) (Public Safety Canada, 2013, Figure C16). During the same period the non-Aboriginal federal prison population increased by a more modest 12% (Public Safety Canada, 2013, Figures C2, C16). Aboriginal people are also over-represented in provincial and territorial prisons, where they comprised 26% of custodial admissions in 2013/14 (Correctional Services Program, 2015). In some provinces and territories with larger Aboriginal populations, particularly Manitoba, Saskatchewan and the Yukon, Aboriginal people made up more than 70% of the total prisoner population (Prison Justice Canada, 2005).

In Australia, the imprisonment of Indigenous people has been increasing since the 1980s and growing more rapidly than non-Indigenous imprisonment rates in recent decades. At 30 June 2014, there were 9,264 prisoners in Australian prisons who identified as Aboriginal and Torres Strait Islander, which was a 10% increase from the previous year. Indigenous people were imprisoned at a rate 13 times greater than their non-Indigenous counterparts (ABS, 2014, Tables 2, 16). In the decade between 2004 and 2014, Indigenous imprisonment rates rose by 37%, while at the same time the non-Indigenous imprisonment rate rose by 9% (ABS, 2014, Table 19). Thus while the use of imprisonment had increased for all people, the increase was far more pronounced for Indigenous people.

Data shows that Māori are over-represented at every stage of the New Zealand criminal justice system. They are four to five times more likely to be apprehended, prosecuted and convicted for a criminal offence than non-Māori, are 11 times more likely to be remanded in custody and are more than seven times more likely to be sentenced to imprisonment (Morrison, 2009, p 18). As at December 2014, Māori comprised 51% and Pacifica peoples a further 11% of the NZ prison population (Department of Corrections, 2015). Māori have consistently made up at least 50% of the prison population since the early 1980s (Clayworth, 2014, p 5). The Māori imprisonment rate has grown as the general imprisonment rate increased from 150 per 100,000 in 1999 to 195 in 2009 (The Treasury, 2009), and further to 199 per 100,000 in 2011 (Clayworth, 2014, p 1). The Māori imprisonment rate is estimated at 700 per 100,000 (Workman and McIntosh, 2013).

Estimating the incarceration rates of Indigenous peoples (American Indian, Alaska Native and Native Hawaiian peoples) in the US is no simple task. Incarceration can occur in local county and city jails, and state and federal prisons. The National Prisoner Statistics Program that reports on state and federal prison rates does not routinely publish information on Indigenous peoples – they are included in a catch-all category of 'other', as in: white, black, Hispanic and 'other'. We do know, however, that Native American federal offenders increased by 27% over the five years to 2013, and 90% of these in 2013 were sentenced to imprisonment (United States Sentencing Commission, 2013, p 1). The Prison Policy Initiative (Sakala, 2014) has used the US Census 2010 to calculate incarceration rates in each state and nationally, based on people detained in federal, state and local facilities. It was estimated that the imprisonment rate nationally for American Indian/Alaska Native peoples was 895 per 100,000, compared to 450 for whites, 831 for Hispanics and 2,306 for blacks. American Indian/Alaska Native peoples were over-represented compared to the white population in 43 states of the US. The proportion of American Indian/Alaska Native peoples in prison in some states is particularly high, including Alaska (38%), South Dakota (29%), North Dakota (29%) and Montana (22%) (Sakala, 2014).

Criminal victimisation rates for Indigenous peoples are also much higher than the rates found in the general population. In Aotearoa New Zealand, Māori were 13% more likely to experience criminal victimisation than the average rate of victimisation (Ministry of Justice, 2010, p 59). A study by the Bureau of Justice Statistics found that American Indians are much more likely to become victims of crime than any other group, experiencing crime at a rate of one in 10, or twice that of the general population (Perry, 2004). In Canada, some 37% of Aboriginal people reported being a victim of crime compared to 26% of non-Aboriginal people, and Aboriginal people were more than twice as likely to report being victims of non-spousal violent crime as non-Aboriginal people (Perreault, 2011, p 7).

Criminal victimisation is particularly high for Indigenous women in the settler colonial states. To take Australia as an example, Indigenous women are:

- more than 10 times more likely to be a victim of homicide than other women;
- 45 times more likely than non-Indigenous women to be a victim of domestic violence;
- 10.7 times more likely to be victims of violent crime than non-Indigenous women;
- more than twice as likely to be the victim of sexual assault than non-Indigenous women (ATSISJC, 2006, pp 97-101; Memmot et al, 2001, pp 38-44).

One might conclude from this data that the mass incarceration of Indigenous people has not enhanced the relative safety of individuals within Indigenous communities. Many Indigenous and non-Indigenous commentators argue that the roots of the current crisis can be found in colonial dispossession (Trudgeon, 2000), the social and historical contexts of Indigenous crime (Ross, 1998), and new forms of domination – particularly through administrative, economic and legal controls that have created new types of enforced dependency on government (Altman and Hinkson, 2007). The high levels of incarceration and victimisation need to be contextualised by dramatic increases in the general prison populations across the settler colonial societies at a time when long-term reported crimes rates have been falling (Cunneen et al, 2013, pp 41-2; Boyce et al, 2013, p 4; The Treasury, 2013). However, as we discuss more fully in the following chapters, despite various policy initiatives aimed at ameliorating the over-representation of Indigenous people in the criminal justice system, the situation has not improved. Indigenous imprisonment rates have either increased alongside more general increases in imprisonment (and consequently their level of over-representation has remained steady), or their rate of incarceration has accelerated more quickly than the general rate (and therefore their level of over-representation has increased). As we argue in this book, one of the key failings of both the settler colonial state, and many criminologists, has been to not take Indigenous responses to these problems seriously.

Enhancing criminology through Indigenous knowledges and methodologies

In many respects, the response of criminology to Indigenous knowledge about social harm – and their experiences of it – mirrors that of other social sciences and the policy sector in general: more often than not it is subsumed within Eurocentric, standardised policies and interventions through a process of 'indigenisation' (Havemann, 1988; Tauri, 1998, 2012).[3] Agozino (2003), Tauri (2012, 2014) and Cunneen and Rowe (2015) argue that the discipline of criminology is a significant contributor to the failed settler colonial response to the wicked problem of Indigenous over-representation. We acknowledge here the various influences that postcolonial writers such as de Sousa Santos (2006), Fanon (1963, 1967), Nandy (1983), Quijano (1999, 2007), Said (1993, 1996), Spivak (1985) and those within the emerging Critical Race Theory (CRT) school (see Schneider, 2003; Delgardo and Stefancic, 2007; Coyle, 2010) have had on our understanding of the centrality of the colonial project in defining, describing, enumerating and evaluating the 'native' or, in shorthand, the epistemic violence of colonialism (Spivak, 1985).

However, we argue that despite some common concerns around a focus on race and prioritising the voices of the oppressed, the work of many postcolonial and CRT advocates has largely sidelined the Indigenous experience. Speaking of the development of 'whiteness studies' in the US in the 1990s and early 2000s, Moreton-Robinson (2004, p viii) stated that 'the problem with American literature is that it tends to locate race and whiteness with the development of slavery and immigration, rather than the dispossession of Native Americans and colonisation'. In a similar vein, and as we discuss in Chapter Two, despite CRT centring the intersection of race, ethnicity and gender as a key component for critical analysis of contemporary western crime control, the Indigenous experience has been largely absent (see Delgado and Stefancic, 2007).

---

[3] Indigenisation is a process through which attempts are made to increase the number of Indigenous peoples directly contributing to the operation of the criminal justice system, as opposed to their significant contribution as 'clients' of the system via their rates of offending, victimisation and imprisonment (see Havemann, 1988).

In Chapter Two of this book we challenge the absence of this experience, both in mainstream criminology and more recent critical paradigms, by offering an alternative to the standard criminological narrative. We do this through an elaboration of a set of principles for the development of a specifically Indigenous approach to criminological work. The approach is distinguished by the core principles of endorsing committed objectivity through acceptance of the research role of 'objective outsider', and a belief in the ability of Indigenous peoples to carry out empirical research that will result in meaningful outcomes for their communities (Agozino, 2003; Smith, 1999). The role of objective outsider when matched with another key principle discussed in Chapter Two – to *give back* to Indigenous peoples by 'speaking truth to power' – means that the critical gaze of the Indigenous criminologist is never fixed solely on exposing issues that *arise out of* Indigenous individuals and/or communities, but also on the impact that the intersections between settler colonial structures (such as police, courts, child protection and education), policies and legislation have on Indigenous peoples (Tauri, 2014).

This is not to say that 'real' research on the Indigenous life-world precludes the use of the favoured methods of administrative criminology, such as closed surveys/questionnaires or statistical analysis. As Kukutai and Walter (2015) and Walter and Andersen (2013) argue, there is nothing inherently 'un-Indigenous' about employing, for example, statistical methods to shed light on the Indigenous context. Rather, issues arise when these methodological approaches to knowledge construction are treated as inherently 'value neutral' and 'apolitical', thus hiding what 'emerges from, and [is] given meaning through, the dominant frameworks of the settler state societies that produce and use them' (Kukutai and Walter, 2015, p 317). As Cunneen (2006) argues, any attempt to understand the Indigenous experience of criminal justice in the settler colonial world, must involve a critical analysis of the activities of the powerful, such as policy makers, criminologists and criminal justice institutions. We argue further that any such empirical inquiry must also deal with one of the significant epistemological and methodological blind spots of the discipline: the absence of the process of colonialism in criminological theorising of Indigenous over-representation.

Silencing colonialism

Traditional criminology has long had a problem with understanding the importance of colonialism[4] in structuring ideas about crime and punishment (Agozino, 2010). It is a concept that has been largely missing from the discipline (Cunneen, 2011a). The disregard for colonialism as an explanatory factor in settler colonial contexts is not confined to criminology. Martin (2014, p 238) notes that by neglecting colonialism, 'Anglo-white society [can] re-write history as if these events had never occurred ... what emerges is a sense of triumphalism among the dominant population which is so seamless, pervasive, and pronounced'. As argued in Chapter Three, the silence around colonialism effectively removes the possibility of understanding the contemporary position of Indigenous people within settler colonial societies. The result of this silencing is an averting of the critical criminological gaze from the role the discipline played in the colonial endeavour (see Agozino, 2003). On a theoretical and practical level, it has resulted in decontextualised and dehistoricised accounts of Indigenous criminality and victimisation that explain these complex phenomena as simple manifestations of individual, aberrant Indigenous behaviour.

Sumner argued that an historical perspective on criminal law 'must inevitably turn us towards colonialism ... crime is not behaviour universally given in human nature and history, but a moral-political concept with culturally and historically varying form and content' (Sumner, 1982, p 10). Blagg exposes the limitations with taking American or European criminological traditions as our starting point for a critical analysis of the Indigenous context as 'they all tend to operate without a theory of colonialism and its effects' (Blagg, 2008, p 11). We go further and align with Agozino (2003, 2010) in arguing that the relative absence of discussions of colonialism in criminology is itself an *effect* of colonialism. That is, it is part of the process of

[4]   The term 'colonialism' (from which the process term 'colonialisation' derives) refers to those 'situations in which states impose sovereignty on foreign peoples, even when there is little or no permanent settlement by the foreign rulers' (Gillen and Ghosh, 2007, p 14). This definition of colonialism, roughly synonymous with imperialism, requires the qualifier 'settler colonialism' when there is an extensive and permanent migration and settlement. The process of colonisation, colonialism, combines military, political and cultural force, with the expressed intent of creating hegemony over the colonised (Fanon, 1967; Agozino, 2003).

eradicating an Indigenous past, and silencing Indigenous experiences of settler colonialism.

Part of the process of decolonising criminology is to see that criminology is a product of a particular set of narratives within western social sciences formed during the later 19th and early 20th centuries (Agozino, 2003). They were a set of narratives developed in relation to the experiences of the European Diaspora particularly in the US, and 'in the construction of complexly stratified societies within and around the urban conurbations of western cities' (Blagg, 2008, p 202). The criminological imagination falters when confronted with Indigenous genocide and dispossession, and with Indigenous peoples who demand that their radical difference, their laws and customs, their alterity to the West be recognised (Morrison, 2004; Blagg, 2008; Cunneen, 2011a).

The constraints of criminology's eradication of colonialism from its conceptual and theoretical frameworks is a key theme explored throughout this book. The value of an intersectional analysis that places colonialism at its centre can be ascertained from analysing Indigenous women's experience of colonial/settler colonial crime control (Baldry and Cunneen, 2014). As discussed in Chapter Five, Indigenous women's experience of settler colonial criminal justice is one where the rationality and rehabilitative ideal that supposedly characterises *penal modernity* is set aside for a response based on the principles of infantalisation and sequestration. As we argue in Chapter Five, a complete understanding of this situation is not possible without recourse to the colonial context. Many of the narratives about Indigenous women that permeate criminology (for example as the victims of rapacious Indigenous men, or as incapable mothers) had their antecedents in a sociopolitical context common in colonial discourses, aptly portrayed by Jacobs (2009, p 112), who writes:

> nearly all white women portrayed Indigenous women as the degraded slaves of their cruel and lazy men. Making such colonial connections, Daisy Bates believed "the subjection of women in Africa, India, etc, is not to be compared to the dreadful slavery of the wild Australian woman and the young girl throughout their whole lives".

Jacobs (2009, p 113) goes on to state that: 'Bates' depiction of Aboriginal women as slaves became common currency among white women activists'. It is a depiction and sentiment that, one could argue, form the justificatory rhetoric that accompanies much of the punitive criminal justice policies in Indigenous communities, such as the Australian government's Northern Territory Emergency Response (see Chapter Five).

Sovereignty, self-determination and Indigenous rights

Western liberal democratic states see themselves as based on popular sovereignty. The source of their political legitimacy is popular consent and support – a notion of consent often at odds with Indigenous views of the colonial process and its outcomes. These states also see their criminal justice systems guided by principles of the rule of law and as essentially neutral, fair and universal in their application. Yet it is clear that many Indigenous peoples believe that settler colonial criminal justice systems are ineffective in their operation and oppressive in their outcomes. The process of reasserting Indigenous collective rights may require significant institutional change on the part of state criminal justice agencies, especially when a central component of the Indigenous critique of policing and the criminal justice system has been that Indigenous rights have been ignored, in particular rights to self-determination, self-government and authority over the maintenance of social order.

The differing recognition of Indigenous rights in settler colonial states

It is important to note, however, that both historically and in more recent periods, there are differences in the legal frameworks that developed among settler colonial states in regard to the recognition (or not) of Indigenous rights to self-government and self-determination. These differences have important implications for understanding both contemporary criminal justice systems and the way Indigenous peoples have engaged with settler colonial states.

Perhaps the most complex of the colonial legal frameworks that have developed has been in the US. Since the Marshall decisions of the US Supreme Court during the first half of the 19th century, it has been recognised that Indian nations are 'distinct, political communities, having territorial boundaries, within which their authority is exclusive' (*Worcester v. Georgia*, 31 U.S. 515 [1832] at 557). The nations have an inherent right of tribal sovereignty and are entitled to self-government. They are 'domestic, dependent nations' (*Cherokee Nation v. Georgia*,

30 U.S. 1 [1831] at 16).[5] Indian governments are entitled to exercise legislative, executive and judicial powers, subject to the powers of the US Federal Government. As McCarthy (2004, p 45) notes:

> The Supreme Court long ago upheld the right of reservation Indians to make their own laws and be ruled by them. The Court has recognized the authority of tribal governments to provide for the protection of health and safety of reservation residents and the political integrity of the tribe. However, the exercise of Indian jurisdiction and the sovereign powers of Indian tribes may be removed by the US Congress.

Various US federal laws have limited the exercise of jurisdiction on Indian country. The *Major Crimes Act 1885* gave power to the federal government to enforce major crimes (including murder, manslaughter and rape) that occur in Indian country. Tribal jurisdiction was curtailed in 1953 when Public Law 83-280 was introduced, which gave six states (Alaska, California, Minnesota, Nebraska, Oregon and Wisconsin) criminal jurisdiction over tribal members and other people on reservations, and permitted other states to opt for similar jurisdiction. The *Indian Civil Rights Act 1968* also affected tribal jurisdiction with the import of the protections of the US *Bill of Rights* including criminal law protections with due process guarantees. The end result of these changes is a highly complex 'jurisdictional maze' of criminal justice on Indian country, depending on 'a variety of factors, including but not limited to: where the crime was committed, whether or not the perpetrator is an Indian or non-Indian, whether or not the victim is an Indian or non-Indian, and the type of crime committed' (Indian Law and Order Commission, 2013, p viii).

In Canada, Aboriginal rights are recognised in section 35 (1) of the Constitution, which states that 'the existing aboriginal and treaty rights of the aboriginal peoples of Canada are hereby recognized and affirmed'. Milward (2012, p 32) notes that there are three distinct categories of rights here: inherent Aboriginal rights, land rights and treaty rights. He goes on to argue that inherent rights are communal in their character and are distinct rather than general (for example they do not provide for a general right to self-government). They relate to 'practices, traditions and customs that were integral to distinctive

---

[5]   For a discussion of these decisions, see the RCAP (1996a, pp 180-1) and Canby (2009, pp 15-18).

Aboriginal societies before contact with Europeans' (Milward, 2012, p 32). The interpretation of treaty rights may provide greater recognition of Aboriginal people's autonomy over internal affairs including dispute resolution. However, it has also been noted that treaty interpretation by the courts does not necessarily give meaningful recognition of Aboriginal understanding of the treaties (Milward, 2012, p 39).

More contemporary self-government agreements between Canadian federal and provincial governments and Aboriginal peoples are also relevant here. For example, the Nisga'a Final Agreement (2000) provides for Nisga'a right to self-government and for the establishment of police, courts and community corrections. Similarly in the Tsawwassen First Nation Final Agreement (2007), the Tsawwassen government can make laws, inter alia, for public order, peace and safety. Tsawwassen law may provide for the imposition of penalties, including fines, restitution and imprisonment not greater than the general limit set for summary offences in the Canadian *Criminal Code*. It is important to note, then, that both constitutional recognition and the development of modern agreements with Aboriginal people leave intact the overall sovereignty of the Canadian state. As Milward (2012, p 41) notes, various Supreme Court decisions have reaffirmed 'the principle that sovereignty remains vested with the Crown'.

In Aotearoa New Zealand the 1840 Treaty of Waitangi influences government legislation and administration in relation to Māori. However, for more than a century the Treaty of Waitangi was routinely ignored. The US Marshall judgements were 'cited and rejected in the New Zealand courts [who] refused to acknowledge any residual tribal sovereignty existing parallel with that of the Crown' (McHugh, 2001, p 195). McHugh (2001, pp 201-4) notes that it was the pan-Māori protest movements and the language of Māori sovereignty during the 1960s and 1970s that challenged the view that the Treaty of Waitangi was of little consequence (see also Poata-Smith, 1996). Today, while the foundations of New Zealand sovereignty cannot be directly contested in the courts, it is accepted that the exercise of sovereignty can be scrutinised. The Waitangi Tribunal was established in 1975. The Tribunal makes recommendations on claims brought by Māori relating to actions or omissions of the Crown that potentially breach the promises made in the Treaty of Waitangi.

While differing English and Māori versions of the Treaty provide different accounts of whether sovereignty was surrendered by the Māori, the Treaty has a 'quasi-constitutional' role and provides a structure and process for Māori influence (Brennan et al, 2004). We note in Chapter Four that a recent decision of the Waitangi Tribunal has been important in upholding the right of Māori to self-government and the effect that this has on Māori self-policing initiatives (Waitangi Tribunal, 2014).

The place of Indigenous people in Australia within English law was determined during the early part of the 19th century, at least to the satisfaction of the British. Although the object of some debate, various judgements confirmed that Aboriginal people were subject to colonial courts (*R v Lowe* [1827] NSWSC 32, *R v Murrell* [1836] NSWSC 35). In *Murrell*, Burton J held that the 'various tribes' had not attained either the numbers or the status of 'civilised nations' that could be recognised as sovereign states governed by laws of their own. Upon settlement and possession of the land there was only one sovereign, the King of England, and only one law, English law. Aboriginal people in the colony became the subjects of the King. According to the law of the coloniser, Indigenous people in Australia were without sovereignty and without law. Their land had been peacefully annexed to the British dominions.

Australian governments and courts have consistently denied Indigenous sovereignty, and in the absence of a treaty, any rights that might flow from such a legal document. The Australian High Court found that Aboriginal people 'have no legislative, executive or judicial organs by which sovereignty might be organised' (*Coe v Commonwealth* (1979) 24 ALR 118 at 129). Subsequent decisions confirmed that 'English criminal law did not, and Australian criminal law does not, accommodate an alternative body of law operating alongside it' (*Walker v New South Wales* (1994) 182 CLR 45 at 50). Further, 'what the assertion of sovereignty by the British Crown necessarily entailed was that there could be thereafter no parallel law-making system in the territory over which it asserted sovereignty' (*Members of the Yorta Yorta Aboriginal Community v Victoria* (2002) 194 ALR 538 at 552).

A consequence of the different ways in which the settler colonial societies came to understand and recognise Indigenous sovereignty, and the authority that resided with these powers, has seen significant variation in the extent to which Indigenous peoples have been able to influence the application and processes of the state's criminal law.[6] Thus, while acknowledging similarities in the demand for recognition of sovereignty, self-determination and self-government among Indigenous leaders across Canada, the United States, Aotearoa New Zealand and Australia, these political demands will be played out within specific

---

[6] For discussion of legal recognition of residual powers of self-government among Indigenous peoples in North America, see Anaya (1996, pp 16-18) and in contrast to Australia, see Reynolds (1996, pp 124-35).

legal and constitutional frameworks. Further, specifically in regard to criminal jurisdiction, existing constitutional and treaty arrangements will influence the nature and level of Indigenous control over justice institutions. We discuss these issues further in later chapters.

Sovereignty

We noted earlier that the settler colonial states have reaffirmed their sovereignty over Indigenous peoples even while recognising to varying degrees Indigenous rights. However, it is important to note that sovereignty can have multiple meanings: it is an elusive concept dependent on context (Brennan et al, 2004, p 310). Indigenous aspirations for sovereignty fundamentally challenge a unitary vision of the criminal law and, by extension, positivist criminology which draws its objects of attention from the definitions of state law. Sovereignty in the context of Indigenous political claims can refer to the historical claim that Indigenous people have never relinquished sovereignty. Or it can be used to refer by Indigenous people to the residual and unextinguished rights to self-government and autonomy that were recognised to varying degrees through treaties in New Zealand and North America. More generally, the political claim of a right to self-determination implies the right and ability to exercise some level of sovereign power – even if within the boundaries of existing nation states. Sovereignty can refer to a kind of residual distinctiveness and identity: 'we were sovereign peoples'; or to a more specific capacity to make social, political and economic decisions. For some Indigenous leaders it is the starting point, the bedrock on which other Indigenous rights can be developed and acknowledged (Behrendt, 2003, p 99). Sovereignty is about power and authority and it is seen as a point at which negotiation can begin. As Dodson (1997a, p 58) notes in the Australian context, there 'has never been genuine negotiation with Indigenous peoples, there has never been agreement between Indigenous and non-Indigenous Australians as to the terms of our citizenship in this nation'.

Indigenous sovereignty is not necessarily about creating separate enclaves or secession. As Curry (2004, p 147) notes, Indigenous sovereignty is 'something to do with the whole country that once belonged to Indigenous peoples and which now contains them. And it has something to do with the terms of engagement that will govern their membership of the state that now governs that country.' Among the necessary features of Indigenous sovereignty identified by Curry (2004, pp 148-49), of particular importance for a discussion within criminology is the expectation that Indigenous sovereignty will require a retrospective re-imagining of the terms of engagement between colonial settlers and Indigenous peoples, and will require changes to how non-Indigenous institutions conduct themselves, and to the laws of the larger society. Respect for Indigenous self-determination and self-government can lead to the creation of territorial units with primary Indigenous control over administration. However, it can also lead to 'the principled collaboration in, and sharing of, administrative functions in areas affecting Indigenous interests' (Castan and Yarrow, 2006, p 135). We note that the realisation of self-determination within domestic jurisdictions may be a complex task (Milward, 2012, p 2).

While sovereign power remains central to settler colonial states, trends towards globalisation have also seen states deal with competing modes of governance. Although 'the liberal-democratic nation-state retains a central role in redistributing elements of sovereign power and national jurisdiction' (Stenson, 1999, p 67), there has also been a 'redistribution' of sovereign powers. In the criminal justice area, we can see sovereign power moving out of the state to international bodies for courts and policing (United Nations and regional-based courts, regulatory bodies, investigatory bodies and so forth). Sovereign power can also be seen as moving downwards to more regional and local spheres of government and governance, such as multi-agency crime control partnerships (Stenson, 1999, p 68).

The redistribution of sovereignty may also provide avenues for the development of shared jurisdictions or shared sovereignty (for example Jackson, 1988). The challenge that Indigenous claims to sovereignty and self-determination pose are both theoretical and practical. The theoretical challenge is to understand that basic categories and definitions of crime are fundamentally circumscribed by historical and political contexts. The very legitimacy of the institutions used to control crime is not universally accepted. The praxis issue this raises is how we develop legal institutions that are capable of dealing with multiple jurisdictions and differential citizenship claims (Cunneen, 2005a). In other words, how do criminal justice system institutions develop in a manner that can deal fairly with competing citizenship demands and maintain legitimacy for different social groups? Developing answers to the challenge of differential citizenship is a necessary alternative to the 'one nation' view of citizenship that sees equality narrowly defined as 'sameness' and fails to recognise the unique status of Indigenous peoples within modern states.

Declaration on the Rights of Indigenous Peoples

The framework for understanding, developing and promoting Indigenous human rights has advanced significantly since the adoption of the *Declaration on the Rights of Indigenous Peoples* by the United Nations General Assembly in 2007. All the settler colonial states that are the subject of this book have ratified the convention (although with some delay). It is a normative document that establishes the 'minimum standards for the survival, dignity and well-being of the indigenous peoples of the world' (Article 43). There are four key principles that underpin the *Declaration*. These are: self-determination; participation in decision making and free, prior and informed consent; non-discrimination and equality; and respect for and protection of culture (ATSISJC, 2011, p 18). Each of these principles provides a guide for both reflecting on and assessing the shortcomings of the criminal justice systems of settler colonial states and Indigenous demands for reconceptualising justice.

The four principles provide a framework for much of the discussion in this book. Put briefly, every issue concerning Indigenous people is implicated in the concept of self-determination. 'Self-determination is a process. The right to self-determination is the right to make decisions' (ATSISJC, 1993, p 41). At a community or tribal level, is the right, inter alia, to exercise control over decision making, community priorities, how communities operate and processes for resolving disputes (ATSISJC, 2011, pp 109-10). Participation in decision making requires participation in both internal Indigenous community decision making, as well as external decision-making processes with government, industry and non-government organisations. Decision making must be free, prior to any activity occurring, informed of all the options and consequences, and based on consent. These requirements underpinning decision making are particularly apt when assessing how governments 'consult' with Indigenous peoples. The principle of non-discrimination and equality is particularly important given the histories of racial discrimination against Indigenous people and the gendered forms of inequality and marginalisation that were entrenched with the colonial project. Respect for and protection of culture is fundamental for the survival of Indigenous peoples. For a decolonising and postcolonial criminology, a fundamental understanding is that Indigenous culture is a source of strength and resilience, and cultural safety and cultural security are foundational to restoring and maintaining social order in Indigenous communities (ATSISJC, 2011, pp 123-34).

Overall, the political claim to self-determination has significant implications for state-based criminal justice systems – particularly when narrow definitions of universalism are seen to preclude the potential for the development of differential approaches to justice. However, rather than seeing Indigenous claims as a *problem*, a decolonising and postcolonial vision might see the potential fragmentation of centralised criminal justice systems as an opportunity for progressive change and development.

Conclusion

As stated earlier, a primary goal of this book is to work towards the development of a distinctly Indigenous criminology. To that end, each chapter deals with an issue that we believe is fundamental to that endeavour. These are not the only issues of import to its construction, and in time Indigenous scholars and our non-Indigenous collaborators will develop further theoretical and empirical insights into the range of issues affecting Indigenous peoples including, for example: the impact of poverty and racism on criminalisation from a critical Indigenous perspective; a deeper understanding of the role of Indigenous governance in responding to social disorder; the experience of Indigenous transgender, gay, lesbian peoples of settler colonial 'justice'; and a deeper questioning of the applicability to colonised peoples of fundamental criminological concepts. In terms of this book, the various chapters focus on the following issues.

In Chapter Two, *Towards an Indigenous criminology*, we focus on the added-value that Indigenous knowledges and methodologies bring to understanding Indigenous experiences of settler colonial criminal justice. By doing so, we seek to expose the shortcomings of the way in which mainstream criminology and the policy sector construct Indigenes as 'problem populations'.

Chapter Three, *Understanding the impact of colonialism*, builds on the foundations laid in Chapter Two through an exploration of the relationship between colonialism and the contemporary over-representation of Indigenous peoples in criminal justice systems. In particular, it discusses the major similarities and differences between colonial strategies in settler colonial societies and the enduring effects of colonialism on crime, criminal justice and Indigenous resistance. It develops a specific Indigenous criminological framework that is underpinned by an historical, structural and biographical appreciation of the experiences of colonialism and settler colonialism.

In Chapter Four, *Policing, Indigenous peoples and social order*, the focus moves to the impact of specific settler colonial justice policies and strategies, namely policing, and Indigenous responses to the problems arising from them. In recognition of our previous argument for the need to be mindful of Indigenous agency and resistance, we focus here on the organic forms of social control and policing that have emerged in Indigenous communities, often connected to long-standing forms of Indigenous order maintenance. These include processes such as women's night patrols and local community justice groups. The chapter discusses these innovations and the way they differ from dominant Western institutions of criminal justice.

Building on one of the key issues discussed in the previous chapter, Chapter Five, *Indigenous women and settler colonial crime control*, demonstrates that while there are commonalities in the contact of Indigenous men and women with criminal justice systems, there are also significant differences especially in the experiences of women. In particular, Indigenous women have much higher crime victimisation rates than non-Indigenous women, particularly in relation to domestic violence and homicide, and are experiencing more rapidly increasing imprisonment rates, especially over the last two decades. This chapter seeks to expose the fundamental weaknesses of the criminal justice systems response to Indigenous women, to make real these flaws to enable the development of effective responses.

Chapter Six, *Reconceptualising sentencing and punishment from an Indigenous perspective*, begins with a critical analysis of dominant Western forms of penality, which have led to the large-scale over-representation of Indigenous peoples in settler colonial prison systems. Alongside the dominant settler colonial approaches to the 'Indigenous problem' of sentencing and punishment (in particular, imprisonment) have arisen a number of 'innovations', including various hybrid court models such as sentencing circles and Gladue courts (Canada), peace-making courts (US), Rangatahi courts (NZ) and Aboriginal (Koori and Murri) courts (Australia). In addition, Indigenous alternative approaches to punishment, particularly around the concept of healing, provide an important Indigenous counterpoint to Western sentencing concepts of deterrence and rehabilitation. The chapter explores the tension between the dominant, state-centred approaches to penality and Indigenous models and processes of working with offenders, families and communities.

Chapter Seven, *Indigenous peoples and the globalisation of crime control*, builds on a number of themes developed in the book. In particular, it explores the impact on Indigenous peoples – and their endeavours for enhanced jurisdictional autonomy and self-determination – of the apparent increase in the globalisation of crime control policies and interventions, in particular restorative justice interventions such as the Family Group Conferencing forum. Using empirical research undertaken with Indigenous peoples, we argue that the globalisation of restorative justice has been based on indigenising state-centred interventions, which in turn has impeded Indigenous peoples' ability to self-determine.

Lastly, in Chapter Eight, *Critical issues in the development of an indigenous criminology*, we present the argument that an Indigenous criminology will play an important role in a radical rethink about the way we 'do' justice in the settler colonial context. There are several elements to what this 'rethinking' will involve. Certainly one will be making central the role of colonialism in the analysis of both the reasons for Indigenous offending and the limitations of the way the criminal justice system responds to Indigenous peoples. Another element will be challenging the discourses of risk and dysfunction that surround so much criminological treatment of Indigenous people and reinforce more punitive state interventions. Counterpoised against these discourses is the fundamental importance of Indigenous knowledges and methodologies in opening up new spaces for Indigenous criminological inquiry. Finally, the UN *Declaration on the Rights of Indigenous Peoples* provides an international framework for the recognition of Indigenous peoples' rights. Key principles underpinning the *Declaration* (such as the right to self-determination) need to be foundational to the development of an Indigenous criminology.

TWO

Towards a critical Indigenous criminology

The focus of this chapter is knowledge; in particular, the way(s) in which knowledge – and its production and dissemination – on the one hand provides the basis for the subjugation of Indigenous peoples in settler colonial contexts, while on the other hand supporting contemporary modes of Indigenous resistance and empowerment (Smith, 1999; Nakata, 2002; Sefa Dei, 2002; Alfred, 2005; Wane, 2013). The purpose of this chapter is twofold: first, to engage the discipline of criminology in a critical conversation about the predilection of the discipline to sideline Indigenous experiences in the formulation of knowledge about crime and social harm; second, to affirm the validity of Indigenous knowledge in understanding crime and social harm, and in the development of effective responses to these phenomena. Our second goal will only ever be partial, given the complexity and multiplicity of Indigenous experiences and perspectives.

Epistemologically, we consider the discursive project of an Indigenous criminology as a way to rupture the sense of comfort and complacency that exists in conventional criminological approaches to the construction, validation and dissemination of disciplinary knowledge in Western educational and policy settings (Sefa Dei, 2002). For this reason we explicitly reject the position taken by some criminologists, such as Weatherburn (2014), that we have learnt nothing from Indigenous research and scholarship on the causes of crime, or responses to it. Instead, we adhere to Hampton's (cited in Gilchrist, 1997, p 70) argument that 'it may not be a shortage of research that hampers but a shortage of research that is useful from [Indigenous] points of view'.

Criminology, knowledge and 'othering' the Indigenous

In his inaugural professorial lecture at Queen's University, Belfast, Phil Scraton (2005, p 3) stated that '[n]o group conceives itself as *the One*, the *essential*, the absolute, without conceiving and defining the *Other*. The Other is the *stranger*, the *outsider*, the *alien*, the *suspect community*: Otherness *begets* fear, *begets* hostility, *begets* denial' (emphasis in original). There have been many 'others' through the relatively short histories of contemporary social democracies, African Americans in the US, the proletariat and lumpen proletariat residing in capitalist economies, the traveller communities of Europe, and women (or at least certain categories of women) residing in Western patriarchies (Young, 2003; Scraton, 2005 pp 3-4). To this list of suspect 'others' we can add Indigenous peoples in the settler colonial jurisdictions of Canada, Australia, Aotearoa New Zealand and the US (Tauri, 2013a).

That criminology, or at least specific variants of the discipline, plays a role in the 'othering' of Indigenous peoples has only recently received serious consideration by researchers. In the main, critical commentators have primarily been Indigenous (Agozino, 2003; Kitossa, 2012; Tauri and Webb, 2012), or drawn from a small group of non-Indigenous collaborators (for example Blagg, 2002; Cunneen and Rowe, 2014; Deckert, 2014). Most recently, they have been joined by those working to develop a critical criminology informed by the precepts and conceptual paradigm of Critical Race Theory (CRT) (see Schneider, 2003; Coyle, 2010; and discussion later). In comparison, 'Western' criminology, as it is generally practised in settler colonial contexts, appears to be largely immune to the exhortations of Agozino (2004) and Tauri (2014) that it seek to extricate itself from the significant, and seemingly imposed, epistemological blind spot suffered by the discipline; namely its role as a *colonial project* in the continued subjugation of Indigenous people.

Drawing on Douglas (1966) and Sibley (1995), the Italian theorist Ruggiero challenges contemporary Western criminology's obsession with purity/impurity; the latter symbolically (and, for Indigenous peoples and other 'outsiders', often physically) positioned in a space he calls the 'inferno of the social elsewhere', the inhabitants of which are 'immediately recognisable for the halo of sludge surrounding them and for the subhuman features which they [have] slowly acquired during a long residence in hell' (Ruggiero, 2000, p 1). Ruggiero (2000, p 1) further argues that '[traditional criminology] makes filth, sewers, and excrement, in brief that "inferno" delimited by imaginary geographies, its main terrain of analysis and development'.

Similarly, the Nigerian criminologist Biko Agozino (2003) has suggested that from the outset, the discipline was *intellectually bankrupt* due to its empirical gaze being firmly fixed on the geographical space inhabited by the damned. At the same time, the inquiring gaze is, as much as possible, turned away from the immoralities and ethical contradictions of the propertied classes and the political elite. Of course, one can point to Sutherland (1949), Merton (1938) and others for evidence that from time to time members of the discipline gaze upon the privileged few, the '1 percent' so prominent in the rhetoric of the recent Occupy Movement (Razsa and Kwanik, 2012). Furthermore, the rise of Marxist, feminist, postmodern, counter-colonial and, most recently, critical race criminologies has also resulted in further scrutinising of the conduct of the powerful (Spitzer, 1974; Simpson, 1989; Agozino, 2003; Coyle, 2010). Yet despite the growing evidence of the perfidy and illegality of state conduct in various forms (Kramer and Michalowski, 2005; McCulloch and Stanley, 2012; Burton, 2013), *administrative and authoritarian* criminologists, to whom the policy makers look for empirical validation of their endeavours, continue to reserve their empirical gaze for the inhabitants of Ruggiero's geographical wasteland.

Although, as Ruggiero argues, the geographical boundaries may not be as clear cut as they arguably once were, the discipline nonetheless continues to create theoretical and conceptual binaries such as crime/criminal, offender/victim, moral/immoral and exclusion/inclusion that result in *real consequences* for those deemed worthy of the negative connotations associated with these binaries (Ruggiero and Welch, 2009). As individuals and as an academic collective, criminologists often contribute to the political enterprise of inclusion/exclusion through the very act of *doing* criminology, for example when they accept contracts from the policy sector to carry out research that limits Indigenous peoples' input into the design and administration of research *on them* (Tauri, 2012). In the Indigenous context, all too often criminologists conduct research *on* Indigenous issues while *proselytising from afar*, utilising, for example, highly structured surveys, statistical modelling, and such like, while rarely (and sometimes never) descending into the spaces described by Ruggiero, in order to experience directly the life-worlds they present themselves as experts on (Tauri, 2013a).

Compared to the standard, hegemonic representation of the evolution of criminology (Moyer, 2001) founded in the early 19th-century humanist, enlightenment ideals of Beccaria and his contemporaries, Beirne (1993) and Lynch (2000) argue that criminology is an oppressive construct. This position is perhaps most starkly articulated by Agozino (2010, p i), who describes the discipline as 'a social-control freak' that is 'obsessed with … domination over others in otherwise democratising global communities'. Channelling Foucault and Halleck, Lynch (2000, pp 146-7) further argues that 'the history of criminology has been the story of humanly created methods of oppression told from the oppressor perspective'. In Lynch's view, criminology developed as one of the 'sciences of oppression', whose central focus was controlling the supposedly free and unfettered creativity of the criminal classes – Ruggiero's 'damned'. Thus, according to Agozino (2010) and Lynch (2000), criminology can be viewed as a method of legitimising mechanisms of oppression that target the dangerous class(es), which we argue here includes the Indigenous Other:

> In short, criminology is one of the disciplines that established the conditions necessary for maintenance of the status quo of power. It can only do so by oppressing those who would undermine the status quo. In this sense, criminology must be viewed as a *science of oppression*. (Lynch, 2000, p 149, emphasis added)

Within administrative/authoritarian criminology, the colonial devastation of Indigenous peoples is legitimated by an imaginary that 'establishes incommensurable differences between the coloniser [represented here in the form of administrative, in particular 'authoritarian', criminologies] and the colonised [represented here by Indigenous scholars, their communities and their epistemological frameworks]' (Castro-Gomez, 2002, p 276). A key colonial project within the academy, and we argue especially within criminology, is the ideologically driven dismissal of Indigenous knowledge about the social world as 'subjective', 'unscientific', and/or at best 'folk epistemology' (Moyle and Tauri, 2016). Castro-Gomez (2002, p 276) describes this project as an exercise in creating the 'other of reason', which in turn paves the way for excluding *other ways of knowing* from the Western, criminological lexicon (Tauri, 2012).

The (re-)emergence of authoritarian (colonialist) criminology

The re-emergence of the influence of administrative and authoritarian criminologies on crime control policy development is well documented: Y2K, 9/11 (Chunn and Menzies, 2006), the increasing influence of the neo-liberal ethos in the development of social, economic and crime control policy in Western, 'liberal' jurisdictions (Wacquant, 2009a, 2009b), and the steady growth in globalised markets for crime control products (Jones and Newburn, 2001) combined to empower the authoritarian neo-liberal state. Given a long-standing alignment with state crime control and its focus on disciplining unruly, problem populations (Colvin and Pauly, 1983), perhaps it is not surprising that particular formulations of academic criminology – those that seek to be of relevance to state crime control – should have experienced these developments with some intensity (Tauri, 2009b). As Chunn and Menzies (2006, p 665) argue: '[s]ix years into the new millennium, the roots of criminology are once more showing. And the "liberal boot" described by R.S. Ratner more than two decades ago ... has more and more assumed an eerily familiar shade of blue'.

The obituary on critical criminology was long ago prophesised, with Foucault (1977), Smart (1989, 1990) and Sumner (1994) all lamenting the sacrifice of the discipline's supposed emancipatory and transformative potential to the drive for policy relevance (see Tauri, 2009b). However, the recent, (re)consummated marriage between administrative criminologies and formal criminal justice complicates both the anticipated demise and the development of a critical, Indigenous-centred approach to the study of social harm (the focus of the last section of this chapter). In particular, the epistemological Eurocentrism of the discipline, and the parasitic relationship that many of its adherents enjoy with settler colonial crime control, renders difficult the development of respectful, empowering relations with the academy (Tauri, 2013a). The limitations have also been recognised by critical, non-Indigenous members of the academy, including Hillyard et al (2004, p 9), who condemn disciples of administrative criminology for their self-limiting methodologies and resulting uninformed analysis of the Indigenous (and more broadly, the ethnic minority/new migrant) experience. But perhaps the most damaging claim made against academic (administrative) criminology is the inherent belief of its members in their *right to dominate the construction and dissemination of crime control knowledge*, because of an adherence to the illusion of an epistemology that enables 'dispassionate' reason and the rule of objectivity (see Young, 2011).

For Indigenous scholars, and Indigenous communities everywhere, the dangers of the discipline's drive for policy relevance in the contemporary moment relate directly to the significant role its adherents played in the process of colonisation (Agozino, 2003; Tauri, 2012). On this issue, Doxtater (2004, p 618) makes the prescient observation that:

> Western knowledge rests itself on a foundation of reason to understand the true nature of the world, yet it also privileges itself as the fiduciary of all knowledge with authority to authenticate or invalidate other knowledge (when it gets around to it). Colonial-power-knowledge conceptualizes intellectual colonisation in Foucaultian terms, in this case with a Western knowledge fiduciary acting as guardian over its Indigenous knowledge ward. I suggest that the resulting

contradiction embroiders some Western knowledge expertise with unreasonableness through its ignorance of other knowledge.

Building on the main theme of Doxtator's argument, Cunneen and Rowe (2014, p51) write that '[w]ith relatively few exceptions in criminology (for example, Agozino, 2003, 2004; Blagg, 2008; Cunneen, 2011a, 2011c; Morrison, 2006; Tauri and Webb, 2012) … the colonial subjugation of Indigenous knowledge has not been analysed to any great extent'. However, what critical analysis has been completed reveals two overwhelming, and related issues:

- that academic criminology is complicit in the silencing of Indigenous experiences and perspectives in the pursuit of crime control knowledge;
- that many Indigenous peoples experience criminology as a component of the *epistemic violence* of settler colonial crime control.

According to Bhargava (2013, p 413), 'epistemic injustice [is] a form of cultural injustice that occurs when the concepts and categories by which a people understand themselves and their world is replaced or adversely affected by the concepts and categories of the colonisers'.

The construction of Indigenes, at both the individual and community level, as 'the criminal other' and therefore a danger to the wider community and to state hegemony, is an ongoing process that transcends current academic debates about neo-colonialism/postcolonialism, and arguments about similarities and differences between modernist/ postmodernist penalities (for example see Garland, 2001; Pratt, 2000, 2002). Some things 'stay the same' regardless of how much we attempt to present the contemporary social context as a world of ebbs, flows and ongoing change (Castells, 1996). Arguably, the *Durkheimian rationality* – the purposefully instrumentalist construction of deviant others and its relationship to modes of social control – remains constant regardless of whatever epoch we live in: it is the means and technologies through which this is achieved that differ. Criminology, as a core discipline of the social sciences of the Western academy, is no different in this regard. A 'technology of social control' (Agozino, 2010) conceived during the planned colonial genocide against Indigenous peoples, the discipline, very much like the settler colonial state it nourishes, has repeatedly demonstrated an almost unworldly capacity for *shape changing* (Alfred and Corntassel, 2005). It presents itself to Indigenous peoples as an 'independent' arbiter between them, their communities, and the settler colonial state, while at the same time partnering with the state in the development of policies, legislation and interventions constructed to disempower and criminalise Indigenous peoples (Cunneen, 2011b; Tauri, 2012).

Towards a critical Indigenous criminology

If, as Jock Young (2011) argued, our forays into social inquiry require that we seek to accurately describe the social context by *engaging* (as Ruggiero (2000) infers and Linda Smith (1999) demands), then our epistemology and our methodology must be such that they privilege the perspectives and experiences of the Indigenous Other (see also Cohen, 1988). Our research endeavour must be emancipatory; meaning that it supports Indigenous peoples in their attempts to decolonise their lived experience of settler-colonialism (Agozino, 2003; Glass and Kaufert, 2007. For emancipation (in whatever form that takes) to be possible, there first needs to be a process of *epistemological cleansing* that a number of critical Indigenous scholars have recently referred to as 'decolonising the research field' (see Smith, 1999; Zavala, 2013). Smith (2005, p 88) describes this process as the 'purposeful agenda for transforming the institution of research, the deep underlying structures and taken-for-granted ways of organising, conducting, and disseminating research and knowledge'. We believe that in order to begin this process within criminology, empirical research *with* Indigenous peoples must be based on a set of epistemological principles designed to enable researchers (both Indigenous and in particular non-Indigenous) to employ an *Indigenous emancipatory methodology*.

If, as we have argued previously, administrative, Western criminology is not constructive for *knowing* the interrelated issues of Indigenous offending/victimisation and the responses they deem suitable to it, then is there an Indigenous approach that can provide better understanding of social phenomena such as crime or social harm? We argue that there is. And although it will share similar characteristics with other emancipatory approaches, including Marxist, feminist approaches, and most recently peace making and critical race criminologies, there are key principle and objectives that arguably distinguish a critical Indigenous criminological approach. In the following section we seek to reveal these objectives and principles through discussion of case studies of 'real world' research carried out by Indigenous scholars and critical, non-Indigenous collaborators *with* Indigenous peoples.

Smith (1999, p 125-34), in a section in her book titled 'An Agenda for Indigenous Research', argues that the Indigenous research agenda is being advanced through two significant pathways:

> The first one is through community action projects, local initiatives and nation or tribal research based around [treaty and human rights] claims. The second pathway is through the spaces gained within institutions by Indigenous research centres and studies programmes.

The approach to the study of Indigenous peoples' experiences of crime control that we advocate here shares similar ontological and epistemological features with the recently formulated Participatory Action Research (PAR) process, an approach to social inquiry based on the 'systemic testing of theory in live-action' and where 'the main purpose of research is to *change* the experience of research participants for the better' (Dupont, 2008, p 201; emphasis in original). Adherents to the PAR process regard research participants as co-researchers and use a dialectic process that recognises ways of knowing beyond rationality. They favour critical subjectivity over the notion of a verifiable truth, place action on an equal footing with the quest for knowledge, and ally themselves with marginalised individuals and communities with the purpose of improving their well-being and social conditions to the highest degree possible. If we are to build meaningful responses to the social harms experienced in and by Indigenous communities, then we must begin by making space for gathering meaningful knowledge; which in turn requires the discipline of criminology to make space for 'us'. As Linda Smith (1999, p 193) writes:

> When Indigenous peoples become the researchers and not merely the researched, the activity of research is transformed. Questions are framed differently, priorities are ranked differently, problems are defined differently, and people participate on different terms.

The principles of a critical Indigenous criminology

Agozino has challenged criminologists who advocate that we employ the kind of scientific approach to research discussed earlier, one based on an objective stance that ensures distance between the 'knowledgeable researcher' and the research subject. In contrast, Agozino (2003) urges a researcher/participant relationship that rejects this 'false dichotomy between objectivity and commitment'. Instead, Agozino (2003, p 157) endorses *committed objectivity* as a position that 'capture[s] the inextricability of the articulation of the processes of commitment and objectivity' that are key to carrying out meaningful social inquiry. Rather than seeking to detach from the context of social inquiry, a critical Indigenous criminological approach advocates for researchers who can speak with empirical authority about the life-world of Indigenous people. Building on the key principles of objectivity and 'standpoint' advocated by Cunneen and Agozino, speaking with authority is predicated on *purposely standing in the social context* from which their experience derives, because, as Deutscher (1983, p 2) explains, '[e]very detachment is another kind of involvement – the idea of complete objectivity as complete detachment is a complete fraud'.

We now discuss three 'principles' for Indigenous criminological research – or guides for developing Indigenous criminological knowledge – in more detail.

- The first principle is the necessity of 'committed objectivity' in this endeavour.
- The second principle is 'speaking truth to power' and the need to 'give back' to the communities from which you have received and then taken knowledge.
- The third principle is that Indigenous criminological research with Indigenous peoples should be 'real', meaning it must come *from within* Indigenous peoples and their communities.

Committed objectivity is essential for researching the Indigenous context

A powerful example of the committed objectivity approach in practice is the Stó:lo First Nation criminologist, Dr Wenona Victor's (2007) research and advocacy work on the resurrection of her First Nation justice system, known as *Qwi:qwelstóm*. Wenona's research on Stó:lo justice related to two aspects of her life: as a Stó:lo woman seeking to play a meaningful role in bringing justice to her people after decades of failure on the part of the formal system to deliver anything remotely empowering; and as a postgraduate student undertaking research that would enable her to become 'qualified' in the academic sense, but perhaps more importantly, knowledgeable in the Stó:lo understanding of the term, to participate directly in the reinvigoration of *Qwi:qwelstóm*, and therefore in the empowerment and emancipation of Stó:lo as a people. Wenona's role as a member of the First Nation, and as someone assisting directly in the construction of *Qwi:qwelstóm* would, in the strict world of empiricist criminology, be too close to the sources to be able to carry out 'objective' criminological inquiry. The nature of this potential violation of the rule of objectivity is not lost on Wenona herself, or her co-author on a paper published about her research in 2007, Ted Palys, who wrote in the footnotes (Palys and Victor, 2007, p 13) that:

> ... in two instances we quote Wenona from an account of the early development of the programme that she wrote some years ago. Other times she is simply part of the 'we' when Stó:lo teaching and perspectives are being described, and is the 'I' when the programme goals and processes she played a role in creating and managing are described.

Palys and Victor (2007) relate that in 1993 the Stó:lo House of Justice, composed of members of the Nations House of Leaders and House of Elders, 'was empowered with the mandate to develop and implement alternative justice programmes to help the Stó:lo Nation re-establish healthy communities and achieve the full potential of all Stó:lo citizens'. One of the programmes to come from this task, and Victor's research that informed it, was *Qwi:qwelstóm*, one of the few that is available to all 24 communities that make up Stó:lo.

Hired in 1999 to assist in the development of justice programmes for the First Nation, Wenona was already undertaking research on this issue as part of her MA thesis on traditional forms of Stó:lo justice. Originally contracted to deliver Family Group Conferencing, but finding that 'there was nothing Indigenous about this model of justice whatsoever!' (Palys and Victor, 2007, p 7), Wenona and Stó:lo moved towards the developing sentencing circle model, and training was subsequently arranged in that supposedly Indigenous justice forum. Once again, training was arranged, this time in the use of sentencing circles, and again Stó:lo participants found that the process (and the training) did not meet their needs. Luckily the person arranged to deliver the training, Judge Barry Stuart, had asked that the session be held in a traditional setting and not a hotel (as the Family Group Conferencing training had been), and so it was moved to the *Yakweakwioose* Longhouse, a move that proved precipitous to the eventual development of their own processes, as Victor recounts (Palys and Victor, 2007, p 12):

Our experience at the Longhouse taught me a valuable lesson – that we have all that we need right here. I mean no disrespect, but we don't need the Māori, we don't need a fancy hotel to legitimise what we are learning, and no disrespect, but we don't need a judge either to 'teach' us about circle. We have our own culture, our own teachers, our own Elders, our own language and our own learning environment … The message is clear: If you are going to revitalise your culture don't do it in the *Xwelitem* [European] world.

So Wenona, already a part of the process of working to bring about *Qwi:qwelstóm*, found her role as student and researcher becoming entwined with the political process of empowerment through 'justice'. Her previous experience of researching for her Master's degree meant that she had already engaged with those working with Elders. This meant that she already knew how to conduct herself when interviewing the Elders when the formal process of developing *Qwi:qwelstóm* began (Palys and Victor, 2007, p 12). The research approach used open-ended interviews: 'Each interview began with the question, "Traditionally, prior to courts coming to our territory, what did we do to resolve conflict without out communities?", and then went in whatever direction the Elder deemed appropriate' (Palys and Victor, 2007, p 9). For the next year, Wenona engaged with as many Elders as possible, working towards the completion of her thesis, and the development of the policy and practice framework that would enable the resurrection of *Qwi:qwelstóm*. During that time she reports on the numerous cultural teachings the Elders passed on to her, and especially how she felt 'honoured the Elders knew her to be "worthy" of them' (Palys and Victor, 2007, p 10).

However, there was an issue: in none of the interviews had an Elder ever spoken about crime, criminals or punishment, and Wenona began to wonder how she would complete her Master's. Then she had an epiphany that she recounts (Palys and Victor, 2007, p 10) as follows:

Then one day, that all important paradigm shift occurred, a lesson in decolonising one's mind, an epiphany if you will. Justice to the Stó:lo within a Stó:lo worldview does not look anything like the justice one finds within the Canadian criminal justice system. The criminal justice system may focus on 'crime', 'prosecution', 'prison' and 'punishment', but to the Stó:lo 'justice' is centred upon the family and includes: (1) the role of Elders; (2) the role of family, family ties and connections; (3) teachings; and (4) spirituality. As we describe below, each of these elements is now present in and guides the *Qwi:qwelstóm* process.

Working from Agozino's (2003) argument for committed objectivity, and the desirability for researchers who can speak with empirical authority about the life-world of Indigenous peoples, one can see the added value of an Indigenous scholar like Wenona Victor not only being an *insider*, a member of the Stó:lo community, but also as an institutionally linked and trained researcher tasked with gathering knowledge – much of it sacred – from Elders. The question that critical criminologists need to ask is: would it have been possible for a completely objective, detached 'outsider' to have gained the trust of the Elders? Perhaps. Certainly it has happened before on a number of occasions in other criminological research undertaken on Indigenous issues. However, we argue that the opportunity for the epiphany that took place is limited for those not embedded in the Stó:lo social context, who do not have the trust and guidance of the Elders, and who do not have a direct stake in the policies and justice initiatives informed by the type of knowledge derived from Wenona's research.

Indigenous criminological research gives back by 'speaking truth to power'

A principle that is common to Indigenous-inspired ethics for conducting Indigenous research, is the need to 'give back' to the communities from which you have taken knowledge; even if you are, as Wenona Victor was, a member of that community (Smith, 2005). Some of the ways in which Indigenous researchers give back that have been identified in the literature include:

- taking on the political role as agents of truth that speak to power;
- as organic intellectuals involved in unmasking dominant ideologies and colonising practices of the state and other institutions, including the academy (see Bogues, 2005).

Edward Said (1996, p 11) perhaps best sums up the important role of the (Indigenous) intellectual in this regard, when he describes the role of the politically motivated researcher as one focused on 'confront[ing] orthodoxy and dogma ... whose *raison d'être* is to represent all those people and issues that are routinely forgotten or swept under the rug', while challenging the foundations of the dominant systems of thought and hegemony that confront, in this case, Indigenous peoples. Bogues' dictum (2005, p 91) is that intellectuals employ:

> [a] critical practice that grapples with the historical moments, that seeks to wrestle with theory in efforts to expose not the hypocrisy of power but its assumptions and its language-games of naming, [and that] constructs a set of knowledges that might be useful in any emancipatory project.

The committed objectivity inherent to a critical Indigenous criminology recognises the political bases of *all* research. For example, Agozino (2003, p 166) states: '[i]t is always good for those who have a voice to speak up for the silenced rather than hide behind the mask of scientific objectivity to speak only about silences'. He further indicates that the process of advocacy must involve engagement with the (Indigenous) Other because 'it will be even more commendable for scholars to speak in solidarity *with* the oppressed rather than simply speak *for* them as their silence implies voicelessness' (Agozino, 2003, p 166, emphasis in original). While laying bare the political nature of Indigenous standpoint approaches, Agozino (2003) also exposes the contradictions inherent in those who argue that 'scientific' approaches are divest of subjectivity, or unswayed by 'politics'. He argues (Agozino, 2003, p 167): '[s]ocial scientists may pretend that they are studying race relations ... with point-of-viewlessness, but their findings eventually inform political practices of different tendencies'. For example, the stance taken in this book is *political* in the sense encouraged by Agozino, and also Cunneen (2006), in that it:

- privileges the perspectives, experiences and issues of Indigenous peoples;
- critically analyses the activities of the powerful, such as policy makers, criminologists and criminal justice institutions;
- offers solutions to criminological and policy praxis that empowers Indigenous peoples in their attempts at self-determination and/ or to again a measure of jurisdictional autonomy so they might practice their 'law'.

This approach has clear linkages to the developing Critical Race Criminology, which itself derives from the Critical Race Theory (CRT) movement that took form in the late 1990s and early 2000s (see Delgado and Stenfancic, 2007; Coyle, 2010). CRT shares many similarities to Indigenous approaches to social harm and crime, including the importance of intersectional analysis for facilitating 'a more in-depth understanding of the subtleties of blatant and more hidden forms of race, class and gender' inequalities (Schneider, 2003, p 88). A CRT approach to studying inequalities seeks to understand the social world and work progressively to change it for the better (Delgado and Stefancic, 2007), just as Indigenous approaches aim to present concrete representations of the Indigenous experience and achieve meaningful justice outcomes for Indigenous peoples.

Staying with the emancipatory theme, those using CRT pursue outcomes that are both 'pragmatic and utopian, as they imagine a different world and different values' (Schneider, 2003, p 88), in much the same way that Moana Jackson (1988) envisions a parallel/ separate system of justice for Māori, or Victor (2007) worked for the resurrection of an autonomous justice process for the Stó:lo First Nation. CRT encourages individual and group activism, and is inherently political and subjective as it seeks to question how the status quo maintains inequality through the construction and utilisation of race and racist policies, and its adherents share with critical Indigenous scholars and their non–Indigenous collaborators a 'scepticism toward dominant legal claims to neutrality, objectivity, colour blindness, and meritocracy' (Matsuda et al, 1993).

The CRT and Indigenous criminological perspectives match up in many respects with regard to key principles and especially in a critical analysis of the role of the state in perpetuating inequalities and the marginalisation of minorities. Many scholars from both approaches see the purported 'race neutrality' of Western democratic justice systems, based on 'white', colonialist understandings of justice, crime, and so forth, as perpetuating the privilege of white hegemony, and the disempowerment of ethnic minorities (Coyle, 2010). CRT-informed approaches challenge the ahistoricism of much of mainstream criminological analysis, and instead insist on contextual/historical analysis of law and criminal justice (Delgado and Stefancic, 2007).

While there is clearly much commonality in the approach of CRT advocates and Indigenous scholars, the fact remains that those employing CRT have had 'little to say about race, crime and justice' (Delgado and Stefancic, 2007, p 134), and even less so about the situation of Indigenous peoples residing in settler colonial jurisdictions. While the central tenets of CRT including the powerful representation of the *ordinariness* of racism and critique of the hegemony of white-dominated institutions such as law, there is a distinct lack attention to Indigenous issues per se.

For a theoretical and methodological approach to be 'of value' to Indigenous peoples, much more is required than recognition of the political bases of social and criminological research, as our colleagues in the CRT clearly assert; it is also about the important issue of *positionality*. Or, to employ Bogues' exhortation discussed earlier, it is necessary for social scientists to 'take a position'. The encouragement for Indigenous criminologists and critical non-Indigenous colleagues to undertake 'political' research, to take a position, mirrors what has been occurring across other academic disciplines since the early 1990s, including education (Rigney, 2001), psychology (Powis, 2007) and sociology (Howard-Wagner et al, 2012), wherein the call for Indigenous researchers to be public intellectuals and advocates for the Indigenous experience and perspective is now firmly entrenched.

The benefits of an overtly political stance when pursing Indigenous criminological research is validated in the empirical work of prominent Māori legal and justice philosopher Moana Jackson, in particular his 1988 report *Māori and the Criminal Justice System: He Whaipaanga Hou*. Jackson's research on Māori experiences of crime control represents the only significant empirical project of its kind undertaken in Aotearoa New Zealand. The study was carried out over three years (including 14 months of consultation towards the development of the final report) and involved individual interviews, focus groups and *hui* (meetings) with a range of Māori with experience of the justice system, including police, correctional officers, policy workers, inmates and ex-prisoners, their families, community workers, service providers, members of Elders' councils for various *Iwi* (tribes), and academics and researchers (Jackson, 1988; see part 1 of the report that deals with methodology). In all, it is estimated that Jackson's research involved 3,000 Māori from throughout the country.

Jackson's research broke the methodological mould that had framed research on Māori, by government agents or predominantly *Pākehā* (European) researchers and academics, up to this point. In choosing to involve a range of Māori participants, in particular offenders and inmates, employing community-centred methods, and involving participants in the development of the methodology, including the topics and questions for discussion, Jackson firmly established the political context of this work, which was to privilege the voices and experiences of Māori (Tauri, 2015b). One could argue that in doing so, Jackson laid the foundations for what has become known as Kaupapa Māori Research, an epistemological and research approach now most famously associated with Linda Smith and her 1999 work *Decolonising methodologies*. The work that Jackson, his associates and participants put into developing a Māori-centred methodology – one based in placing Māori, their culture, their experiences, as the centre of research – cannot be underestimated, as the following summary by JustSpeak (2012, pp 12-13) attests:

> Jackson observes that a *Pākehā* [European] research method has in the past tried to employ overly simplistic causal explanations, for instance linking historical injustice to offending. More complex lines of causality are needed and made possible by a Māori research method; history must be connected, for example, to trauma and dysfunction, which is then used to explain offending.

Jackson's work gave voice to decades of Māori dissatisfaction with crime control policies and activities. What was new about his work was also what made it unpalatable for government ministers and policy makers: Jackson and his participants' analyses of crime were directed towards a range of antecedents, including a detailed examination of the marginalisation of Māori by government institutions, most notably from the social welfare and justice systems. Jackson's participants contended that Aotearoa New Zealand's criminal justice system reflected a *Pākehā* theoretical and practice bias, and that this bias was evident in research into Māori criminal behaviour. It was suggested that policy makers and members of the academy did not consider Māori experiences of colonisation to a degree necessary for informing the development of effective policy: in effect, the policy sector, served by mainstream criminology, ignored the structural antecedents of the growing over-representation of Māori in the justice system, preferring instead individual-focused explanations and solutions (Tauri, 2015a). Importantly, the policy sector was criticised for assuming that criminal behaviour by Māori could be dealt with in the same way as offending by other population groups.

While participants observed that Māori offenders in the criminal justice system had, like many non-Māori, experienced poor education, difficulties in family upbringing, long periods of unemployment and other factors which increased the likelihood of offending behaviour, for Māori these issues were impacted by a history of marginalisation from Aotearoa New Zealand society through the process of colonisation. Participants argued that Māori social deprivations were the result of state policies that had negatively impacted on Māori social structures, through the active suppression of Māori culture, and their economic and political autonomy (see Walker, 1990). To understand Māori offending, Jackson (1988, p 26) argued that theoretical explanations and policy responses had to contextualise Māori experiences in relation to a history of colonisation:

> The monocultural basis of *Pākehā* research into Māori offending has prevented recognition of these socio-cultural dynamics and the appropriate mechanisms needed to understand them. This has resulted in a raft of 'explanations' of Māori crime which reflect considerable monocultural and theoretical bias, but little effective explanation. Thus the Māori offender has merely been defined as an urban misfit, a cultural maladept, an educational retard, or the victim of behavioural labelling, while the socio-cultural forces underlying such descriptions have been largely unrecognised.

This emphasises the importance of understanding how colonisation shapes contemporary social relations and contexts, in contrast to analyses that focuses on individual pathology and ignores wider social relations in Aotearoa New Zealand society. Jackson believed that Māori philosophies were relevant to understanding offending, and he argued (1988, p 17) that *tikanga* (philosophy) would:

> provide some insight into the complex questions of why some Māori men become criminal offenders and how the criminal justice process responds to them. It approaches the topic from within a Māori conceptual framework and seeks to explain Māori perception of the causes and consequences of criminal offending.

Most controversially of all, Jackson and many of his participants made the major political error of suggesting that as the formal system criminalised Māori as much as anything else, the state should consider providing Māori with a meaningful measure of jurisdictional autonomy via a parallel system of justice.

At the time, government ministers and policy makers largely ignored Jackson and his research participants' argument for increased Māori jurisdictional autonomy. Instead, the primary policy response largely revolved around the controlled integration of 'acceptable' Māori concepts and cultural practices into confined areas of the justice system (see Tauri, 2011). For example, in reviewing *He Whaipanga Hou*, the Courts' Consultative Committee (1991) (comprising members of the judiciary, lawyers and community representatives) recommended to the then minister of justice that culturally appropriate responses to Māori offending were achievable through existing state mechanisms. The Committee expressly recommended against transferring criminal justice-centred processes into distinctly Māori settings. The Committee especially argued against *marae* (meeting houses) being used for court cases (thus ignoring evidence that historically Māori utilised *marae* as a site for dealing with social harm – see Jackson, 1988). It was argued that court trials could not be easily transposed to the *marae* setting while ensuring that the integrity of the state process remained 'intact'. However, officials did express the view that *marae* could play a minor role in the formal justice system through the delivery of community diversion and rehabilitative programmes designed by the state for the benefit of Māori offenders sometime in the future.

Yet as time has moved on since the publication of Jackson's work, the benefits and subsequent influence have become apparent. The state has since moved to utilise *marae* to deal with Māori justice matters, first, as indicated above, as a site for the delivery of rehabilitation programmes and restorative justice interventions (Tauri, 2005), and of late through the establishment of the Rangatahi youth courts (see discussion in Chapter Six on sentencing). Among the suite of recommendations contained in the 1988 report were a number that at the time were ignored or dismissed out of hand as being, in the words of the then justice minister, 'separatist'. These included: referring cases to Māori providers, holding meaningful hearings on *marae*; cultural advisory groups for justice agencies, in particular the (then) Department of Justice; affirmative action to secure employment of those with knowledge of *te ao Māori* (Māori culture, language, and so on); and meaningful bicultural training (Jackson, 1988). Since then, all of these recommendations have in some form or other been implemented, although the extent to which they mirror what Māori want – or indeed the extent to which they make positive contributions – is an issue for agencies to ponder. The point is that Jackson's highly 'politicised' research changed the criminal justice landscape in Aotearoa New Zealand immeasurably and at least opened up the space for Māori-centred research and responses to issues of crime control (Tauri, 2004).

Indigenous criminological research with Indigenous peoples should be 'real'

Arguably, some members of the Western academy have become adept at faking the appearance of respectful consultation/research (Tauri, 2014). The anthropologist C. Menzies (2001, p 21) exposes the strategy of 'faking it', when he writes that:

> It is unfortunate that there are still many researchers who continue to conduct research on Aboriginal people as opposed to with us. Some of these researchers have even mastered the technical form of respectful consultation, but without the necessary depth and the real respect that is required.

Elsewhere, we have exposed the nature and extent of this problem as it recurs across much of the criminological research on the 'Indigenous problem' (Tauri, 2012, 2014). More importantly, the negative impact of 'faking it', in terms of meaningless Indigenous strategies, biculturalised interventions and such like, is *very real* and often damaging for the Indigenous communities upon whom they are forced (Victor, 2007; Tauri, 2012). Therefore, it is essential that we ensure that the knowledge about Indigenous peoples that we assemble and disseminate, reflects their experiences and has a positive impact on their lives. For this to happen, we need to ensure that our work is 'real', meaning it must come *from within* Indigenous peoples and their communities (Smith, 1999). According to Schmidt (2009, p 52) there are two main criteria that researchers must observe if they wish to research or work *with* Indigenous peoples: (1) 'the process by which the research is carried out must contribute to community empowerment and (2) the community must perceive the choice of research topic or question as relevant'.

In order to be of use to our Indigenous collaborators in the research endeavour, we must avoid a common occurrence in the work of the Western academy and the policy sector, namely a propensity for relegating Indigenous knowledge to the 'symbolic'. MacDonald (2010) discusses this disempowering tendency in relation to the construction of multicultural policies in settler colonial contexts. Referring to the work of Stanley Fish, MacDonald distinguished between 'boutique' and 'strong' versions of multiculturalism, where the 'boutique' was 'the multiculturalism of ethnic restaurants, weekend festivals, and high profile flirtations with the other'. However, MacDonald then states that while proponents of 'boutique' multiculturalism:

admire or appreciate or enjoy or sympathise with or (at the very least) recognise the legitimacy of the traditions of cultures other than their own, they have strict limits of tolerance, and will always stop short of approving other cultures at a point where some value at their centre generates to act that offends against the canons of civilised decency as they have been either declared or assumed. (MacDonald, 2010, p 5)

This boutique approach to multiculturalism results in the '[s]hallow recognition of Aboriginal cultures, languages, governance systems, and spiritual practices [that] parallel a similar shallow recognition of these analogous group characteristics among new immigrants' (MacDonald, 2010, p 6). In similar fashion, a significant amount of criminological research and a significant number of resulting publications are of the boutique kind – from research into the impact of Aboriginal culture, and experiences of 'colonialism' on sentencing decisions based on judges' notes (and not the experiences and opinions of Aboriginal participants; see Bond and Jeffries, 2011), to explorations of the antecedents of 'Aboriginal violence' that ignore the structural violence of colonialist policies (see Weatherburn, 2014).

Conclusion

As demonstrated in this chapter, the place of Indigenous knowledge in criminology is a precarious one. This precariousness stems from the historical development of criminology as a discipline of social control within the colonial context. Indigenous peoples have long been marginalised within and by the criminological enterprise. The marginalisation takes many forms, including: a propensity to view Indigenes and their life-worlds through the prism of deficit and dysfunctionality; the dismissal of Indigenous epistemologies and 'ways of knowing' – their strategies of knowledge construction, as 'unscientific', 'ideological', 'subjective'; and the results of our research being considered of little criminological value.

The vacuity of the last position was exposed in our discussion of the work of Moana Jackson and Wenona Victor, research that resulted in the exposure of the bias and criminalisation of Māori in Aotearoa New Zealand's criminal justice system and, for the Stó:lo First Nation in Canada, the basis for the reinvigoration of their own justice practices. The result, we argue, is a tendency within criminology towards universalism, a belief that Eurocentrically derived theories, policies and interventions work for everyone and everywhere. It is an approach that manifests itself in a theme that threads through so much of the criminological musings on the 'Indigenous problem', namely that the tools of the master can fix problems that have emanated from the master's house, including the significant over-representation of Indigenous peoples in the criminal justice system of settler colonial states.

We are not advocating that Indigenous scholars do not work in criminology, or that Indigenous-centred, empowering research is not possible. Instead, we believe that to begin the process of indigenisation we – Indigenous scholars and our critical, non-Indigenous collaborators – must turn our critique to the discipline itself and expose the role it plays in Indigenous marginalisation. Relatedly, we need to build critical knowledge of Indigenous experiences of settler colonial crime control through research that speaks truth to power and reveals the criminalising impact of state-dominated crime control.

THREE

Understanding the impact of colonialism

The impact of colonialism on Indigenous peoples is poorly understood in mainstream criminology and often ignored in leading textbooks (Martin, 2014). A fundamental problem has been the absence of a colonial framework within contemporary criminology. Our argument, however, is that the colonial experience and its ongoing effects is critical to understanding how criminal justice systems interact with Indigenous peoples today, and is therefore central to the development of an Indigenous criminology.

Commonalities in the experiences of Indigenous peoples in the British settler colonial societies include the loss of land, social, economic and political marginalisation, and the contemporary phenomenon of over-representation in criminal justice systems. This common experience stems from the history of colonisation and the profound disruption caused to pre-existing societies. Every part of Indigenous society was attacked during the colonial process. Early contact often involved open warfare, to be replaced later by extensive government controls. Government policies and practices variously attempted to 'civilise', Christianise and assimilate Indigenous peoples through the establishment of reservations, forced removal of children and education in residential schools, the banning of language, cultural and spiritual practices, and the imposition of an alien justice system (Pratt, 1992; Stannard, 1992; RCAP, 1996b; Cunneen, 2001; Dunbar-Ortiz, 2014). The devastation to families, communities and nations caused by government policies was widespread.

However, as noted previously, although the overarching sovereignty of colonial states remains in place, there are differences in the way Indigenous rights were recognised in the settler colonial societies. Both Canada and the US had a long history of signing treaties with Indigenous people up until the 1870s. Aboriginal rights are also recognised in section 35 of the Canadian Constitution. In Aotearoa New Zealand, the 1840 Treaty of Waitangi influences government legislation and administration in relation to Māori. In Australia, governments and courts have consistently denied Indigenous

45

sovereignty, and in the absence of a treaty, any rights that might flow from such a legal document.

We argue in this chapter that the over-representation of Indigenous people in crime and victimisation statistics needs to be contextualised within a much broader framework of the effects of colonisation. The long-term social and economic marginalisation, the denial of citizenship rights for Indigenous peoples, and the limited recognition of Indigenous law and governance are important in explaining over-representation in criminal justice systems. In other words, colonial systems of control are not merely of historical interest, but they also have material effects on the contemporary position of Indigenous people. Furthermore, Indigenous resistance to colonial systems of control have ongoing relevance. The political demands by Indigenous peoples to exercise self-determination, including through recognition of Indigenous law and greater control over criminal justice decision making, have long-term implications for criminal justice in settler states.

Settler colonialism

Colonialism involves subjecting particular groups of people, with pre-existing links to land and resources and independent cultural and political processes, to the control of another group. Colonialism involves the exercise of power, violence and a range of strategies to expedite subjugation, including cultural and social domination (Thomas, 1994). These processes generate resistance by those being dispossessed and expropriated. As Dunbar-Ortiz (2014, p 8) notes: 'People do not hand over their land, resources, children, and futures without a fight … In employing the force necessary to accomplish its expansionist goals, a colonising regime institutionalises violence.' The imposition of colonial systems of criminal justice was a part of this process. Criminal law became an important tool *both* for legitimising the use of force *and* in imposing a range of cultural, social and institutional values and processes.

There were historical variations between the settler colonial states. For example, in Canada and the US, strategic military alliances between Indian nations and colonialists were important considerations at least until the beginning of the 19th century. As noted above, there were also important differences in the recognition of Indigenous rights. However, setting these contextual differences aside, colonialism set in motion a process of invasion, settlement and nation-building across the four countries that fundamentally altered the lives of Indigenous peoples in the newly occupied territories. Settler colonialism was a particular type of colonialism, whereby the primary economic objective is securing the land and where sovereignty is asserted usually on the basis of 'discovery'. Settler colonialism was a form of the colonial experience whereby Indigenous peoples had to be either eliminated, or contained and controlled in order to make land available as private property for the settlers who had come to stay (Wolfe, 2014). The substantial loss of land contributed directly to the material conditions of Indigenous socioeconomic disadvantage. Further, many argue that settler colonialism is fundamentally genocidal, either directly through extermination in the violence of the initial colonial onslaught, or later through processes of assimilation designed to bring about the destruction of Indigenous societies and cultures (Stannard, 1992; Dunbar-Ortiz, 2014). By their very presence, Indigenous people threatened (and continue to threaten) both assertions of colonial sovereignty and the coloniser's right to land (Evans, 2005, p 61).

Colonial processes disrupted modes of governance through which Indigenous peoples lived. The colonial imposition of imperial law and governance on pre-existing Indigenous nations has profound implications for understanding the Indigenous relationship with nation-states today. Colonial law imposed criminal and penological concepts that were foreign to Indigenous peoples. As Quince (2007, p 341) has noted, in Aotearoa New Zealand there were fundamental differences between colonial and Indigenous concepts of law:

- individual responsibility compared to collective responsibility for wrongdoing;
- the removal of the victim from the judicial process;
- the concept of the state as the injured party rather than the collective group;
- the separation of the criminal process from the community;
- the distinction between civil and criminal law and penalty;
- differences in the justifications for, and types of, punishment (for example, imprisonment compared to restitution and reparation).

Although Indigenous nations differed between themselves in cultural values and law, in general they were often in opposition to the values represented by colonial criminal law.

Race and the civilising mission

A legitimating and motivating discourse of the colonial project was the 'civilising mission' to change native 'savages' to civilised Christians. The civilising process was often brutal. For example, American Indians were placed on church missions that resulted in significant loss of life. While many deaths were caused by European-introduced diseases, the conditions on these missions also directly contributed to the large number of deaths (Stannard, 1992, p 138). The civilising process was also to be partly accomplished through the forced removal and 're-education' of Indigenous children in residential schools and institutions (NISATSIC, 1997; Milloy, 1999; TRCC, 2012a, 2012b). We return to the long-term outcomes of forced child removals later in this chapter.

The 'civilising mission' was founded on ideas of racial superiority and inferiority. These ideas provided an overarching basis to law and policy towards Indigenous people throughout much of the 18th, 19th and 20th centuries (Malik, 1996; Wolfe, 2010), and was a precondition of colonial genocides and denial of human rights. The suspension of the rule of law and the use of terror and violence by colonial authorities against Indigenous people were contextualised and legitimated within racialised constructions of Indigenous people as inferior, lesser human beings. Racialised views of Indigenous people changed over time: from concepts of the 'noble savage', to barbarism, to views about Indigenous races being 'doomed' to extinction aided by 'pseudo-scientific theories ... that rested ultimately on ethnocentric and racist premises' (RCAP, 1996b, p 139; see also Williams, 1989, McGregor, 1997, Belich, 2001).

Racial discourses were also gendered. Indigenous women were separated from other women because of perceived biological and culturally defined racial differences: sexually promiscuous, incompetent mothers, and so forth (Green and Baldry, 2002). Indigenous women were also subjected to colonial control by being locked up in disproportionate numbers in women's 'factories' and in mental asylums and punished further by having their children removed because they were seen as negligent parents. The rape of Indigenous women was commonplace across the colonies, and was integral to the colonial conquest of Indigenous people (Smith, 2005). In the US, white men could rape Indian women with impunity because Indian women had no legal standing before the courts (Baker, 2007, p 328). Indigenous women continue to be over-represented in penal institutions and to suffer particularly because of their cultural difference and marginalised status (Ross, 1998; Baldry and Cunneen, 2014).

In short, racialised and gendered constructions of Indigenous people facilitated institutionalised discrimination, irrespective of whether policies were designed to eradicate, protect or assimilate the 'Native'. Furthermore legal protections could be suspended and otherwise unlawful behaviour by the colonialists could be ignored in the higher interest of the betterment, protection or control of colonised peoples.

Violence, genocide and the rule of law

Western liberal democratic states define their criminal justice systems as neutral, fair and universal in their application and founded their legitimacy on these principles. Equality before the law and equal protection of the law are seen as the defining features of the rule of law – which itself is understood as a universal principle and a fundamental good. Yet it is clear that colonialism institutionalised selective notions of universality and equality before the law. Historians have argued that the rule of law was suspended in relation to Indigenous peoples (Kercher, 1995; Evans, 2005; Dunbar-Ortiz, 2014). During the colonial period, Indigenous people, even where they were ostensibly equal subjects, often fell outside the protection of the law. The suspension of the rule of law was largely justified by racialised constructions of Indigenous inferiority: to be protected by rule of law required a requisite level of civilisation (Evans, 2005).

At various times, active resistance by Indigenous people to colonising powers led to open warfare. There is not the space here to explore the dynamics of this warfare, nor the historical variations that existed across the settler colonial states. However, it is clear that imperial justifications for colonisation, even by way of discovery and settlement, allowed for the conduct of war against resisting Indigenous peoples (Finnane, 2005). For example, there were well-documented massacres of Indigenous people in Australia in the late 18th, 19th and early 20th centuries – the last recorded massacre occurred in 1928 in the Northern Territory (NT) (Cunneen, 2001, p 55). There was never any doubt at the time that the Indigenous people and the colonisers were indeed at war in parts of south-eastern Australia in the early 19th century (Goodall, 1996), Tasmania during the 1820s and early 1830s (Reynolds, 1995), and Queensland and the NT during the mid to latter half of the 19th century (Reynolds, 1993; Roberts, 2005). In Aotearoa New Zealand, Māori resistance and conflict over colonial expansion lead to the New Zealand Wars of 1845-72 (Belich, 1986). At the height of the conflict, the colony relied on 18,000 British troops and local militia to quell the resistance at a time when the total Māori population of men, women and children was no more than 60,000 (Belich, 1986, p 15).

In some cases, wars against Indigenous people can be seen as genocide. Moses (2000) argues in the Australian context that particular campaigns undertaken by Native Police against Indigenous nations in Queensland during the latter part of the 19th century were genocide – they were clearly undertaken with the intention of physically destroying a whole group of people. On the other side of the continent, in July

1895, Western Australian senior state officials noted that: 'There can be no doubt from these frequent [police] reports that a war of extermination in effect is being waged against these unfortunate blacks in the Kimberley district' (quoted in Cunneen, 2001, p 50).

In relation to genocide and American Indians, Stannard describes the 'European habit' of killing women and children during hostilities with American Indians as 'flatly and intentionally genocidal. For no population can survive if its women and children are destroyed' (Stannard, 1992, pp 118-19; see also Churchill, 1997). As US General Sherman wrote in 1873: 'We must act with vindictive earnestness against the Sioux, even to their extermination, men, women and children ... during an assault, the soldiers cannot pause to distinguish between male and female, or even discriminate as to age' (cited in Dunbar-Ortiz, 2014, p 10). His words were put into practice in massacres such as Wounded Knee in 1890, when upwards of 300 unarmed Lakota Sioux men, women and children were killed by US troops (Dunbar-Ortiz, 2014, pp 154-7). The massacre reflected a much longer-term strategy of 'total' war against American Indian nations, both east and west of the Mississippi (Dunbar-Ortiz, 2014, pp 92-4). These wars in the US, as they were in other settler colonial societies, were fundamentally over control of the land.

It is clear that colonial processes meant that the rule of law as a constraint on arbitrary power and state violence, and as a guarantee of equality before the law, was suspended in relation to Indigenous peoples. It was a 'rubbery attitude to the law' where basic notions of the rule of law could be cast aside (Kercher, 1995, p 6). Punitive expeditions were ordered, collective punishment was exercised, armed 'pacification' parties were used against Indigenous people, and at various times martial law – and (in some settler colonial states) war – was declared. Men, women and children were killed. If Indigenous people were indeed British (or American) subjects, then the official and unofficial killings that took place were mass murders (Kercher, 1995, pp 7-9). The law of the coloniser was always applied ambiguously, anomalously, strategically (Evans, 2005; Shenhav, 2012): colonised peoples were 'both within the reach of the law and yet outside its protection' (Anghie, 1999, p 103).

Civilisation and criminal law

Indigenous law was viewed disparagingly by British colonialists. Defined as 'customary' law, it was regarded as distinctly inferior to colonial law – a view that reflected both ethnocentrism and the effects of 'a narrow positivistic doctrine of jurisprudence', which served to denigrate Indigenous systems of law (Jackson, 1992; Sheleff, 1999, p 83). In discussing American Indian law, Zion noted that 'the term "custom" implies something that is somehow less, or of lower degree than "law". There are connotations that a "custom" is somehow outside the "law" of government, which is powerful and binding' (Zion, 1988, p 121). Legal positivism – the dominant jurisprudence of the English legal system – reinforced the view that law is inherently linked to the institutions of the modern political state (New Zealand Law Commission, 2001, p 18). The delegitimisation of Indigenous law was part of the 'civilising' process designed to bring the superior political and legal institutions of the West to the native. At times, colonial authorities recognised aspects of Indigenous law, but when they did so, the broader sovereignty from which Indigenous law derived was generally ignored.

Furthermore, when colonial authorities recognised the ongoing existence of Indigenous 'customs', it was seen as a temporary measure whereby the processes of assimilation would eventually bring about their demise and replacement with the criminal law of the colonial power. In Aotearoa New Zealand, Pratt (1992) has shown that *becoming* British subjects required a complete reconstitution of Māori life, and the reshaping of justice practices was fundamental to this process. While the British recognised the ongoing nature of Māori forms of punishment through the establishment of Native Courts and other measures from the 1840s, these were seen as temporary measures to aid in the assimilation of Māori. Indeed by the end of the 19th century, different court processes and punishments for Māori were abolished, and Māori systems of punishment no longer had formal recognition (Pratt, 1992, pp 27-68).

The colonising impact of settler law had a number of consequences. First, it meant the continued subjection of Indigenous peoples to legal processes that are systemically racist – they are built on the denial of the legitimacy of Indigenous law. Second, it has led to equating *justice* with the law of the colonising power – both in general public consciousness and sometimes within Indigenous communities themselves (Jackson, 1994, pp 117-18). Indigenous rights become defined by the colonial legal system. Speaking of Indigenous Hawaiians, Haunani-Kay Trask comments that: 'by entering legalistic discussions wholly internal to the American system, Natives participate in their own mental colonisation' (cited in Watson, 2000, p 5). Similarly, Jackson notes that Māori may be compelled to seek a culturally 'sensitive process' within an ideological framework that forces them to adopt the consciousness they wish to transform (Jackson, 1994, p 118).

The imposition of the criminal law of the coloniser went hand in hand with the denial of the legitimacy of Indigenous law. The colonial state continues to choose whether and which Indigenous laws can be recognised. However, it is clear that many Indigenous peoples see state criminal justice systems as oppressive, and insist on Indigenous law as a rightful alternative to an imposed system of law (Zion, 1988; Jackson, 1994).

Protection, assimilation and criminalisation

Criminalisation and punishment were central to the operation of the colonial state in its governance of Indigenous peoples, particularly when open warfare was replaced by more regulatory forms of control. During the 19th century, colonial states moved towards policies of protection and assimilation of Indigenous peoples. In the US and Canada, the aim from the 1830s was increasingly to 'civilise' Indians. In Canada this outcome was to be achieved initially through 'educational, economic and social programs delivered primarily by the Christian churches and missionary societies' (RCAP, 1996b, p14). When the Dominion of Canada was formed in 1867, the first prime minister told parliament that Canada's goal was 'to do away with the tribal system and assimilate the Indian people in all respects with the inhabitants of the Dominion' (quoted in RCAP, 1996b, p 179). This policy was translated into federal legislation with the Indian Act 1876. In the US, Congress established the Federal Bureau of Indian Affairs (BIA) in the Department of War in 1834 and then transferred it to the Department of Interior in 1849, marking a change towards assimilation and detribalisation (Fleras and Elliot, 1992, pp 146-7). The Dawes Act (or General Allotment Act) 1887 sought to change Indian life by destroying the communal social organisation based on tribal affiliations. It was to achieve this outcome by dividing tribal lands into individual land-holdings and selling the remainder of reserve lands to white settlers. A significant proportion of the Indian land base passed into non-Indian hands between 1887 and 1934, wreaking havoc on traditional Indian social organisation (Fleras and Elliot, 1992, p 144).

In Aotearoa New Zealand, policies sought the assimilation of Māori people into the developing settler society through legislation such as the Native Land Act 1865 and the Native School Act 1867. Māori people 'were regarded for the most past as a "social problem" who either "had problems" because of cultural differences or "created problems" in competition over power and resources' (Fleras and Elliott, 1992, p 180). In Australia, colonial governments introduced comprehensive 'protection' legislation in the latter part of the 19th century that enabled extensive regulation of the lives of Indigenous people. A central feature of the legislation was Indigenous segregation on government and church-run reserves and missions, particularly for those who were unable to demonstrate the level of civilisation required to exercise citizenship rights.

Although legislation and policy aimed at Indigenous people was couched in the language of protection and assimilation, the model was based on the institutions of the criminal justice system, often through police, civil 'protectors' or Indian agents exercising a range of administrative, policing and judicial functions. The extensive regulation of the lives of Indigenous people and the corresponding denial of basic human rights became inextricably linked with the day-to-day administration of Indigenous affairs. The 'tutelage' necessary to be civilised and assimilated required extensive regulatory control and criminal sanctions. Indeed, criminal sanctions were a core part of *enforcing* assimilation.

In Canada, the Indian Act of 1876, and subsequent Acts, shaped various educational, social and economic policies designed to extinguish rights and assimilate Indigenous people: 'traditional customs and forms of organisation were interfered with in the interest of remaking Aboriginal people in the image of the newcomers' (RCAP, 1996b, p 140). The Indian Act enforced conformity; for example, non-Aboriginal concepts of marriage and parenting were to prevail, with penalties imposed for non-compliance (RCAP, 1996b, pp 184-5). The government had the power to make and enforce regulations, which had the force of law, 'with regard to the full spectrum of public and private life in communities' (RCAP, 1996b, p 185). Indians could only leave their reserves if they had a written pass from the local Indian agent of the Department of Indian Affairs (DIA). This was used, inter alia, to prevent participation in cultural ceremonies, prevent political organisation and stop parents from visiting their children in residential schools (RCAP, 1996b, p 296). In Australia, protection legislation allowed government-appointed protectors and superintendents (often police) to extensively regulate all aspects of Indigenous peoples' lives: whether their children would be removed to an institution, their rations, who they could marry, where they could work and for what salary, access to savings, which areas were prohibited and where the person would reside (Cunneen, 2001, pp 66-75).

In Australia, Canada and the US, aspects of Indigenous culture were criminalised. In the US, the BIA was at the forefront of enforcing assimilation. 'Cultural activities such as feasts and dances, as well as various religious practices were defined as Indian Offenses by the Commissioner of Indian Affairs in 1883' (Fleras and Elliot, 1992, p 147). Courts of Indian Offenses, composed of Indians appointed by BIA agents, were set up to enforce these laws and to replace traditional forms of dispute resolution. In Canada, Indigenous ritual life and social organisation could be declared to be criminal behaviour (RCAP, 1996b, p 186). In the 1880s the Sundance and Potlatch ceremonies were outlawed. These were 'two of the most visible and spiritually significant aspects of coastal and plains culture … participation in potlatch was made a criminal offence, and it was also illegal to appear in traditional costume or dance at festivals' (RCAP, 1996b, p 183). Other offences exclusively applied to Indians, for example in relation to consuming alcohol.

In Canada during the 1880s, agents from the DIA were given the same powers as magistrates, and could conduct trials wherever they thought necessary. Although their jurisdiction was originally limited to the Indian Act, this was extended during the 1890s to include certain sexual offences, prostitution and vagrancy when committed by Indian people (RCAP, 1996b, pp 288-9). It has been noted that all Indian agents were automatically:

> granted judicial authority to buttress their other powers, with the result that they could not only lodge a complaint with the police, but they could direct that a prosecution be conducted and then sit in judgment of it. Except as accused, Aboriginal persons were excluded totally from the process. (Hamilton and Sinclair, 1991, pp 303-4)

In Australia, reserves and missions administered their own penal regimes outside, and parallel to, existing formal criminal justice systems. For example, the Queensland *Aboriginals Preservation and Protection Act 1939* established local policing and court functions under the control of reserve superintendents. Superintendents could constitute a court exercising broad powers; legal representation for accused was only by permission of the court (the superintendent); and Indigenous police on the reserves were under the supervision of the superintendent, as was the local prison. Sentences of imprisonment were common and indeterminate sentences could be imposed for Indigenous people said to be 'uncontrollable'. Until well into the mid-20th century, Aboriginal people still needed permission to leave the reserve. Indigenous people on reserves came to be called 'inmates' and those who escaped were charged with 'desertion' (McGrath, 1993, p 107). Perhaps the most notorious of all Queensland reserves, Palm Island became the principal place of punishment for Indigenous people in that state – a 'peculiar mix of prison, protectorate and concentration camp' (Finnane and McGuire, 2001, p 292).

Protection was based on a penal model of administration and control. The breadth of discretion afforded to superintendents, protectors and Indian agents meant that there was very little restraint on the exercise of power. While reservations and missions became a key site of colonial penality specific to Indigenous peoples, they were also subject to the mainstream colonial systems of criminal justice. It is notable that the two systems operated in tandem. In Australia, for example, Indigenous prisoners on expiration of their formal sentence were then 'deported' indefinitely to be confined on reserves; while others seen as troublemakers or 'offenders' were simply removed to reserves without criminal charge or conviction (Finnane and McGuire, 2001, pp 290-2). Penal sanctions were applied liberally and without external scrutiny. Indigenous people did not appear in the records of the official prisons of the day, but were, nonetheless, as imprisoned as if they had been locked up in the formal prison system.

Punishing Indigenous peoples

Racial discourses on Indigenous people were central to penality, and systems of punishment that differentiated between the colonisers and the colonised were foundational to the colonial state. Racial understandings of Indigenous people played a constitutive role in defining penal strategies and different types of punishment. The use of the death penalty in both the US and Australia is illustrative of this differentiating process. In Australia in 1871, reflecting changing sensibilities around punishment, the Western Australian parliament passed legislation banning public executions and requiring that they take place within the walls of the prison. However, the legislation was amended to allow for the public execution of Aboriginal people. Although falling into disuse, the law remained in force until repealed in 1952 (Markovich, 2003). Aboriginal people were significantly over-represented in death sentences (Finnane, 1997, pp 129-30) and two thirds of those hanged in South Australia during the mid-19th century were Aboriginal (Kercher, 1995, p 12).

In his study of the history of American Indian executions, Baker (2007, p 317) notes that these deaths were:

clearly nested within a socio-political context of genocidal colonialism calculated to dispossess American Indians of their *Indianism* by removing them from their sacred tribal territories, disrupting their traditional cultures, and continuing their marginalized status in US society today.

The most notorious mass execution of Native Americans occurred in 1862 in Minnesota, when 39 people were executed by the federal government in the aftermath of the Lakota-Sioux uprising. The defendants were tried and convicted for civilian crimes by a military commission (Baker, 2007, p 338). Native Americans continue to be over-represented in death penalty statistics. In recent decades, one estimate puts the number of Native American executions between 1977 and 2002 at 13.3% of all executions, although they comprise only 1.7% of the national population (Perry, 2009a, p 269). In the executions between 1973 and 2007 the victims were overwhelmingly white and the Native American defendants 'largely suffered from severe alcoholism, drug abuse and mental illness' (Baker, 2007, p 353).

Criminal law and penality reflected different cultural understandings of Indigenous people. Modernity and the development of modes of punishment that disavowed corporal punishment and public execution were seen as inapplicable to Indigenous people because of their perceived racial and cultural characteristics: the appropriate punishment for Indigenous people was a salutary public spectacle of violence.[1] For example, in Australia the extended use of physical punishments and restraints (lashings, floggings, chaining) for Aboriginal offenders continued until well into the 20th century (Finnane, 1997). Often the cultural ideas underlying more brutal forms of punishment were justified in terms of benevolence. When introducing the amending legislation allowing public executions for Aboriginal people noted previously, the Western Australian Attorney-General stated that (Hocking, 1875, p 28):

> The object of this measure was to strike terror into the heart of other natives who might be collected together to witness the execution of a malefactor of their own tribe ... The Bill had been framed in no vindictive spirit, but in the belief that it would operate beneficially.

---

[1] See also Davis (1998, p 98) for parallels with the punishment of slaves in the US.

Public execution was thus recast as a form of tutelage, as part of the civilising process for Indigenous people. At the same time, the spectacle of punishment for European offenders was being redefined and relocated behind prison walls.

The criminogenic effects of colonialism

The erasure of colonialism as an ongoing process with tangible criminogenic effects still pervades academic studies of Indigenous offending (for example Weatherburn, 2014). It is not that colonialism is 'unknown' to criminologists, but rather, it is that they actively deny its importance (see Agozino, 2003). This denial of colonialism contrasts directly with the work of Indigenous academics and activists that place the long-term colonial experience at the centre of explaining the contemporary position of Indigenous people in settler states (for example Dunbar-Ortiz, 2014; Tauri, 2014). We now consider specific examples of how the effects of colonialism materially impact on the contemporary marginalisation of Indigenous people, that is, on the day-to-day conditions under which Indigenous people live, and how the effects of colonialism can be seen to directly contribute to crime and victimisation. In other words, we consider the criminogenic effects of colonialism.

The loss of an economic foundation through colonisation clearly impacted on Indigenous peoples and created social and economic disadvantage among the colonised (Jackson, 1988). At a general level, then, colonialism can be considered criminogenic to the extent that it actively produces dispossession, marginalisation and cultural dislocation. However, the two examples explored further in this chapter are more specific. They arise directly from government *policies* aimed at regulation and assimilation. They are:

- the effects of the forced removal of Indigenous children from their families and their placement in institutions and residential schools;
- the long-term impact of government fraud and corruption in bringing about the contemporary immiseration (the forcible imposition and maintenance of structural conditions of extreme poverty) of Indigenous people.

Residential schools and the stolen generations

One process for 'civilising' Indigenous people was through the focus on children: their removal and placement in institutions, prohibitions on language and culture, and their instruction in English. Various policies designed to implement these outcomes were introduced in Australia, Canada and the US during the 19th century, lasting until the second half of the 20th century. In Aotearoa New Zealand, similar educational policies were introduced through the Native School Act 1867, although without the same extensive removal of Māori children.

Canadian Prime Minister Harper, in his official apology to Indigenous people for these policies, stated that the objectives of the system 'were based on the assumption Aboriginal cultures and spiritual beliefs were inferior and unequal. Indeed, some sought, as it was infamously said, "to kill the Indian in the child"' (Prime Minister Stephen Harper, official apology, 11 June 2008). In its intention to 'kill the Indian', the Canadian residential school policy was violent and abusive even as a concept (Milloy, 1999, p xv). The policy lasted for more than a century from the 1870s to the 1980s and was a church–state partnership with the DIA providing the funding, setting the standards and exercising legal control over the children who were wards, and various Christian churches operating a nationwide network of schools (Milloy, 1999). Authorities would frequently take children to schools far from their home communities as part of a strategy to alienate them from their families and tribal culture. In 1920, under the Indian Act, it became mandatory for every Indian child to attend a residential school and illegal to attend any other educational institution. More than 150,000 First Nations, Métis and Inuit children were placed in these schools. There are an estimated 80,000 former students still living (TRCC, 2012b, p 2). In the US the main period of the Indian residential school movement was from the 1860s to the 1980s. The number of American Indian children in the boarding schools reached a peak in the 1970s. As in Canada, Indian children were removed from their culture, language and identity. More than 100,000 Native American children were forced to attend these residential schools (Smith, 2004, p 89).

By the early 20th century, most states of Australia had developed a systematic policy of Aboriginal child removal utilising both church and state-run institutions (NISATSIC, 1997, pp 25-149). The Australian removal policies rested on specific assumptions about race, 'blood' and racial hygiene. According to social Darwinist ideas, so-called 'full blood' Aboriginal people were bound to die out because of their biological inferiority. However, the concern for the state was the apparently rapidly growing population of 'mixed blood' children. These children became the target of intervention. Through permanent removal from their families and communities, it was believed that this group of children would, over generations, be biologically absorbed into the non-Indigenous population. Their Aboriginality would be 'bred' out. Legislation provided the foundation through which an administrative edifice would define Indigenous people as 'full blood', 'half caste', 'quarter caste' and so on (McCorquodale, 1986).

Long-term outcomes of Indigenous child removal

In Canada, the US and Australia, authorities saw the removal process as essential to eradicating Indigenous cultures. It is important to recognise the contemporary multiple effects of policies of child removal. The system in all three countries was characterised by 'denial of identity through attacks on language and spiritual beliefs, frequent lack of basic care, the failure to ensure safety of children from physical and sexual abuse, [and] the failure to ensure education' (RCAP, 1996b, p 187).

The US Brookings Institution report on Indian Residential Schools found that the schools were a 'menace to both health and education'. Malnutrition, 'grossly inadequate care', 'routine institutionalisation', and heavy labour by children were all documented (Meriam, 1928). The report found that the work by children in the boarding schools would violate child labour laws in most states (Meriam, 1928). The Committee on Labour and Public Welfare (1969) referred to Indian education as 'a national tragedy'. The Committee found 'serious deficiencies in guidance and counselling programs', an environment that was 'sterile, impersonal and rigid' with an emphasis on discipline and punishment, with teachers and administrators seeing their role as 'civilising the native'. Indian boarding schools were 'emotionally and culturally destructive' (Committee on Labour and Public Welfare, 1969, pp 100-3). Documented cases of sexual abuse at reservation schools continued until the end of the 1980s (Smith, 2004, 2007).

In Australia, a 1997 federal inquiry found that basic legal safeguards that protected non-Indigenous families were cast aside when it came to the removal of Indigenous children (NISATSIC, 1997). Practices included deprivation of liberty, deprivation of parental rights, abuses of power, and breach of guardianship duties. In relation to international human rights, the policy of forced removals breached prohibitions on racial discrimination and genocide (NISATSIC, 1997).

Various reports in Australia, Canada and the US have noted that the consequence of removal was a range of complex trauma-related psychological and psychiatric effects, many of which have been intergenerational. These include poorer educational, health and employment outcomes, domestic violence, greater likelihood of arrest, loss of parenting skills, unresolved grief and trauma, violence, depression, mental illness, and other behavioural problems including alcohol and other substance abuse (Hamilton and Sinclair, 1991; NISATSIC, 1997; Smith, 2004; TRCC, 2012a, 2012b).

Indigenous people have demanded recognition of the harm caused by the forced removals. It has been explicitly recognised through formal apologies in Canada and Australia. The US Congress apologised to Native Americans for the 'official depredations, ill-conceived policies … [and] for the many instances of violence, maltreatment and neglect' (Public Law 111-118, sec 8113). However, Congress did not refer to Indian residential schools. In Canada, the Indian Residential Schools Settlement Agreement was reached in 2006, with the federal government and the churches involved agreeing to pay individual and collective compensation to residential school survivors. A Truth and Reconciliation Commission was also established. In Australia, some states have introduced compensation schemes for 'stolen generation' members, although there has been no federal reparation package. In both the US and Australia, lawsuits filed by Indigenous people for abuse that occurred in institutions have met with only limited success.

Government fraud, Indigenous trust funds and forced labour

Colonial states were involved in vast frauds against Indigenous people who were under their care and protection. These included missing trust moneys, stolen wages, widespread corruption, mismanagement and bribery. The precondition for this fraudulent activity was the extensive state control over Indigenous people. State agents engaged in activities defined *at the time* as unlawful (such as breaches of fiduciary or guardianship duties), and in many cases were clearly criminal (acts of fraud).

In the US, fraud, corruption and bribery were endemic to the BIA. Local BIA officials had discretionary control over money, goods, trading licenses, and supplies provided by the Bureau. 'Substantial portions of the supplies and annuity payments owed to the tribes were routinely siphoned off by traders, in cooperation with corrupt federal Indian agents' (Piecuch and Lutz, 2011, p 384) and by the 1860s the BIA 'was rife with corruption' (Pierpaoli, 2011, p 101). Such corruption was acknowledged publicly at the time.[2] Over the next 100 years, various US House of Representatives and Congressional reports identified the defrauding and gross mismanagement of Indian trust funds arising from the Dawes Act 1887. After a protracted 13-year lawsuit in 2009 there was a $3.4 billion settlement to a class action relating to the mismanagement of hundreds of thousands of American Indian trust accounts (Riccardi, 2009; also Kidd, 2006, pp 28–35).

In Australia, governments put in place legislative and administrative controls over the employment, working conditions and wages of Indigenous workers – more in the interests of capital than protecting Indigenous people. For example, in 1901 in Queensland the Indigenous wage was set at less than one eighth the 'white wage'. Aboriginal workers could be jailed for up to five years for breach of employment contracts compared to a maximum of three months for non-Indigenous workers (Haebich, 2000, p 210). The 'regulation' of Aboriginal labour amounted to forced labour in some cases. Many Aboriginal workers in Western Australia were not paid wages and were primarily remunerated through rations such as flour, tea, tobacco and clothing – a practice still occurring in the 1960s. The exploitation of Aboriginal workers in the pastoral industry was often considered as 'unpaid slavery' at the time (Haebich, 1992, p 150). Australia was in contravention of various International Labour Organisation (ILO) conventions. For example, in 1930 Australia had signed the Forced Labour Convention, which prohibited working for rations.

Widespread negligent, corrupt and dishonest practices led to the withholding of moneys from Aboriginal wages paid into savings accounts and trust funds. Corruption by police 'protectors' and other state officials saw the diversion of Aboriginal money from trust funds into the pockets of the protectors (Kidd, 1997, 2000). A Senate Standing Committee [the Standing Committee] inquiry into Indigenous 'Stolen Wages' found 'compelling evidence that governments systematically withheld and mismanaged Indigenous wages and entitlements over decades … Indigenous people [were] underpaid or not paid at all for their work' (Standing Committee, 2006, p 4). In some cases, the practices were still in place in the 1980s. The Senate inquiry found that Indigenous people had been 'seriously disadvantaged by these practices across generations' (Standing Committee, 2006, p 4), and this created a cycle of poverty.

---

[2] See, for example, editorials in the *New York Times* on 12 December 1868 and 10 years later on 8 January 1878 describing extensive fraud in the BIA.

Given the depth of contemporary Indigenous detriment across all social, educational, health and economic indicators (SCRGSP, 2014), and the active role played by the state in controlling Aboriginal access to wages and entitlements, the outcome of this colonial process was one of *immiseration*. Contemporary problems of overcrowded housing, low incomes, chronic health issues, lower life expectancies, poor educational outcomes, child protection concerns – precisely the factors known to be associated with higher levels of violence and offending – can be related in various degrees to state control of Indigenous lives. The long-term impact of government policy in the realm of financial controls over Indigenous people has been devastating.

Civil rights and Indigenous resistance

The progressive developments associated with the rise of liberal democracy and the welfare state during the course of the late 19th and 20th centuries must be reconsidered against the backdrop of racially defined exclusionary practices that prevented Indigenous people from participation in and enjoyment of the social and political benefits of citizenship. Legislative controls and restrictions existed on movement, residence, education, healthcare, employment, voting, workers' compensation and welfare/social security entitlements. Indigenous organisations were to struggle for the recognition of civil rights throughout the 20th century. This struggle reflected the core conflict at the heart of the settler colonial states. As the Canadian Royal Commission on Aboriginal Peoples noted, this was 'the fundamental contradiction of building a modern liberal democracy upon the subversion of Aboriginal nations and at the expense of the cultural identity of Indigenous peoples' (RCAP, 1996b, p 607).

The expansion of formal citizenship rights was a slow process during the course of the 20th century:

- In Canada, The Indian Act 1951 removed some of the more overtly discriminatory aspects of the 1876 legislation. Some Indigenous cultural practices such as the potlatch ceremony were legalised, as well as prohibitions on raising money for political purposes and drinking alcohol in hotels (Fleras and Elliott, 1992, p 75). Indigenous people did not have the right to vote in federal elections until 1960. Prior to 1960 they could only vote if they gave up their Indian status.
- In the US, citizenship was not extended to all Indians until 1924, religious freedom did not extend to Indians until the 1930s, and the Indian Civil Rights Act was not passed until 1968.

- In Australia, Indigenous people were largely excluded from the right to social security: including old age, invalid and widow's pensions, child endowment and maternity allowances. These discriminatory restrictions were not completely lifted until 1966 and it was not until 1962 that Commonwealth amendments to electoral laws removed any remaining prohibitions on voting at the federal level (Chesterman and Galligan, 1997).

The resurgence and rise of the modern Indigenous political movement dates from the 1960s. An important point is that criminal justice issues, particularly the struggle against police brutality and imprisonment, were a core part of the catalyst for Indigenous political organisations during this period. Reform of policing and criminal justice was central to the movement for civil rights. In 1968, what was to become a leading national organisation, the American Indian Movement (AIM) was formed in Minneapolis. It established street patrols in Indigenous housing projects to address the problem of police violence, and established the Legal Rights Center to provide legal representation (Dunbar-Ortiz, 2014, pp 184-5). At the same time as AIM was establishing itself, another group of American Indians were engaged in the 19-month occupation of Alcatraz Island in San Francisco Bay. Alcatraz was a highly symbolic target. Many American Indians who resisted colonial expansion had been imprisoned there during the latter part of the 1800s. The occupiers' demands included a memorial as a 'reminder that the island had been established as a prison initially to incarcerate and execute California Indian resisters to the US assault on their nations' (Dunbar-Ortiz, 2014, p 184). Although their demands were not met, the Alcatraz occupation was important in highlighting to the broader American public the American Indian demands for self-determination.

In inner-city Sydney, Australian concern over police brutality and discriminatory arrests of Aboriginal people led to the establishment of the first Aboriginal Legal Service (ALS) in 1970. The ALS was from the beginning much broader than simply a legal service provider. It became a key advocacy organisation for Indigenous self-determination and human rights, and represented, according to one of the founding Aboriginal activists, 'the birth of the modern day Aboriginal political movement' (Foley, 1988, p 109).

The development of modern political Indigenous resistance in Canada can be marked by the Canadian federal government's *White Paper* on Indigenous rights. The 1969 *White Paper* firmed the government's position that it would not negotiate treaties with

Indigenous nations because this could only be undertaken between sovereign nations. A coalition of Indigenous leaders and organisations offered their own Indigenous policy statement, the *Red Paper*. The Red Paper challenged the government paper, and facilitated direct engagement between representatives of the federal government and Indigenous leaders (Cardinal, 1999). The White Paper/Red Paper incident directly contributed to the rise of the contemporary Canadian Indigenous rights movement, and related cultural revival (Ryser, 2012), with the formation of a number of national Aboriginal associations and separate provincial organisations being organised as a result (Clement, 2005). The rise of the Red Power movement, although evident before 1969, began to gather force from the early 1970s onwards, and resulted in numerous protests and occupations across all parts of Canada (Lannon, 2013).

At a political level, Indigenous organisations were fundamentally concerned with fighting for Indigenous sovereignty and self-determination. For example, in 1972 both AIM and the ALS were instrumental in establishing Indian and Aboriginal 'tent embassies' in Washington and Canberra, respectively, which were powerful symbols of Indigenous nationhood within the colonial states. In Aotearoa New Zealand, the growth in Māori activism in the 1970s centred around the reassertion of Māori identity and demands for civil rights and land. The reassertion of the fundamental importance of the Treaty of Waitangi represented the political declaration of Māori sovereignty (Poata-Smith, 1996).

As a response to Indigenous activism, the movement in government policy during the 1970s in Australia, Canada, Aotearoa New Zealand and the US was away from integration and assimilation. The US also changed it's approach of formally withdrawing federal recognition of Indian tribes (known as the policy of 'termination'). The policy frameworks in settler colonial states shifted to an official policy of Indigenous self-determination. However, 'self-determination' was to be defined by government, not by Indigenous nations. It gave rise to an emphasis on consultation, negotiation and partnerships, but in reality denoting 'nothing more than a federal promise that local [Indigenous] concerns and wishes will be considered in the design and implementation of [Indigenous] policies' (Fleras and Elliott, 1992, p 165). There was thus a substantial gap in the understanding of self-determination between government policy and the political demands of Indigenous organisations. These differing understandings of self-determination also played out in the criminal justice sphere, where Indigenous peoples increasingly argued for the recognition and autonomy of Indigenous law and justice, while government responses focused more on the *Indigenisation* of existing institutional processes and programmes.

Conclusion: defining crime in a colonial context

As many Australian, Canadian, Aotearoa New Zealand and US Indigenous people have noted over the decades: when the theft of the land, mass murder, genocide, dispossession, forced relocations and removals, government fraud and corruption, and racial discrimination are considered, then the answer to the questions of 'who is the criminal?' and 'what is justice?' take on a different meaning (for example Dodson, 1997b; Jackson, 1995; Ross, 1998; Tauri, 1998; Dunbar-Ortiz, 2014).

Developing an appreciation of colonialism within criminology has important ramifications for understanding Indigenous crime, punishment and over-representation in criminal justice systems. The processes of colonisation 'have *direct and immediate* relevance to both criminal behaviour and to processes of criminalisation' (Blagg, 2008, p16). Attempts by the state to eliminate, restructure and reconstitute Aboriginal identity in the interests of the coloniser form the core issue for many Indigenous people, rather than criminal offending *per se* (Blagg, 2008, p 3). It is not the case that Indigenous people are ignored in criminology – quite the contrary, they are the object of intense scrutiny and intervention. Criminologists produce and reproduce data on offending, policing and sentencing patterns comparing Indigenous and non-Indigenous people. However, Indigenous understanding and explanations for their own predicament with regard to colonial law and justice are often ignored.

The denial and attempted eradication of Indigenous laws underpinned the application and development of colonial criminal laws and penal systems aimed at the control of Indigenous peoples. A genealogy of crime and punishment in settler colonial societies must consider the links between criminal justice, punishment and race, or what has been referred to elsewhere as a penal/colonial complex (Cunneen et al, 2013; see also Davis, 1998; Pratt, 1992). Crime and punishment, in a variety of institutional forms, has been a central part of the operation of the colonial state in its governance of Indigenous peoples. Further, as argued in this chapter, the racialisation of punishment is fundamental to understanding the contemporary over-representation of Indigenous peoples in prison in settler colonial societies. Contemporary incarceration patterns follow a long historical trajectory of imprisoning Indigenous people in a variety of ways, including forts, boarding schools, orphanages, jails, prisons and on reservations (Ross, 1998, p 3). It is not surprising, then, that Native American academic Luana Ross writes: 'It is common for Native people either to have been incarcerated or to have relatives who have been imprisoned. Because we are a colonized people, the experiences of imprisonment are, unfortunately, exceedingly familiar' (Ross, 1998, p 1). Defining and understanding crime through the broader lens of colonisation enables a better appreciation of contemporary Indigenous priorities for reform and change within criminal justice systems. It also enables a more thoughtful consideration of Indigenous solutions to social disorder and dislocation which enhance Indigenous authority and lie outside state priorities of criminalisation.

FOUR

Policing, Indigenous peoples and social order

Indigenous political activism and civil rights struggles in the early 1970s were at least partially concerned with drawing attention to problems with state policing and the criminal justice system. These concerns were to take on an even more urgent focus in the 1980s, particularly in the context of a more punitive political approach to law and order (Clark and Cove, 1999; Cunneen, 2001).

Growing out of Indigenous political pressure, in the late 1980s and early 1990s both Canadian and Australian governments established judicial inquiries that either focused directly on, or substantially considered, the criminal justice system (and particularly police) treatment of Indigenous peoples. Included in this list is: the Australian Royal Commission into Aboriginal Deaths in Custody (RCADIC); the Canadian Royal Commission on Aboriginal Peoples (RCAP); the Nova Scotia Royal Commission on the Donald Marshall, Jr, Prosecution; and the Aboriginal Justice Inquiry of Manitoba (Hickman et al, 1989; Hamilton and Sinclair, 1991; Johnston, 1991; RCAP, 1996a, 1996b). In Aotearoa New Zealand, an important step in understanding the problematic relationship between Māori and the criminal justice system from a Māori perspective was a report to the Department of Justice by Moana Jackson (1988). In the US, while there were no similar judicial inquiries, the struggle around criminal justice and policing issues was galvanised through what many, including Amnesty International (n.d.), saw as the unjust conviction and imprisonment of Leonard Peltier for the murder of two FBI agents in 1975 (Matthiessen, 1992). Peltier, a member of the American Indian Movement, has been in federal prison for 39 years and remains there as at the beginning of 2016, despite a broad and ongoing campaign for his release. The policing of Indigenous people remains as divisive today as it has been in previous decades.

It is perhaps not surprising that state policing of Indigenous people is controversial, given that it is an activity deeply implicated within the wider historical trends of colonisation and nation building (Cunneen, 2001). As outlined in Chapter Three, the historical roots of policing in settler societies were embedded in colonial relations – from enforcing the laws of the coloniser, to acting as a 'civilising' force of assimilation. For example, in the US this involved various approaches, including the appointment of Indian constables to police American Indians, the development of police forces to protect settlers from American Indians and, in the south, many police forces evolving from their roots in slave patrols (Turner et al, 2006). In Canada, a primary reason for the formation of the North West Mounted Police (the forerunner of the Royal Canadian Mounted Police (RCMP)) in the 1870s was the control of the Indian and Métis population (Hamilton and Sinclair, 1991). In the Australian colonies, Indigenous resistance influenced the development of various police units, including border police, mounted police and native police forces (Cunneen, 2001, pp 48-9). Contemporary Indigenous concerns with police discrimination, racism and violence are partly formed from the histories of colonisation – a point forcefully argued in the reports of the RCADIC and RCAP (Johnston, 1991; RCAP, 1996a, 1996b) and one that contemporary police and criminal justice agencies often ignore.

The relationship between criminal justice institutions and Indigenous peoples has been forged within the context of a colonial political process and a colonial 'mentality'. Criminalisation played an important historical role in the processes of control outlined in the previous chapter. Contemporary criminalisation legitimates excessive policing, the use of state violence, the loss of liberty, and diminished social and economic participation. Criminalisation also permits an historical and political amnesia in relation to Indigenous rights. The political, social and cultural rights of Indigenous peoples are easily transformed into seeing racialised groups as a 'law and order' threat (Cunneen, 2005a). A major political impact arising from criminalisation is that it removes the political status of Indigenous people as First Peoples, and denies the validity of Indigenous methods of governance and social control. In place of this inherent political status, Indigenous people are both racialised and criminalised. 'Race' becomes conflated with criminality, and the political right of Indigenous people to control their own lives as legal subjects disappears. It is not surprising, then, that Indigenous political claims to self-determination often focus on criminal justice (see Jackson, 1988), and are thus directly linked to a process of decolonisation: decolonisation of criminal justice institutions and a decolonisation of the discursive construction of Indigenous people as 'criminal'.

During the latter half of the 20th century, overtly discriminatory legislation that denied active citizenship to Indigenous people was replaced by a formal recognition of equality. This transformation has particular ramifications for understanding policing. Full citizenship rights for Indigenous people implied at the very least the application of the principle of equality before the law, with the right to be treated in a non-discriminatory manner. Thus, contemporary policing is different from colonial policing in one important respect: the appeal to the formal 'racially neutral' character of modern policing differentiates it from previous periods of direct involvement in racially discriminatory colonial policies (Cunneen, 2001). Yet there are also the ongoing processes of 'deep colonising' (Rose, 1996). Although the formal relations between Indigenous people and the colonial state changed, colonising practices were still deeply embedded within institutions. This notion of 'deep colonising' resonates with the concept of the 'coloniality of power' developed by Quijano (1999, 2007), who draws attention to the way in which colonial relations are reproduced in the contemporary world through various institutional processes. We see policing and the criminal justice system as fundamental to this process of reproducing Indigenous people as a colonised *and* criminalised group within settler colonial states.

Problems with policing and criminalisation in Indigenous communities were well documented in the inquiries in Canada, Australia and Aotearoa New Zealand noted earlier. Of further importance, all the inquiries (except the Marshall Royal Commission) emphasised the central role of Indigenous self-determination (Clark and Cove, 1999; Cunneen, 2001). For example, the RCADIC (in recommendation 188) required:

> That Governments negotiate with appropriate Aboriginal organisations and communities to determine guidelines as to the procedures and processes which should be followed to ensure that the self determination principle is applied in the design and implementation of any policy or program or the substantial modification of any policy or program which will particularly affect Aboriginal people. (Johnston, 1991, vol 5, p 111)

This recommendation encompassed the philosophical and political basis of action to implement all the RCADIC recommendations. The Manitoba Inquiry recommended that 'federal and provincial governments recognise the right of aboriginal people to establish their own justice systems as part of their inherent right to self-government' (Hamilton and Sinclair, 1991, p 266). The RCAP made similar recommendations in relation to self-determination (RCAP, 1996a, pp 54-76). In addition, all the inquiries mentioned earlier were concerned with systemic discrimination and/or institutional racism in the treatment of Indigenous people by the criminal justice system. The Manitoba Inquiry noted that:

> The justice system has failed Manitoba's Aboriginal people on a massive scale. It has been insensitive and inaccessible, and has arrested and imprisoned Aboriginal people in grossly disproportionate numbers. Aboriginal people who are arrested are more likely than non-Aboriginal people to be denied bail, spend more time in pre-trial detention and spend less time with their lawyers, and, if convicted, are more likely to be incarcerated. (Hamilton and Sinclair, 1991, p 1)

The question of racism in the criminal justice system was fundamental to the Australian RCADIC: racism is 'institutionalised and systemic, and resides not just in individuals or in individual institutions, but in the relationship between the various institutions' (Johnston, 1991, vol 4, p 124). Institutional racism is defined as 'an institution, having significant dealings with Aboriginal people, which has rules, practices, habits which systematically discriminate against or in some way disadvantage Aboriginal people' (Johnston, 1991, vol 2, p 161). The concept of institutional racism provides the broad framework for the discussion on state policing that follows, starting with consideration of the use of discretion.

The adverse use of police discretion

Policing and the criminal law play a large part in Indigenous people's lives. The Law Reform Commission of Western Australia (2006, p 192) found that 'historically Aboriginal people have been subject to oppressive treatment by police. As a consequence, Aboriginal people often distrust and resent police officers.' During the Commission's consultations, many Aboriginal people complained about: their treatment by police; lack of respect by police for Aboriginal people and their Elders and community leaders; poor treatment by police of young Aboriginal people; and lack of sensitivity by police towards Aboriginal victims and lack of appropriate support for victims of family violence. 'Many Aboriginal people believed there was extensive racism within the police service' (Law Reform Commission of Western Australia, 2006, p 192).

One of the key issues in relation to the policing of Indigenous people is the exercise of police discretionary powers. There is a significant body of research that shows the adverse use of police discretion in relation to Indigenous people. As Brown et al (2015, p 259) note, the 'criminal process is riven with discretion at every stage'. The use of discretionary powers is significant for a number of reasons. First, the use of discretion determines the pathway into and through the criminal justice system, affecting for example an individual's criminal record, access to diversionary options and likelihood of imprisonment. Second, the experiences of arrest, detention, bail and pre-trial custody are in themselves a form of punishment, of 'summary justice'.

Police decisions to stop and search

The use of police 'stop and search' powers offers wide discretionary power to police. The inappropriate use of these powers against Indigenous people is a major concern. In the US and Canada, the concerns are often expressed as the *racial profiling* of Indigenous people, which we see as one form of institutional racism:

> Indigenous Peoples refer to 'DWI' or 'Driving While Indian' and often complain about stops and searches by police and sheriffs on roads leading to and from reservations. In South Dakota, widespread reports of racial profiling led to hearings before the state legislature, where Indians testified about their being stopped and searched not only based on race, but also on religious articles hanging from rearview mirrors and regional license plates that identified them as living on reservations. (International Indian Treaty Council, 2014, p 5)

In Canada, the Ontario Human Rights Commission (2004), in its report on racial profiling, detailed the negative impact of racial profiling and racism by police on Aboriginal communities. And in Aotearoa New Zealand, qualitative research found that Māori believed that police 'disproportionately targeted Māori youth for stop and search procedures without just cause' and that police 'harass Māori in an attempt to provoke retaliation in order to justify an arrest when no other rationale for arrest is apparent' (Morrison, 2009, p 36).

In Australia, an example of adverse police discretion in the use of stop and search powers arises with police powers to search for prohibited implements (such as knives) being carried in public. The NSW

Ombudsman found that the majority of all stop and searches were for young people aged 19 years or younger (New South Wales Office of the Ombudsman, 1999, p 128). Further evaluation showed stop and search powers were used far more frequently in Aboriginal areas of the State. In some towns with large Aboriginal populations, between 90% and 95% of the stop and searches were 'unsuccessful' (Chan and Cunneen, 2000, p 39), showing that police were not forming a reasonable suspicion that the individual was carrying a prohibited implement. Police were clearly using the legislation to target young people, and in particular Indigenous young people, in public places.

Police use of move-on powers

Police use of move-on powers and, depending on the state legislation, offences relating to homelessness (sleeping in public places, loitering and vagrancy) have also been problematic for Indigenous people. The Law Reform Commission of Western Australia (2006, p 206) found that:

> Move-on notices are being issued to Aboriginal people in inappropriate circumstances and Aboriginal people are being disproportionately affected by this law. It appears that in some cases Aboriginal people are being targeted by the police for congregating in large groups in public areas even though no one is doing anything wrong ... The Commission is very concerned about the apparent discriminatory treatment of Aboriginal people with respect to move-on notices ... there is a large scope for misuse of police discretion.

In New South Wales, 22% of people given move-on directions were Indigenous people (who comprise approximately 2.2% of the State's total population) (New South Wales Office of the Ombudsman, 1999, p 128). Use of the legislation in areas with large Aboriginal populations showed move-on orders issued at a rate 30 times higher than the State average (Chan and Cunneen, 2000, p 230).

Public order offences

The use of public order offences remains among the most contentious issues in the policing of Indigenous people. In Aotearoa New Zealand, qualitative research revealed Māori perceptions that police were more likely to be deployed in areas where Māori congregated, and they were subject to large-scale police operations as a result (Morrison, 2009, p 36). This form of 'over-policing' becomes particularly apparent when Indigenous people assert their rights. In this context, examples of the escalation of police responses against Aboriginal people can be seen in Canada at Oka (1990) and at Ipperwash (1995), when people asserted their rights over land and resources. In these cases, the affirmation of rights became politically transformed by the state into a policing problem of maintaining public order, with the use of riot police, tactical units and (at Oka) the military (Linden, 2007).

In Australia, despite the decriminalisation of public drunkenness in most jurisdictions, many Indigenous people still come into contact with the criminal justice system because of the public consumption of alcohol. In part these problems are related to the use of 'protective detention', the use of local council or state laws prohibiting alcohol consumption and other restrictions (for example, the Northern Territory's law prohibiting public alcohol consumption within 2 kilometres of licensed premises, and Queensland's alcohol management plans). Some alcohol restrictions only apply to Indigenous people or Indigenous communities. For example, alcohol management plans restrict possession and consumption of alcohol in designated Indigenous communities. Criminal penalties, including imprisonment, apply for breaches of the legislation (Behrendt et al, 2009).

As Rudin (2007, p 35) notes, in Canada, 'the targeting of Aboriginal people for arrest under drunk in public laws might seem like a minor inconvenience, but the reality is that it continues to serve to put Aboriginal people in jail'. Like Australia, some provinces in Canada (such as Ontario) use protective detention to detain people who are intoxicated into police custody. Rudin (2007, p 35) argues that, 'the reality of the exercise of this form of police discretion has been to disproportionately target Aboriginal people'. In both Australia and Canada a number of Aboriginal people have died in police custody while being held in preventive detention. We return later to the issue of deaths in custody.

Public order offences of offensive language and offensive behaviour are also commonly used against Indigenous people. For example, in Queensland, Australia, they are the second most common reason for an Indigenous young person to appear before a juvenile court (Cunneen et al, 2015, p 152). As Brown et al (2015, p 518) note, 'such provisions are inevitably open-ended, with the characterisation of the behaviour left to the discretion of the police in the first instance, and subsequently to the discretion of magistrates'. Extensive research has shown that

Aboriginal people are significantly over-represented in prosecutions for these types of offences (Brown et al, 2015, pp 537-9). Aboriginal people charged with offensive language or offensive conduct are also often charged with other offences. As the RCADIC noted:

> Too often the attempt to arrest or charge an Aboriginal for offensive language sets in train a sequence of offences by that person and others—resisting arrest, assaulting police, hindering police and so on, none of which would have occurred if police were not so easily 'offended'. (Wootten, 1991, pp 144-5)

Juvenile diversion and police discretion

Police are less likely to divert Indigenous youth away from formal court processing. For example, in Aotearoa New Zealand there are disparities affecting Māori youth whereby they are less likely to receive a diversionary option rather than court, and are less likely to be referred to a family group conference than non-Māori youth (Morrison, 2009, p 42).

In Australia, various studies have found that Indigenous young people do not receive the benefit of a diversionary police caution to the same extent as non-Indigenous youth (Cunneen et al, 2015, pp 154-5). Similarly, the evidence suggests that Indigenous young people are not referred as frequently to restorative justice youth conferences as non-Indigenous youth (Cunneen et al, 2015, p 157). Yet a key rationale for the introduction of restorative justice youth conferencing in both Aotearoa New Zealand and Australia was to provide a more culturally sensitive method of responding to offending by Indigenous youth (Morris and Maxwell, 1993; Consedine, 1995; see also Cleland and Quince, 2014, pp 173-80).

Use of arrest v summons

In addition to making decisions as to whether to divert young people out of the juvenile justice system, police also make decisions about whether to process an alleged offender by way of arrest and charge, or to proceed by way of a summons to appear in court (or some other form of court attendance notice). The use of a summons is a less punitive way of bringing a person (adult or juvenile) before the court on a criminal charge, than proceeding by way of arrest. Unlike proceeding by way of arrest, a summons does not normally involve being held in custody or the need to make a bail determination.

In Canada, evidence suggests that Aboriginal youth are 20% more likely to be charged when apprehended than non-Aboriginal youth (Hogeveen, 2005, p 296). Similarly, in many Australian states, Indigenous young people are more likely to be proceeded against by way of arrest and bail, and to be held in police custody, and are less likely to be summonsed to court than non-Indigenous youth. For example in Queensland, the majority of Indigenous young people charged with an offence were proceeded against by way of arrest. For non-Indigenous youth the majority were proceeded against by way of a notice to appear in court (Cunneen et al, 2015, p 155). Similar evidence in differential treatment is also apparent in relation to Indigenous adults (Behrendt et al, 2009, p 121).

Research suggests that courts are more likely to impose custodial sentences on people brought before them by way of arrest, than on the basis of a summons or court attendance notice, even when the seriousness of the charge and the criminal history of the defendant is taken into account. This may be because the process itself influences the court's view of the seriousness of the matter and the nature of the offender. It can also be because once arrested and remanded, defendants may feel pressured to plead guilty, or because of the limited ability to prepare for court appearances that being arrested and remanded in custody places on defendants (Cunneen et al, 2015, p 155). The UN Convention on the Rights of the Child requires that arrest be used as a measure of last resort when deciding to commence criminal proceedings (Article 37 (b)). The problem for Indigenous people is that police tend to use arrest for minor offences involving Indigenous people, and they use it more frequently than they do with non-Indigenous people. The long-term result is to further entrench Indigenous people within the criminal justice system.

Problems with meeting bail conditions and with pre-trial detention

The purpose of bail is to ensure that the defendant will appear in court to face charges, and to protect any victim and/or the community from further offences. The need to determine bail arises after the person has been arrested and charged with a criminal offence. Bail does not arise when a person is proceeded against by way of a summons or court attendance notice. Therefore, because Indigenous people are more likely to be proceeded against by way of arrest, they are more likely to face a bail determination. Two issues are important: first, whether bail will be refused and the person held in custody; and second, if bail is granted, which conditions, if any, will be attached.

In both Canada and Australia, there is some evidence to suggest that Indigenous people are more likely than non-Indigenous people to be refused bail by police or are unable to meet bail conditions (Hamilton and Sinclair, 1991, p 86; Hogeveen, 2005, p 296; Rudin, 2007, pp 53-4; Cunneen et al, 2015, p 155). Aboriginal juveniles in both Canada and Australia are also likely to spend more time in pre-trial detention than non-Aboriginal youth (Hogeveen, 2005, p 296; Cunneen, 2014a). The second issue of importance concerning bail is the nature of the conditions that are imposed when bail is granted. Onerous and oppressive bail conditions may be imposed and then regularly broken. The result is that people are recycled through the courts and prisons. These requirements include curfews, residential requirements, non-association orders or, in the case of juveniles, remaining in the company of their parents when in public. Other reasons why Indigenous people may not be able to meet bail conditions, include (Behrendt et al, 2009, p 122):

- an inability to attend court because of a lack of available transport;
- communication barriers between Aboriginal defendants and their legal representatives;
- a lack of understanding of bail process;
- unemployment and poverty;
- physical or mental disability;
- prior offending histories.

Police use of force and racist violence

The use of excessive force where it is based on the perceived racial characteristics of individuals is indicative of racial profiling and institutional racism. In Canada, the Ontario Human Rights Commission (2004, p 58) detailed the use of violence and racial slurs by police against Aboriginal people: 'concerns regarding the entire criminal justice system's treatment of Aboriginal youth was a recurring theme in the submissions received by the Commission ... there seemed to be a particular sensitivity to how police treat them'.

In Australia, the 1991 National Inquiry into Racist Violence found that racist violence against Indigenous people was endemic, nationwide and very severe. Many of the complaints from Indigenous people involved treatment by police. The Race Discrimination Commissioner found that: 'Aboriginal-police relations have never been good, but they have now reached a critical point due to widespread police involvement, in acts of racist violence, intimidation and harassment' (Moss, 1991, p 5).

Deaths in police custody

The problems of the adverse use of police discretion and institutional racism show their most controversial effects in cases of Indigenous deaths in police custody. A review of deaths in police custody in Aotearoa New Zealand in the period 2000-10 found that almost half the deaths involved Māori (IPCA, 2012, p 3). Thirty per cent of Māori deaths occurred while being restrained by police, which was three times higher than the proportion of European deaths (IPCA, 2012, p 29).

Many Indigenous deaths in police custody arise from people being locked up for minor offences. For example, 22-year-old Ms Dhu died in police custody in 2014 in a Western Australian police lock-up after being arrested for unpaid fines. Kwementyaye Briscoe, 28, died after being taken into Northern Territory (NT) police protective custody in 2012 for being drunk. In 2015, an Aboriginal man died in NT police custody after being locked up for minor alcohol-related offences; the death occurred after new laws were introduced to provide police with powers to detain people for four hours for minor offences that would have normally only attracted a monetary fine.

In discussing the deaths of Aboriginal people held in custody for being 'drunk in public' in Ontario, Rudin (2007, p 35) notes that, 'what makes this process even more objectionable is that there is no reason to believe that placing a person who is very drunk in jail for a period of time to "sleep it off" will actually prevent harm coming to the person'. As argued elsewhere (Cunneen, 2009), many Indigenous deaths in custody arise through a failure to exercise a required duty of care. This failure represents the 'violence of neglect' found in the *inaction* of authorities who have specific responsibilities and duties towards people held in custody. The Australian RCADIC found that there was a significant failure by custodial authorities to exercise a proper duty of care for Indigenous people. The Commission found that there was little understanding of the duty of care owed by custodial authorities, and that in some cases, the failure to offer proper care directly contributed to or caused deaths in custody.

Not all deaths in police custody arise from an absence of duty of care; some appear deliberate. The so-called 'Saskatoon freezing deaths' (in Saskatchewan, Canada) during the 1990s and early 2000s arose from the practice of members of the Saskatoon police arresting Aboriginal people for minor public order offences, driving them out of the city and abandoning them during winter months. A number of victims died from hypothermia. In one case, the victim (Darrel Night) was able to survive. Two police officers were convicted as a result (Wright, 2004, p 1). There was a judicial inquiry into one of the deaths (17-year-old Neil Stonechild), more than a decade after his death had occurred. The Inquiry found that the initial police investigation was 'superficial and totally inadequate' (Wright, 2004, p 212).

The sense of injustice generated by Indigenous deaths in custody has led to serious anti-police riots and protests on a number of occasions. One case from Australia illustrates the point. In 2004, Cameron Doomadgee died in police custody on Palm Island. He had been arrested for a minor public order offence. He was healthy man when arrested. A protest riot occurred after Doomadgee's death, when post-mortem results revealed that he had been violently assaulted, suffering four broken ribs, a ruptured spleen and his liver almost cleaved in two. During the protest, the local police station was extensively damaged and the courthouse was burnt to the ground (Cunneen, 2007a, pp 26-8 and see also pp 24-6 on the Redfern riot after the death of TJ Hickey).

In many respects, Indigenous deaths in custody encapsulate the historical and contemporary problems of Indigenous/police relations:

- the histories of colonial violence that seem to be reproduced through contemporary policing tactics;
- the adverse use of discretion, which sees Indigenous people locked-up in police cells for minor offences;
- the failure to exercise a basic duty of care towards people held in custody;
- the breakdown in Indigenous/police relations which bursts onto the public stage through riots and protests.

Under-policing and violence against women

In what appears at first to contradict the argument thus far – that Indigenous people experience policing as one characterised by heightened surveillance – the phenomenon of under-policing in Indigenous communities has been widely commented upon since the 1990s (see, for example, RCAP, 1996a, p 88). It refers to the lack of response to issues affecting Indigenous communities where law enforcement or legal assistance is required.

How this problem plays out varies to some extent depending on the jurisdiction. For example, the complicated system of policing in

Indian country in the US adds to the problem of under-policing. The International Indian Treaty Council (2007, p 28) has noted:

> For Indian communities, criminal jurisdiction is exercised by three separate governmental systems – federal, state and tribal. To determine which law enforcement agency has the power to respond, one must complete the following analysis: Did the crime occur in Indian Country? Is the victim Indian or non-Indian? Is the offender Indian or non-Indian? What is the nature of the crime? This analysis can be quite confusing and often victims of crimes are unsure as to which authority – tribal, federal, or state – to call for help. It can also be confusing to the authorities investigating a crime. As a result, many Indian victims of crimes in Indian country are left without access to justice.

Under-policing is exacerbated by: the failure to adequately fund tribal justice systems; the sporadic and inconsistent investigation and prosecution by state and federal law enforcement (where applicable) on Indian country; and the particular problems of (interracial) violence and violence against women in urban areas and border towns adjacent to Indian reservations (Perry, 2008, 2009a; National Indian Youth Council, 2013, pp 8-10). One area where under-policing occurs is with hate crimes. Perry (2008) found that in the US only 10% of hate crimes were reported to police. She found that the low reporting was the result of the historical and contemporary experiences with police and the view that police do not take American Indian victimisation seriously.

The problem of under-policing has also been noted in Canada, where Aboriginal people are often seen as 'less worthy' victims by police. Requests for assistance are 'often ignored or downplayed' and 'crimes against them are not investigated as thoroughly or prosecuted as vigorously' (Rudin, 2007, pp 1, 36). The Ontario Human Rights Commission (2004, p 57) noted from its discussions with Aboriginal people that, 'frequently, [they] talked about the uselessness of making complaints to police, human rights commissions or other complaint mechanisms because they would not be taken seriously or, worse yet, would be treated like suspects'.

Perhaps the greatest problem with under-policing identified in all the settler colonial states has been the failure to provide protection for Indigenous women who are victims of violence. The UN Committee on the Elimination of Racial Discrimination (CERD, 2008, 2014) has frequently expressed concern about the incidence of rape and sexual violence against American Indian and Alaska Native women, the insufficient will of federal and state authorities to take action, and in particular the need to ensure Indigenous women's right of access to justice (CERD, 2008, 2014). The National Congress of American Indians (2014, p 2) has noted that 'violence against Indian and Alaska Native women is at epidemic proportions and is one of the most horrific manifestations of the discriminatory legal system in the United States'. One problem arises from prohibitions on tribal police and courts from prosecuting non-Native offenders who commit violent crimes against Indigenous women. Although this changed with the Violence Against Women Reauthorization Act 2013, which restored limited authority to tribal justice systems, there are still many restrictions, particularly for Alaska Natives who are almost totally excluded from the new protections (National Congress of American Indians, 2014, p 3).

The reality of under-policing for Aboriginal women in both Australia and Canada has been highlighted in several reports. In Australia, inadequate police responses to Indigenous women who are victims of violence have the result that women are reluctant to seek assistance from police (Cunneen, 2001; ATSISJC, 2006). Amnesty International Canada (2004), highlighting nine cases of disappearances of Aboriginal women, found that 'many Indigenous families [stated] that police did little when they reported a sister or daughter missing' and that 'police in Canada have often failed to provide Indigenous women with an adequate standard of protection' (Amnesty International Canada, 2004, pp 2, 19). Nine years later, Human Rights Watch (2013) found both abusive policing practices against Indigenous women and girls in Canada, and police failures to either protect Indigenous women and girls in cases of domestic violence and sexual assault, and/or failures to properly investigate disappearances and murders. Abusive police practices included the use of excessive force, assaults, inappropriate use of police dogs, pepper spray and tasers, and rape and sexual assault by police officers (Human Rights Watch, 2013, pp 50-65). Indigenous women did not feel safe approaching the RCMP:

> Police abuse undermines women and girls' safety far beyond the direct physical consequences of any physical mistreatment. The impact is felt in the reticence of Indigenous women and girls to call the police for help when they fear or have experienced violence. (Human Rights Watch, 2013, p 66)

The aptly named Highway of Tears in northern British Columbia alone has an estimated 40 unsolved cases of missing and murdered Indigenous women (Human Rights Watch, 2013, p 67). More broadly, a report by the RCMP (2014, p 7) found that over a 30-year period, there were 1,181 police-reported incidents of Indigenous female homicide victims and unresolved missing Aboriginal female investigations. This number included 225 unsolved cases of either missing or murdered Indigenous women (RCMP, 2014, p 7).

UN human rights committees have also been critical of Canada's approach to protecting Indigenous women, who remain 'disproportionately victims of life-threatening forms of violence,' spousal homicides and disappearances' (CERD, 2012, p 5). The Committee for the Elimination of Discrimination against Women (CEDAW) found a 'grave violation' of the rights of Aboriginal women through insufficient and inadequate measures to protect Aboriginal women from gender-based violence, including disappearances and murders (CEDAW, 2015a, p 47). CEDAW recommended, inter alia, a national public inquiry into the cases of missing and murdered Aboriginal women and girls (CEDAW, 2015a, p 51). At the time, the Canadian government rejected both CEDAW's findings and the need for a national inquiry (CEDAW, 2015b, p 24). In late 2015, the new Canadian Liberal government announced that an inquiry would proceed.

Repeatedly, critical and Indigenous writers have highlighted that the pressing priority in any campaign against violence in Indigenous communities, and specifically violence against Indigenous women, is the implementation and resourcing of many more Indigenous controlled-programmes and mechanisms, and the importance of the principle of Indigenous self-determination. (For example, in the Australian context, see Memmott et al, 2001; Blagg, 2000, 2008; ATSISJC, 2011.) We return to the specific issue of the gendered aspects of colonialism and violence in Chapter Five.

Indigenous community policing

While, as noted earlier, Indigenous activism has been fundamental to challenging the way state police operate, it has also been at the forefront of developing various modes of Indigenous community policing. Indigenous communities have a right to security, and some form of policing is required to legitimately support, ensure and maintain community safety and harmony. While Aboriginal people deserve the same level of community safety as other people, as Blagg (2008, p 91) notes: 'what remains an issue is the way this security is provided: how it is structured and administered; how it is embedded culturally; how, and to whom, it is made open and accountable'.

Indigenous approaches to policing have developed in the vacuum left by ineffective state police who have failed to provide safe communities and are often seen as oppressive. Developing and extending Indigenous policing has become an important part of Indigenous governance and capacity-building. Having said that, developments in Indigenous policing under the financial, legal or regulatory supervision of external state authorities have been fraught with difficulties.

Community police

Indigenous community police have a long history in the various settler colonial states dating back to at least the 19th century, when they were often used in the interests of colonial powers. More contemporary developments, essentially from the 1960s and 1970s, in Indigenous community police and US tribal police have been founded on the principle that community police should be responsible to Indigenous communities – that is, they developed alongside Indigenous demands for sovereignty and self-determination. However, as noted later in this chapter, there have been common problems faced by Indigenous community police across the settler colonial societies.

In Canada, local policing on First Nations reservations has been occurring for decades in various forms. Lithopoulos (2007) describes several models under the First Nations Policing Policy. These involve First Nations self-administered police services, where 'the First Nation develops, manages and administers its own police service' (Lithopoulos, 2007, p 6). Other models include Aboriginal RCMP officers, and RCMP Aboriginal community constables. Evaluations of Aboriginal policing programmes show conflicting results. According to Lithopoulos (2007, p 8), two surveys in Quebec and Six Nations of the Grand River (the largest First Nations reserve in Canada comprised of six Iroquois nations) showed similar levels of community satisfaction with police to that which existed in the broader Canadian population. Other surveys have shown that First Nations people living on reserves do not rate their police service's performance very highly. In addition, there are problems of Aboriginal policing initiatives being under-funded and treated as 'pilot projects', with all the uncertainty that this involves (RCAP, 1996a, p 86).

A system of community police in Aotearoa New Zealand is the Māori warden scheme, which has been in place since the 19th century.

Their responsibilities are established under the Māori Community Development Act 1962. Māori wardens are not police as such; they are volunteers who provide a broad range of services – from tackling school truancy to assisting with community patrols and providing support at various cultural and sporting events. They are responsible to Māori councils. The right of Māori councils to control their institutions, including the Māori warden scheme, was upheld in 2014 by the Waitangi Tribunal. The Māori Community Development Act 1962 provides 'statutory recognition and powers to institutions established by the Māori people for their own self-government' (Waitangi Tribunal, 2014, p xvi). Māori self-government and self-determination are reflected in the legislation. The Tribunal found that, as community volunteers, 'Māori Wardens are called to respond to whatever the most immediate and pressing needs of their communities may be. [The] work that Māori Wardens perform can vary greatly between different areas, and even within a single district' (Waitangi Tribunal, 2014, p 292).

In Australia, there are various examples of Indigenous community police. For instance in Queensland there has been a long history of Indigenous community police on the former reserves. In general, the community police exercise powers conferred on them through legislation that enables community councils to pass by-laws for the maintenance of peace and good order. Community police exercise their jurisdiction within the local by-laws and exercise their powers subject to the direction and control of the state police (Cunneen, 2001, p 219). Over the years, various problems have been identified with the role and functions of community police:

- First, Aboriginal community police can lawfully exercise only very limited powers of arrest. They do not have the same powers as the state police in the same community.
- Second, the community police are under the direct supervision of the state police, rather than the elected Indigenous council, representing a lack of community control over community police. Although under the direct supervision of state police, the supervision itself has been consistently found to be inadequate. At times, community police have been given a substantial range of responsibilities without proper training – in some cases, inadequate training and poor supervision have directly contributed to deaths in custody.
- Third, employment conditions have resulted in poor remuneration and, in some cases, employment on a 'work for the dole' basis (Cunneen, 2001, pp 219-21).

US tribal police

At the outset it is important to recognise that, although 40% of all federally recognised tribes in the US are Alaska Native, Indigenous people in Alaska do not have the same jurisdictional rights as American Indians. Criminal jurisdiction in Alaska is exercised exclusively by the state, with police and judicial services to many of the remote 229 recognised tribes being provided from regional centres. According to the Indian Law and Order Commission (2013, p xiii), this approach has led to severe problems with safety and 'to a dramatic under-provision of criminal justice services in rural and Native regions'. The unique legal and political relationship between tribal nations and the US government also does not extend to Native Hawaiians. Therefore the following discussion on tribal police is focused on American Indian jurisdiction.

We noted in Chapter One the 'jurisdictional maze' that exists on Indian country in the US. Jurisdictional problems impact on the role of tribal police particularly, as we note later in this chapter, in Indian nations subject to Public Law 83-280. More generally, the International Indian Treaty Council (2007, p 27) found that, 'the present criminal jurisdictional scheme in Indian country represents a major intrusion by the federal government onto the self-government powers of Indian nations, impeding Indian nations' abilities to properly protect their citizens'. There are 178 tribal law enforcement agencies. Some 157 of these agencies are general-purpose police departments, and the remainder are special jurisdiction agencies responsible for enforcing natural resources laws (Bureau of Justice Statistics, 2015). They ranged in size from two or three officers to several hundred officers (Wakeling et al, 2001, p 4).

The largest tribal police service is the Navajo Nation Police, established in 1936. It has its own training academy and is closely tied with the broader aims of the distinctively Navajo justice system (see Chapter Six). Luna-Firebaugh (2007) argues that tribal police are an important reflection of tribal sovereignty and self-determination rights: 'A tribal police department, if nothing else, serves as a declaration of sovereignty, of the intent of a tribal government to protect and serve its own citizens, and to render justice' (Luna-Firebaugh, 2007, p 8).

Luna-Firebaugh (2007) and Perry (2009b) note that the problems with tribal police departments (a lack of adequate funds, understaffing, low pay and poor standards of training) make it difficult to address crime and victimisation. More recently, the Indian Law and Order Commission (2013, p 67) estimated a 50% staffing shortfall for tribal police on Indian country, resulting in the 'vast majority of law enforcement and public safety departments in Indian country [being unable] to implement the strategies they know will work'.

The problem is even more exacerbated in areas where Indian nations are subject to Public Law 83-280. Federal investment in tribal justice systems has been limited, and state governments have not been forthcoming with assistance. The Indian Law and Order Commission (2013, p 69) found that:

> Particularly in remote, rural areas, calls for service go answered, victims are left unattended, criminals are undeterred, and Tribal governments are left stranded with high-crime environments ... To the extent that States and localities do provide law enforcement, witnesses testified that there was deep distrust between local non-Indian law enforcement and these Tribal communities, which is evidenced by frequent conflicts, communication failures and disrespectful actions.

Contractual issues in federal funding for tribal police also inhibit tribal self-determination. Federal policies and rules over a range of administrative, legal and financial matters limit the possibilities in developing distinctly Indigenous policing (Barker, 1998, p 29). Perry (2009b, p 102) found that even where there were tribally defined protocols, 'these are in addition to rather than instead of US state and federal codes'. Thus it remains highly variable between tribal governments, and debatable overall, whether tribal policing amounts 'to an autonomous system of social control' (Perry, 2009b, p 102).

Night patrols

One of the key developments in Indigenous self-policing in Australia has been the use of 'night patrols', beginning in the NT in the 1980s and then subsequently extending to most states of Australia. They are operated by Indigenous people at the local community level and work in a variety of settings including urban, rural and remote areas. They focus on assisting people in need and maintaining social order, and receive varied levels of support from state and federal governments.

Priorities for the night patrols are largely set by local Indigenous need; for example, in some areas the focus may be on young people, while in other communities it may be homelessness, or problems with alcohol-related violence. Night patrols are involved in truancy programmes and school breakfast programmes, and transporting people to places such as sobering-up shelters, safe houses, women's refuges, men's places, clinics, hostels, family healing and justice groups (Blagg and Anthony, 2014, p 109; Porter, 2014). Blagg (2008, pp 107-25) describes the services of night patrols as including:

- dispute resolution;
- removal from danger;
- safe transportation;
- connecting people to services;
- prevention of family violence;
- assistance and interventions around homelessness, alcohol and substance misuse and anti-social behaviour;
- keeping the peace at events such as sports carnivals;
- diversion from contact with the criminal justice system.

Night patrols operate through Indigenous cultural authority. Patrols, unlike state police, do not rely on the use or threat of force. Nor do they rely on the authority of Western law. Significantly, Indigenous women have played a substantial role in developing and operating night patrols, and took the initiative in establishing some of the first night patrols in the NT. About 50% of people working in night patrols are women. Blagg (2008, p 114) suggests that, perhaps as a consequence of this involvement, patrols report 'seeing their work in terms of mediation and persuasion rather than force, and fulfilling a preventative/welfare role, rather than a reactive/controlling one'.

Night patrols represent a different vision of policing: external state authority is replaced by local cultural authority; bureaucratised state-centred methods of crime control are replaced by an organic approach to community needs which focuses on assistance and prevention rather than the use of force. Indeed Porter's (2014; and in press) observational study of night patrols in NSW suggests that they are a form of counter-policing.

Conclusion

Policing and the exercise of criminal jurisdiction are inevitably bound up with issues of Indigenous sovereignty, and the right to self-determination. Two decades ago, the Canadian RCAP (1996a, pp 91-2) confirmed the link between the development of Indigenous policing and self-government. A widespread view among Indigenous peoples is that Indigenous sovereignty has never been extinguished: sovereignty continues to be exercised by Indigenous communities, despite the formal declarations of settler colonial law. Ultimately these claims rest on Indigenous pre-existing rights to self-government and contemporary rights to self-determination. Such claims have profound implications for the *right* to police, to enforce law and to maintain order in Indigenous communities.

Developing a new interface between policing and Indigenous people within a context of self-determination is both a theoretical and a practical task. There is no single blueprint for operationalising self-determination in the area of policing and community justice. However, the lesson of successful Indigenous community justice responses is efficient, practical and ongoing support from governments to facilitate communities in the process of finding acceptable solutions. Indigenous people live in many different circumstances with varying levels of autonomy and interdependency with non-Indigenous communities. These contextual variations will affect how the practice of policing and the principle of self-determination interact.

It is clear that the Indigenous domain of law and culture has continued not only to survive but also to develop in many places. Indigenous space continues to be defended and extended. In contrast, non-Indigenous governance through policing and the broad spectrum of government policy and programmes tends to circumscribe and delimit the struggle for Indigenous autonomy. In many cases where Indigenous justice initiatives have flourished with community-controlled policing, there have been successes in reducing levels of arrests and detention, as well as improvements in the maintenance of social harmony. The success of these programmes has been acknowledged as deriving from active Indigenous community involvement in identifying problems and developing solutions.

Indigenous resistance to colonial power has been productive of new spaces for the exercise of Indigenous governance over policing. Throughout Australia, Canada, the US and Aotearoa New Zealand, Indigenous communities have continued to exercise authority, or have developed localised methods of dealing with problems of social disorder. Indigenous practice has provided us with the opportunity and the necessity to rethink the possibilities of a decolonised relationship between police and community. Thus we need to explore the *possibilities* of new forms of policing, and a *rethinking* of policing in the light of Indigenous aspirations for self-determination.

FIVE

Indigenous women and settler colonial crime control

Indigenous contact with the criminal justice system throughout settler colonial jurisdictions shares one common statistical feature with all ethnic groups – the majority of those apprehended, convicted and imprisoned are (primarily young) men (Allard, 2010). However, where the statistical profile differentiates significantly is that Indigenous women are significantly *over-represented* compared to non-Indigenous men and women. Trends over the past decade show that the rate of their over-representation is increasing even more than for Indigenous men. Research also reveals that Indigenous women's experience of crime control policy and imprisonment is arguably becoming more punitive and disempowering (Sisters Inside, 2013).

While one might argue that in other respects their experience of crime and crime control mirrors that of other women, in so far as they experience high levels of physical and sexual victimisation, it can be argued that Indigenous women are further victimised and marginalised through the fact that their experiences and needs rarely impact on the development of crime control policy in settler colonial contexts (Stubbs, 2011). The lack of attention to Indigenous women, their issues and needs is compounded by the fact that they are systematically (and systemically) excluded from the development and application of crime control policies and interventions in settler colonial contexts. However, at the same time they are too often recipients of invasive crime control measures, such as policing and imprisonment (Baldry and Cunneen, 2014).

In this chapter we seek to challenge the marginalisation of Indigenous women within settler colonial crime control, by revealing both the nature and extent of their engagement with the criminal justice system, the impact of the failure of the sector to engage meaningfully with them, and the *intersectional foundations of their interactions with the criminal justice system*. We employ a critical Indigenous paradigm to analyse and expose the colonial ethos that sits at the heart of the state's response to Indigenous (women's) offending and victimisation. Utilising the Northern Territory (NT) Emergency Response ('the Intervention') as a case study, we challenge the hegemonic construction of the

Indigenous experience of criminal justice that permeates much of Western academic and settler colonial government theorising about the nature of Indigenous crime, much of which marginalises and fails to protect Indigenous women (Baldry and Cunneen, 2014; Cunneen and Rowe, 2015). Our objective in this chapter specifically in relation to Indigenous women, is similar to Howard–Wagner and Kelly (2011, p 103) who, writing on the impact of the Intervention on Aboriginal peoples of the North Territory of Australia, set out 'to make visible the persistence of the colonial in the concrete and material conditions of everyday life'.

Indigenous women's engagement with settler colonial crime control

One of the issues in Indigenous justice that has received much attention from both critical scholars and, most especially, from administrative and authoritarian criminologists, is the increasing rates of Indigenous people's contact with police, the courts, and the 'extraordinary growth in Indigenous women's imprisonment rates, which has far outstripped the growth in Indigenous male imprisonment' (Cunneen and Rowe, 2015, p 10). Research reveals that Indigenous women's increasing imprisonment rates are now a common feature of criminal justice in settler colonial contexts (Monture-Angus, 2006; McIntosh, 2011b; Dell and Kilty, 2013; Baldry and Cunneen, 2014; Cunneen and Rowe, 2015; Marchetti and Downie, 2014).[1]

Analysing the Australian context, Bartels (2010, p ix) writes that in 2007-08, Indigenous Australian women 'comprised 29 percent of women in prison compared with 24 percent for men', and that 'Indigenous women outnumbered them as a proportion of the relevant prison population in almost all [Australian] jurisdictions'. By June 2015 the proportion of women in prison who were Indigenous had grown to 35% (ABS, 2015). Sapers (2010) reports similar figures for Canada, where Indigenous people comprise just 3% of the general population, while Indigenous women comprised 33% of the federal female prison population. In September 2013, Māori were approximately 50.6% of the total Aotearoa New Zealand prison population, made up of around 4,000 Māori men (more than 50%) and close to 400 Māori women (more than 60%) (Department of Corrections, 2013). While the figures

---

[1]   Baldry and Cunneen (2014, pp 1-2) report that '[s]uch a task is especially salient given the 20% rise in Indigenous [Australian] women's imprisonment in a single year [2011]'.

show that Indigenous men remain over-represented in settler colonial prisons, the gender disparity is readily apparent and steadily increasing. For example, in 2006 Statistics Canada reported that 23% of the federal prisoner population were Indigenous women, compared to a figure of 18% for Indigenous men.

Bartels (2012) highlights the worsening situation for Indigenous Australian women when she discloses that their number in full-time custody in Australia 'rose by 7% between 2011 and 2012 March quarters, compared with a 5% increase for Indigenous men and 2% for the general female population'. In the Aotearoa New Zealand context, data shows that from 1986 to 2009, numbers of women in prison had burgeoned by 297%, almost twice the rate of growth in men (Workman and McIntosh, 2013). Figures for this jurisdiction also reveal that Māori women were the fastest-growing group in the prison population, particularly in the age group 17 to 24 years. Lastly, turning our attention to the Canadian jurisdictions, we find that a federal Canadian government report obtained by the Huffington Post Politics Canada (2014) revealed that '[t]he number of aboriginal women who were locked behind bars in federal institutions grew a staggering 97% between 2002 and 2012', while 'in comparison, the number of aboriginal men increased by a comparatively small 34% during that time'. The percentage of Indigenous women held on remand had increased from 14% in 1999 to 23% in 2004, while Indigenous men increased from 11% in 1999 to 13% in the same period (Statistics Canada, 2006; see also Comack, 2006 and Saper, 2010a, for critical analysis of the data pertaining to Canada).

Indigenous women's experience of imprisonment

In addition to ongoing increases in the rate of imprisonment, evidence is emerging that Indigenous women are often treated 'differently' once imprisoned on account of being both female and Indigenous, a 'state of being' that renders their experience of imprisonment increasingly problematic. In its 2003 report *Protecting their rights*, the Canadian Human Rights Commission revealed that while Indigenous women represented 29% of the women incarcerated in federal prisons at that time, they accounted for 46% of women classified as maximum security (as reported in Balfour, 2008). Sapers (2010) reports that once they are classified as maximum security, Indigenous women are prevented from accessing standard prison and community services at much higher rates than non-Indigenous women. Hayman (2006) and Pollack (2012) found that the maximum security classification also prevented them from accessing prison programmes specially created for Indigenous prisoners, such as the *Okimaw Ohci* healing lodge introduced by Corrections Canada in the early 1990s. Furthermore, Martel and Brassard (2008, p 340) report that many Canadian First Nation women 'negotiate their passage into prison through Aboriginal self-identification configurations that often have little in common with the prison's vision of Aboriginality'.

Similar issues of gender-related differentiation in service delivery have been identified in the Aotearoa New Zealand context, where a 2002 review of crime control sector by Te Puni Kokiri (the Ministry of Māori Development) found that a *tikanga* (Māori cultural) programme[2] supposedly designed to meet the needs of Māori women prisoners, was in fact largely based on a pre-existing programme for Māori men. The specific needs of Māori women prisoners were not found to be significant factors in the design of the programme (Te Puni Kokiri, 2002). Furthermore, lack of access to 'culturally appropriate' programmes – in particular the department's Māori Focus Units – was highlighted by Māori women prisoners who participated in a Te Puni Kokiri-led research exercise in 2007. This issue was also identified by participants in George et al's (2014) research on the links between historic trauma and Māori women's experience of imprisonment. Lastly, Australian-based participatory research with Indigenous women found that:

- there is only one residential programme available in Victoria that encompasses Aboriginal people's cultural needs – the *Wulgunggo Ngalu* Learning Place, but it is only available to Aboriginal men;
- once in prison, Aboriginal women appear not to be using programmes on offer, largely because there is a lack of culturally appropriate services in prison for them (the Victorian Equal Opportunity and Human Rights Commission (2013); see also Aboriginal Justice Advisory Council, 2002).

[2]   *Tikanga* programmes refer to a suite of programmes developed by the Department of Corrections to meet the specific cultural needs of Māori inmates. We use the term here in a broad, generic way; encompassing programmes that allow inmates to lean *te reo* (the Māori language), *tikanga* (the rules and philosophies of Māori culture and its practice) and 'blended' programmes – predominantly psycho-therapeutic interventions that utilise *tikanga* Māori to enhance Māori inmates' 'responsivity' to treatment.

The situation for many Indigenous women fails to improve when they are released from prison. During research with Indigenous women, the Victoria Equal Opportunity and Human Rights Commission (reported in *Insight*, 2014) found 'that the life chances for these women outside prison are compounded by the lack of pre-prison diversionary options, in provision of support post-release and in the inability to access employment or education or find safe and affordable housing for themselves and their children when released'. Overall, data trends and analysis of settler colonial crime control shows that not only are Indigenous women's rates of imprisonment increasing at higher rates than even for Indigenous men, but also that their experience of imprisonment is increasingly coercive and disempowering (Goldinguy and Mataki, 2014).

Indigenous women, violence and victimisation

It is not only the significant growth in Indigenous women's imprisonment that makes their experiences of crime and crime control both quantitatively and qualitatively different from Indigenous men, and non-Indigenous men and women. We must also consider the significant differences in their experiences as *victims of social harm*, especially physical, family and/or sexual violence (Canadian Centre for Justice Statistics, 2006; Howe, 2009). From a crime and justice perspective, the violent crime rate for all Indigenous people in Canada is significantly higher than the national rate, and Indigenous people are also far more likely to be victims of violent crime than other Canadians (Canadian Centre for Justice Statistics, 2006). For example, Wesley (2012, pp 5-6) found that Indigenous Canadian women are 3.5 times more likely than non-Indigenous women to be victims of violence, and that Indigenous women between the ages of 25 and 44 are five times more likely to die as a result of violence, with the overall mortality rate resulting from violence being 3 times higher for Indigenous women than women who are non-Indigenous (Native Women's Association of Canada, 2004; Dylan et al, 2008; see also Balfour, 2008, pp 101-2 for a discussion of high rates of serious gendered violence in the Canadian context). Similar figures are found in the Australian context. As we noted in Chapter One, Aboriginal and Torres Strait Islander women experience family violence at a rate of 45 times more than non-Aboriginal women, and are 10 times more likely to be killed as a result of domestic violence (Partnerships Against Domestic Violence, 2001, cited in Vincent and Eveline, 2008, p 323). Alarmingly, 69%

of all reported assaults against Aboriginal and Torres Strait Islander women are inflicted by an intimate partner (Cox et al, 2009, p 152).

The significant and increasing over-representation of Indigenous women in prisons, and their high rates of violent victimisation, reminds us of O'Malley's (2000) 'criminologies of catastrophe' — horror stories of a return to pre-modern penal practices, privatisation of crime control and an ever-expanding prison industrial complex. When we focus on Indigenous women's experience of crime control, especially the extensive use of imprisonment, we sense that some criminological catastrophes are less real and fanciful than others. The situation for Indigenous women correlates with Pratt (2000) and Garland's (2001) argument that for some social behaviours (such as sexual offending) and certain population groups (child sexual offenders), the rationality and rehabilitative ideal that characterises *penal modernity* is set aside. In this case, the population group for which it is set aside are Indigenous peoples, and those most affected by this are Indigenous women. The significant and increasing over-representation of Indigenous women in prison adds empirical weight to the argument that we are seeing the majestic return of the colonial project of sequestration as a key governmental platform for controlling the conduct and participation of Indigenous women (and men) in civil society (Baldry and Cunneen, 2014).[3]

If we accept the data presented above, and the argument that Indigenous women's engagement with settler colonial crime control is a criminological catastrophe writ large, then it is essential that we consider two interrelated questions:

- Why are the perspectives and experiences of Indigenous women largely absent from government and mainstream criminological rhetoric and publications on these issues?
- Why is there a lack of focus on the experiences and needs of Indigenous women during the development of government crime control policies and interventions?

[3] The significant increases in rates and real numbers of incarcerated Indigenous peoples, especially of Indigenous women in the settler colonial states of Canada, Aotearoa New Zealand and Australia highlighted here aligns with Wacquant's (2010) notion of the 'hyperincarceration' of Afro-American and Hispanic peoples in the American context (see also Cunneen et al, 2013) and George et al's (2014) notion of the prison ghettoisation of Indigenous peoples, especially Indigenous women.

Settler colonial crime control and the silencing of Indigenous women

The issue arising from analysis of the criminological and governmental literature on the Indigenous crime problem is that, despite Indigenous women's high rates of imprisonment and increasing experiences of violent and sexual victimisation, the focus of policy makers and criminologists is on Indigenous men (Gardiner and Takagaki, 2001/02). Referring to the Canadian context, the Huffington Post (2014) stated that Indigenous women were 'a group largely neglected by ... research'; a position that appears to contradict that of Indigenous scholars such as Linda Smith (1999), who described Indigenous peoples as *the* most over-researched population group in settler colonial contexts. The sentiment being expressed by the Huffington Post is perhaps better understood in the context of the nature and purpose of the research, rather than a reflection of the amount undertaken. It is useful to acknowledge that government-sponsored criminological research rarely focuses on the lived experiences of Indigenous women and therefore lacks critical understanding of the impact of gendered, colonialist policies (Stubbs, 2011; Tauri, 2012).

A number of commentators argue that the specific experiences of Indigenous women as victims and offenders is largely sidelined in the construction of government policies, and in criminological publications (see Goel, 2000; Lucashenko, 1996; Curtis-Fawley and Daly, 2005). The silencing of Indigenous women's experiences of crime control is well documented in the Australian context and extends to the much vaunted Royal Commission of Inquiry into Aboriginal Deaths in Custody (RCIADC) which, despite investigating the deaths of 11 Aboriginal women, made no specific recommendations directly relating to the situation of Indigenous women (Payne, 1993; Brooks, 1996).[4] That the policy document held up as *the* significant, critical commentary on the Indigenous experience of crime control in Australia can neglect Indigenous women to this extent, imparts authority to Cunneen and Kerley's (1995, p 71) acknowledgement of the 'profound silence surrounding the issue of Aboriginal and Torres Strait Islander women in the Australian criminal justice system'.

There are a number of ways in which Indigenous women are silenced in the development of crime control policy. One is the significant focus on Indigenous men in the development of policy and the funding of

[4]   Five of the 339 recommendations mention Indigenous women, but this is in the context of other more general issues.

research (see Te Puni Kokiri, 2007). While Indigenous men make up the majority of Indigenous offenders in all settler colonial contexts, the significant rise in imprisonment of Indigenous women, and research revealing the significant issues they face in dealing with the criminal justice system, renders their silencing inexcusable. While the focus on men is often rationalised as reflecting their higher overall numbers in prison, the same cannot be said of the neglect of women throughout criminology. Silencing and marginalisation is often the result of the Eurocentric epistemology that underpins policy and criminological work on crime and victimisation, which often results in the silencing of certain 'voices' (Tauri, 2012), most notably Indigenous women (Stubbs, 2011). The way in which members of the policy sector and the academy view the world can have significant bearing on the issues they choose to research, and the population groups involved in research itself (Young, 2011). Referring to the subdiscipline of victimology, Cunneen and Rowe (2015, pp 14) note that '[f]or the increasing number of Indigenous victims living and dealing with the consequences of ongoing colonisation, there is much that a mainstream Eurocentric victimological [and more widely, criminological] lens serves to conceal'. Baldry and Cunneen (2014, p 3) further expose the theoretical and epistemological shortcomings of mainstream criminological analysis of Indigenous women's experience of crime control when they state that:

> [the] absence of a clearly articulated race/ethnicity/gender analysis is evident in much of the critical scholarship on the expansion of incarceration over the last several decades: the critical conceptual frameworks of mass imprisonment, the new penology, the culture of control, governing through crime, and the rise of neo-liberalism seem to falter in providing an explanation that brings together both race [ethnicity] and gender.

Recently, postcolonial and Indigenous scholars have criticised the Eurocentric bias inherent in much of the theorising about crime and penal trends in Western democracies (Agozino, 2003; Cunneen, 2006; Tauri, 2012). Of particular concern is the lack of attention paid by policy makers and Western criminology to the impact of coloniality on the contemporary lived experiences of Indigenous people. The work of these scholars and others like them (see Jackson, 1992; Monture-Angus, 2006; Victor, 2007) reveals that the views and experiences of Indigenous women are silenced in part by the fact that members of the policy sector and administrative criminologists largely exclude the impact of colonial policies, neo-colonial policies, structural/epistemic violence, institutional racism and 'white privilege' from their theoretical and analytical frameworks (Kitossa, 2012; Tauri, 2015a). In relation to the place of Indigenous women, Brooks (1996, p 273) argues that '[i]n combination, the stigmas of gender and race virtually guarantee Aboriginal and Torres Strait Islander women the lowest place in law'. One could argue on the basis of existing evidence that much the same can be said of Indigenous women's treatment at the hands of policy makers and criminologists. We argue that what is missing from much of the governmental and administrative criminological discourse is a critical analysis of the impact of colonialism, and the epistemic violence that supports it.[5]

Speaking to the Canadian context, Mohawk academic Patricia Monture-Angus (2006, p 26) demonstrates that the process of the contemporary criminalisation of Indigenous girls and women has clear linkages to the policies of the so-called 'initial phases of colonisation'. Nowhere in federal or provincial policy statements on Indigenous women's offending is room given to exploring linkages between child removals, laws that overturned women's traditional roles in decision making, the application of white laws on marriage and family-related rights, and contemporary manifestations in poor education, health and criminal justice outcomes. As previously discussed, current Canadian criminal justice policies and procedures result in significant levels of incarceration of Indigenous girls and women, 'but also fails to address the trauma, and the resistance to it, that criminalised them in the first place' (Clark, 2012, p 143). Critical explorations like this have resulted in a number of key theoretical insights that are pertinent to the central theme(s) of this chapter, and indeed of this book, including:

> the inextricable connections between the categories of race, gender and class ...; the related importance of nuanced intersectional analysis ...; the enduring underestimation of the effects of colonisation, patriarchy and violence on the lives of victimised, criminalised and incarcerated Indigenous women. (Cunneen and Rowe, 2015, p 13)

[5] For the purposes of our argument, the term 'epistemic violence' refers to the 'violence of knowledge', which includes, among others, the ability of non-Indigenous policy makers and scholars to define both Aboriginality and the lived experiences of it, and institutional violence, or the governmental practice of the social control and subjugation of problem populations through the application of crime control policies and interventions (Kitossa, 2012).

As revealed by Canada's Commission on the Social Determinants of Health (2008, p 40), '[t]he inequity [in daily living conditions] is systematic, produced by social norms, policies and practices that tolerate or actually promote unfair distribution of and access to power, wealth and other necessary social resources'. Czyzewski (2011, p 1) argues that 'this statement acknowledges that there are larger causes of causes, or distal determinants, of unhealthy life conditions'.

In the international field of the recognition and study of the social determinants of health, the importance of an intersectional approach to analysis of contemporary health outcomes for Indigenous peoples is recognised. For example, the Commission on the Social Determinants of Health (2008, p 24) argued that: '[r]esearch and dialogue at the international level has demonstrated a common element exists for all Indigenous peoples and affects every issue confronting them as a collective: the history of colonisation and the associated subjugation of Indigenous peoples'. Similarly, the Commission acknowledged the unique social exclusion circumstances of Indigenous peoples, based on factors that are influenced by human conditions and actions (in other words, socially influenced), and that colonialism should be inserted into the debate on how contemporary inequalities and social conditions emerged (Czyzewski 2011). Czyzewski (2011, p 3) takes this argument further, when she writes:

> There are and have been direct effects of colonialism or colonial policies on Indigenous health, the introduction of contagious diseases like smallpox; the extinction of the Beothuk; or the gamut of negative experiences within the residential schooling system, to name a few. However, the above disparities also reflect the protracted effects of land dispossession and sedentarisation on cultural continuity, access to traditional economies, as well as physical separation from mainstream monetary economies, to name a few. In other words, these health gaps hint at the distal effects of colonial legislation.

Clark (2012, p 143) further underlines the argument when she writes that '[i]n reality, policy processes are central to the colonisation of Indigenous peoples, locally and globally, historically and currently'. Yet it has been the Indigenous experience that coloniality is rarely the focus of governmental analysis of issues that arise for or within Indigenous communities (Churchill, 1997; Tauri, 2009a). Arguably, the absence of coloniality – the science of colonial oppression – is a symptom of governmental aversion to self-critique, but also a purposeful strategy of avoiding the reality of what Schon (1973) calls the 'messy social world'; a world in which the lived experiences of people are the result of complex intersections of class, ethnicity (race) and gender. This messy reality is no more obvious than when we consider the drivers of Indigenous women's interactions with policy making and crime control.

The intersectional reality of Indigenous women and crime control

In recent times a number of critical Indigenous and postcolonial theorists have challenged shortcomings with governmental and conservative social scientific theorising on Indigenous issues, by constructing explanatory frameworks that place the Indigenous lived experience at the centre of social inquiry and that recognise the complex, intersectional nature of Indigenous people's experience of coloniality (Baldry and Cunneen, 2014). A useful concept that has arisen from the critical analysis of the settler colonial state, particularly for critical exploration of Indigenous women's interactions with crime control policy, is Crenshaw's concept of intersectionality. Analysis of the intersection between gender and race (ethnicity) arguably provides a nuanced framework to analyse: the significant and steadily increasing imprisonment of Indigenous women; high levels of family and sexual violence experienced by Indigenous women; and the silencing of Indigenous women's experiences in the construction of crime control policy (discussed earlier).

Structural intersectionality relates to '[t]he way in which the location of women of colour at the intersection of race and gender makes [their] actual experience of domestic violence, rape, and remedial reform [and arguably, policy] qualitatively different' (Crenshaw, 1991, p 1245) than that of white women, men and Indigenous men. The results of structural intersectionality, involving the impact of criminologically inspired crime control, leads to high levels of unemployment, poverty, homelessness, drug and alcohol addiction and low educational attainment, which hinder 'their ability to create alternatives to abusive relationships' (Crenshaw, 1991, p 1245). According to Kuokannen (2014, p 3):

> Crenshaw's approach enables a detailed examination of the ways in which structural factors such as dispossession, displacement and poverty of Indigenous peoples are

gendered and have different effects on men and women, and how these processes have contributed and reinforce intragroup hierarchies and patriarchal oppression in Indigenous communities.

An intersectional approach to an analysis of Indigenous women's imprisonment enables an understanding of the grounded link between the epistemic, structural violence and oppression of coloniality (Kitossa, 2012; Woolford, 2013) and the contemporary, individual experiences of offending and victimisation of Indigenous women. For example, the Aboriginal Justice Advisory Council's (2002, p 5) qualitative research on Aboriginal women's experiences of prison found that:

> Aboriginal women in prison had long and serious histories of abuse. 70% of the women surveyed said that they had been sexually assaulted as children and most had also suffered other types of childhood abuse. 78% of the women stated that they had been victims of violence as adults and 44% said they had been sexually assaulted as adults.

The complexity of the drivers of Indigenous interaction with crime control policy, and the need for an intersectional theoretical and analytical framework that includes a critical analysis of the impact of coloniality, is highlighted by Watson's (2009, p 5) revelation of the representation of Indigenous Australian culture and gender politics within the legal system:

> In the process of translating Aboriginal law the Australian courts have contributed to the harm that is done to Aboriginal women while at the same time constructing Aboriginal men as inherently violent and inferior to white men (Razack 1994 pp 899-900). The courts' reading of Aboriginal law and culture is that it is permissive of violence, a reading which is translated by a non-Aboriginal process, and one that excludes in its consideration the impact of more than 200 years of colonial violence. When considering traditional culture and law the courts have mostly failed to understand the effect of colonialism on Aboriginal relationships to kin and country, as though those relationships have remained intact and unaffected by modernity.

In defence of his argument that analysis of the lived experiences of Indigenous peoples requires consideration of the effects of colonialism, MacDonald (2010, p 50) asks: 'has colonialism a place in analysis of contemporary social conditions of Indigenous people?' MacDonald answers in the affirmative, stating that analysis of the contemporary lived experiences of Indigenes is incomplete without critical analysis of *coloniality* – that 'technology of power' applied in settler colonial contexts to bring about the subjugation of Indigenous peoples (see Quijano, 1999; Castro-Gomez, 2002). MacDonald (2010, p 50) then asks: '[i]f colonisation is to be understood as a process, how should it be understood?' He suggests that a useful analytical tool is to view it as a 'cultural process':

> An analysis of the reasons for this escalation [in Aboriginal suffering] ... requires that we understand colonisation as a cultural process ... Not solely one of social control and political-legal transformation. Colonisation [in support of coloniality] as a processual experience does not unfold in predictable ways: it is experienced differently in different times and places; it provides opportunities for some and suffering for others.

A common response of administrative and authoritarian criminologists to arguments for the inclusion of colonialism or coloniality in analysis of the contemporary situation, is to ask a series of delimiting questions, including how to measure the impact of policies over time and historical epochs and how to isolate the impact of specific policies or interventions to ascertain their impact on social conditions (Tauri, 2012). To begin to understand these connections, let us consider for a moment the link between family violence, reporting and policing. The historical bases of the current negative relations between police and Indigenous communities in settler colonial jurisdictions are well established (see for example Royal Commission into Aboriginal Deaths in Custody, 1991). Furthermore, in many colonial contexts, especially Australia, colonial police were heavily involved in the application of assimilatory social/welfare policies such as child removals; practices that have had a profound impact on contemporary relations with high levels of distrust between Aboriginal communities and police (Haebich, 2000; Cunneen, 2001; Moses, 2004). One area where this impact can be seen is in the reporting and response to family violence. Indigenous women subjected to family and/or sexual violence often do not report incidents to police or other state functionaries (such as those involved in child care and protection services), because 'of a direct fear, if police are called, that their children will be removed. [This example] is a graphic example of how the effects of colonial policies structure contemporary Indigenous decision-making' (Cunneen and Rowe, 2015, p 21).

The usefulness of intersectionality, whether at the level of linkages between ethnicity, gender and class, or between historical epochs of colonial policy making targeted at Indigenous people (including protection, assimilation, integration and reconciliation), lies in:

> its capacity to allow us to see complex dynamics of power operating simultaneously, but [also] from its connection to Indigenous worldviews, which are ... inherently intersectional ... it is the way we have always thought. Prior to colonisation Indigenous communities had multiple categories of gender, holistic understandings and approaches to health, strong matrilineal traditions, and complex systems of governance, treaty making and peace making. (Clark, 2012, p 140)

Arguably, intersectionality enables theorisation and analysis of the current modalities of coloniality and their impact on Indigenous peoples (Clark and Hunt, 2011). It provides an explanatory framework 'that helps us understand the complex and intersecting vectors of power shaping the historical-material conditions of Indigenous communities' (Grande, 2004, p 29), and especially of Indigenous women.

An intersectional approach also enables us to challenge long-held 'truths' about the relationship between Indigenous men, women and crime control, as demonstrated by Baldry and Cunneen (2014, pp 4-5):

> The complexity of the intersection between race and gender is shown by the fact that Indigenous women's rate of imprisonment is now more than 50% higher than the non-Indigenous male rate (ABS, 2012, p 58). The often taken-for-granted 'truth' that men are more likely to be imprisoned than women is simply false when race and gender are considered simultaneously: Indigenous women are far more likely to be imprisoned than non-indigenous men.

The lack of focus on, first, the impact of coloniality on contemporary social conditions of Indigenous peoples and, second, the intersectional reality of lived experiences, especially for women, results in the development of policy and criminological responses to the 'Indigenous problem' that arguably cause more harm than good for Indigenous communities. A recent example of the negative impact of non-intersectional policy construction, especially the silencing of Indigenous women, is the Northern Territory Emergency Response (known as the 'Intervention'), introduced by the federal Australian government in 2007.

The Northern Territory 'Intervention', Indigenous women and intersectionality

> The logics and rationalities of colonial power are not separate from and antagonistic to those of modern state formations but are indeed available to them. (Brown (2005, p 44)

The 'Intervention' introduced by the Australian federal government via legislation in 2007 (and updated and remodelled in subsequent legislation) failed to consider the intersectional reality of their lives. Subsequently, many of the policies and programmes included in the Intervention failed to address the specific needs of Aboriginal women. Furthermore, we argue that effects of the design and implementation of the Intervention highlight the need for consideration of the impact of coloniality on Indigenous women, if we are to formulate policy responses that empower them and their communities.

The 'Intervention'

In 2006, a number of incidents merged that resulted in the construction of a national emergency regarding child abuse in Aboriginal communities in Australia's Northern Territory (NT). The emergency was given impetus in 2007 with the release of the *Little children are sacred* report (Wild and Anderson, 2007). While the report recommended addressing child abuse through community-based mechanisms, it nevertheless became a key platform for supporting the developing federal government intervention. Within two weeks of the release of the report, the federal government announced that it would be moving to take direct control of 73 Aboriginal communities in the Northern Territory (Anthony and Blagg, 2012).

Legislation was enacted in the form of the Northern Territory National Emergency Response 2007. Through this and other legislation, the federal government introduced a number of policy responses that extend the reach of mainstream policing and governance to remote Aboriginal communities in the NT with the intention of 'normalising' the conduct of Indigenous peoples, including (Bielefeld, 2014):

- bans on pornography;
- criminalisation of the transportation, sale and possession of alcohol in prescribed areas;
- extended police powers for apprehending intoxicated people;
- removal of the consideration of cultural and customary law in bail and sentencing procedures for Indigenous defendants;
- measures to enable quarantining of at least 50% of Indigenous peoples' welfare-related income;
- harsher penalties for school truancy.

All of these measures specifically targeted Indigenous peoples residing in the NT and required the federal government to suspend Australia's Racial Discrimination Act 1975 so that it no longer afforded protection to Indigenous peoples affected by the Intervention (Anthony and Blagg, 2014) – a remove reminiscent of policy responses to Indigenous peoples during the late 19th century and early 20th century 'protection' legislation (see Chapter Three).

Through the introduction of the 2007 legislation, the government resurrected and implemented colonial era policies of 'protection' that were designed to break Indigenous people's links with their culture and move them towards assimilation into mainstream society. This move provides evidence in support of Castro-Gomez's (2002, p 276) argument that 'coloniality is not modernity's "past" but its "other face"', and that colonial strategies for disempowering and controlling Indigenes can be resurrected as colonial projects that have been repackaged to suit contemporary political and socioeconomic conditions (Woolford, 2013; Tauri, 2014).

In a 2015 article, Cunneen and Rowe (2015, p 23) stated that the Intervention was 'a contemporary example of "patriarchal white sovereign" power being used to "regulate and manage the subjugation of Indigenous communities" in the name of protecting Indigenous women and children from sexual assault and violence'. In much of the government and 'expert' rhetoric surrounding the Intervention, women (in particular) were presented as victims of a culture based on violent repression and disempowerment, wielded by Indigenous men who are largely unaccountable and empowered through a traditional, patriarchal cultural context.

The problem of domestic and sexual violence towards women (and children), the foundations for rationalising the Intervention, was stripped bare of the historical and contemporary impact of colonial policies (Anthony, 2012; Nicholson et al, 2012). Instead, the current situation in the NT (and elsewhere across the continent) was the result of the conduct of 'traditional' Aboriginal men, and therefore 'the product of dysfunctional cultural traditions and individual bad behaviour' (Moreton-Robinson, 2009, p 68). Taking this argument further, Cunneen and Rowe (2015, p 24) wrote that 'Indigenous pathology was to blame for the situation of violence and abuse, [and certainly] not the strategies and tactics of patriarchal white sovereignty'.

To date, there is little evidence to suggest that the policies introduced through the Intervention made Indigenous peoples safer, especially women and children (Altman and Russell, 2012; Cox, 2012). Far from protecting Indigenous women and children, extensive social and crime control mechanisms were introduced that significantly increased surveillance and intervention for people residing in the affected communities, most notably matters related to medical records, school attendance and social security entitlements. These supposed 'strategies of social support' resulted in instances where Indigenous people, especially women, were drawn further into the social welfare and criminal justice jurisdictions of the NT. With regard to the direct impact on Indigenous women, Cunneen and Rowe (2015, p 26, emphasis theirs) relate that:

> The Intervention introduced significant changes to social policy governed by increased state regulatory processes, such as housing tenancy leases, requirements around anti-social behaviour, school attendance, and social security income management ... Research has indicated that Indigenous women in particular have been negatively impacted upon because of these changes (Cunneen et al, 2014). For example, in relation to housing, school attendance requirements, social security payments and income management, Indigenous women are *more likely* to identify a problem than Indigenous men.

We do know that it has directly led to increased level of Indigenous incarceration (Anthony and Blagg, 2012; Baldry and Cunneen, 2014), in particular an increase in imprisonment of Aboriginal peoples by

34% – with a much greater increase for women (59%) than for men (24%) (ABS, 2012). Baldry and Cunneen (2014, p 16) argue, in relation to the effects of the Intervention, that 'it is clear that recently the proportional increase in imprisonment has been more than twice as high for Aboriginal women compared to men' (Baldry and Cunneen, 2014, p 16). Similarly, Anthony and Blagg (2014, p 110) argue that:

> it is particularly disturbing, although not surprising, to note the significant increase in the number of Indigenous women being incarcerated in the NT post-Intervention. In the NT, 93 per cent of female prisoners are Indigenous, according to NT 2013 Annual Corrections Report (NT Department of Correctional Services, 2014: 15). The report finds a 31 per cent increase in the number of sentenced Indigenous female receptions and a 30 per cent increase in the number of un-sentenced Indigenous female receptions into adult correctional centres during 2012-13 compared with the previous year (NT Correctional Services, 2014, p 21). This matches the longer-term increases of 33 per cent in NT female imprisonment between 2003 and 2013.

Given what we know about the impact of imprisonment on Indigenous women in this and other settler colonial contexts, the significant rise in rates of imprisonment resulting from the Intervention is of significant concern, especially since 'there is a likelihood of multiple experiences [of imprisonment] over a lifetime particularly for Indigenous people and specifically for Indigenous women' (Baldry and Cunneen, 2014, p 5).

Given the rationale used by Australia's federal government to justify implementation of the Intervention, namely the protection of Indigenous women and children from violence and exploitation, these findings are particularly damning. While research fails to show that Indigenous women are 'safer', it does indicate that the Intervention reinvigorated the use of sequestration, via 'penal excess' in the NT that resulted in a significant rise in the number of Indigenous women being imprisoned. This situation aligns with O'Connor's (1994) invocation of the term 'the new removals' to describe high rates of Indigenous youth residing in Queensland's youth residences, and Cunneen's (1997a) characterisation of imprisoned Indigenous Australians as the 'new stolen generation'. Research carried out by Cunneen et al (2014, p 229) demonstrates how real this feeling of a return to colonial attitude and policies is for NT Indigenous peoples who:

felt that the NTER had brought an increase in child removal
… and that this was corroborated by the rapid rise in child
protection notifications and substantiated cases between
2007/08 and 2009/10 … The historical continuity with
the Stolen Generations was seen as self-evident.

In relation to the impact of the Intervention, Bielefeld (2014, pp 713-
14) argued that:

> In terms of actually addressing domestic violence where
> it is present, a 2012 government-commissioned report
> has indicated that income management is not effective
> in achieving this aim. Bray et al note that, in some areas,
> violence has increased because of income management and
> the Basics Card. Likewise, in the 2009 NTER Redesign
> government consultations in Tennant Creek, it was recorded
> that '[d]omestic violence was fueled by peoples' inability
> to control their money' and that income management 'can
> fuel violence in families'.

In relation to the Intervention protecting Indigenous women from
violence, Altman's (2009, p 1) analysis revealed that 'domestic violence
related incidents are up; and breaches of domestic violence orders are
up, despite a far greater police presence [in the NT post-Intervention].
The most disturbing data … [relates to] personal harm incidents
reported to police: all categories are up except for sexual assault reports
that are slightly down'. Finally, in support of Altman's position, Cox
(2012, p 1) summarises the evidence thus far of the failure of the
Intervention to protect Indigenous women when she argues that:
'[s]tatistics collected on school attendance, education, crime, health and
child welfare should be able to offer evidence of changes in wellbeing
and safety. However, this data – collected since 2007 – has shown scant
improvement in wellbeing.'

It is worth reiterating that various federal governments have argued
that the key outcomes of the Intervention were to significantly decrease
child sexual and domestic violence, to enhance safety of Indigenous
women and children, and to 'normalise' Indigenous communities
through increased participation in the market economy of Australia.
According to Anthony and Blagg (2014, p 111) this last aim 'took
precedence over the safety of Indigenous women, unless prison has
become the new site for "saving" Indigenous women'.

Conclusion

> Women have been a footnote in [a] male-dominated system.
> And if women are the footnote, then Aboriginal women
> are the footnote to the footnote. Patricia Monture-Angus
> (cited in Boulton, 2003, para 4)

The case study of the NT Intervention provides us with clear evidence that the settler colonial state continues to employ assimilatory and punitive frameworks when responding to 'contemporary Indigenous problems' such as domestic violence and child sexual abuse. As the findings of research on the impact of the Intervention demonstrate, this can result in the further disempowerment of Indigenous peoples, and especially Indigenous women. The lack of consultation before and during deployment of the Intervention, the sidelining of Indigenous cultural practice in the formal court system, a lack of analysis of the failure of 'white justice' and 'white policy' to enable Indigenous self-determination, and the impact of colonialism – all attest to the continuation of coloniality as the governmental approach to controlling Indigenous peoples.

Supposedly introduced to protect Indigenous children from violence and exploitation, the Intervention resulted in: more Indigenous women being imprisoned; little evidence of a decrease in domestic violence or other gendered social harms; and more Indigenous children being removed from their Indigenous mothers. The reasons why this occurred are as complex and 'intersectional' as the social issues the Intervention was designed to solve, but unfortunately little evidence exists that any of these were included in the design phase. We argue that the lack of attention to the impact of colonialism on Indigenous communities, family structures, gender and political relations, cultural practices and the intersectional nature of Indigenous women's lived experiences, is evident in the policies that make up the Intervention. The violence and abuse experienced by Indigenous communities, and especially Indigenous women, is very real, and the causes (as well as the solutions) are complex. In comparison, the Intervention provides evidence that much of the policy work and criminological theorising and analysis of these issues in the settler colonial context is not grounded in the intersectional reality of their lives. One reason for this is that far too much 'governmental' work lacks consideration of the intersectional drivers behind Indigenous women's disenfranchisement, or of the impact of racist, colonialist policies and interventions. Until such time as the policy sector and administrative/authoritarian criminology take seriously the intersectional drivers of Indigenous disenfranchisement, especially for Indigenous women, the settler colonial state will continue to replicate failed colonialist policies of the past.

SIX

Reconceptualising sentencing and punishment from an Indigenous perspective

Previously we outlined the over-representation of Indigenous peoples in prison in settler colonial societies. In this chapter we examine the sentencing and punishment of Indigenous peoples. We begin by analysing the way non-Indigenous courts have responded to the sentencing of Indigenous people through two contrasting examples of Australia and Canada. We then discuss what are generally referred to as 'Indigenous sentencing courts'. These courts have developed in different ways in Australia, Canada, NZ and the US, and the scope of their incorporation into mainstream criminal justice systems varies. However, there are commonalities to the extent that the courts take into account some aspects of Indigenous culture when sentencing. The third area we turn our attention to briefly is the development of a distinctly Indigenous approach to justice reinvestment in Australia, and contrast that with the US, where justice reinvestment has largely ignored issues of Indian imprisonment. Finally, we reflect on *healing* as an Indigenous response to social harm. Essentially existing outside the formal court and correctional systems, healing approaches have grown over recent decades as both an alternative to the philosophical underpinnings of Western punishment, as well as providing practical alternatives to mainstream non-Indigenous correctional policies and practices.

We should be clear that we are not interested here in the debate as to whether the courts impose harsher or more lenient sentences on Indigenous peoples. There have been numerous studies of this type focusing on either 'race' or Indigeneity in the US (Alvarez and Bachman, 1996; Steffensmeier and Demuth, 2000; Office of Hawaiian Affairs, 2010), Britain (Hood, 1992) and Australia (Gallagher and Poletti, 1998; Bond and Jeffries, 2011). The studies have found various results. Some have methodological flaws or limitations, for example in the variables that are taken into account; and some are theoretically challenged, for example in their understanding of 'race' and its broader effects. For an overview of these issues in the US, see Wolpert (1999) and Davis (2003); in New Zealand see Morrison (2009); and in Australia see Cunneen (2006) and Anthony (2013).

The view that discrimination in sentencing can be established through a few simple criteria is simplistic:

- First, the focus on discrimination or bias is often caught within a binary 'equality paradigm', where the standard against which Indigenous people are judged is the treatment of the (white) majority. In other words, the dominant non-Indigenous justice system remains in a position of centrality – which closes off the possibility that different treatment, or indeed a different Indigenous system, is what is required.
- Second, a focus on discrimination in sentencing ignores the range of discretionary processes that occur – from the identification of offenders by police through to the various pre-trial processes leading up to the point of sentencing.
- Third, there is the presumption that the law is a neutral object existing impartially outside the actions of individuals who apply it. As we argued in Chapter Three, this misconstrues the nature of colonial law and the nature of social and political power. The criminal justice system, including sentencing and punishment, plays a significant role in constituting social groups as threats and in reproducing a society built on various modes of exclusion and confinement (Cunneen, 2001).

Sentencing and punishment have engaged with various concepts of Indigeneity. Some understandings might be seen as positive affirmations of Indigenous culture, largely because of the struggle of Indigenous people to change colonial criminal justice systems; other understandings are essentially negative views of particular 'racial' and cultural characteristics that are seen as criminogenic. We examine how the ideas and definitions of Indigeneity become imbued with meaning in the sentencing process: in some cases, being Indigenous is seen as a potentially positive cultural attribute likely to lead to rehabilitation and reform, while in others it is seen as embodying a negative set of experiences, outcomes and cultural traits.

One of the recurring themes of this book is the impact of neo-liberalism in creating a more punitive turn in penality and its impact on Indigenous peoples. The emergence of neo-liberalism has coincided with the realignment of approaches in punishment, which emphasise deterrence and retribution, and individual responsibility and accountability. The values of neo-liberalism include: individualisation of rights and responsibilities; the valorisation of individual autonomy; and the denial of cultural values that stand outside of, or in opposition to, a market model of social relations (Findlay, 2008, p 15). The ascendancy of these values has reinforced a particularly negative view of cultural difference and runs counter to Indigenous claims for self-determination. Indeed, cultural difference itself is used to explain crime and the need for particular types of punishment, with a focus on changing Indigenous culture and promoting greater assimilation (Cunneen, 2007b; Anthony, 2013). We argue that neo-liberalism has led to less sympathetic attitudes to Indigenous self-determination in the settler colonial context.

Sentencing Indigenous people in Australia

As we noted in Chapter One, Aboriginal people in Australia were seen as not belonging to 'civilised nations' that could be recognised as sovereign states governed by their own laws. They were subjects of the Crown under a unitary system of colonial law. Since 1975, racial discrimination has been prohibited by the Australian Commonwealth's Racial Discrimination Act. Sentencing principles apply equally, irrespective of the race or cultural background of an offender. The Australian High Court in *Walker* held that:

> It is a basic principle that all people should stand equal before the law. A construction which results in different criminal sanctions applying to different persons for the same conduct offends that basic principle. (*Walker v The State of New South Wales* [1994] 182 CLR 45 at 49, per Mason CJ)

Australian courts have consistently held that Aboriginality is not a mitigating factor in sentencing (Australian Law Reform Commission, 2006, p 720), most recently in the High Court decision *R v Bugmy* (2013) 302 ALR 192. However, this does mean that a judge cannot take into account matters related to the offender's background when sentencing. As an Indigenous person, that might include socioeconomic disadvantage, health problems, removal from family and so on. Such considerations are consistent with the principle of individualised justice. The circumstances where Aboriginality is relevant to sentencing can be categorised into three broad areas: factors relevant to the background of Indigenous offenders; factors relevant to the communities from where the offender and/or victim came; and factors relevant to traditional law and custom (New South Wales Law Reform Commission, 2000, pp 43-51). For example, circumstances of an Indigenous offender that may be relevant in a particular case include:

- whether a custodial sentence is unduly harsh, given the background and circumstances of the offender;
- the offender's residence in a remote community and problems associated with living on reserves or in remote areas;
- the unique difficulties faced by Indigenous people adjusting from a remote traditional community to an urban environment;
- the endemic nature of hearing loss among Indigenous people and its consequent social and psychological effects;
- discrimination, exclusion and disadvantage in the background and upbringing of an Indigenous offender, including harsh treatment, dispossession and separation from families.

In *R v Fernando* (1992) NSWCCA58 at 62-63, Justice Wood found that the Aboriginality of an offender does not necessarily mitigate punishment but may explain the particular offence or the circumstances of the offender. He set out the so-called *Fernando principles*, which recognise social disadvantage and the role of alcohol and violence in some Aboriginal communities, and their impact on Aboriginal offending. Justice Wood noted that 'the problems of alcohol abuse and violence ... to a very significant degree go hand in hand within Aboriginal communities' (*R v Fernando* at 62). The endemic problems in Indigenous communities including poor self-image, absence of education and work opportunities and 'other demoralizing factors' need to be recognised by the court when sentencing. However, whether the principles will be taken into account or not will be determined by the court in each individual case. Superior court decisions have restricted the application of *Fernando* (Flynn, 2005). Furthermore, *Fernando* appears to have been interpreted in a way that offers little application to Indigenous women – despite their rapidly growing imprisonment rates (Cunneen et al, 2013, pp 104-6). In one of the few cases (*R v Trindall* [2005] NSWCCA 446) where the *Fernando principles* were raised by defence lawyers in relation to an Aboriginal woman, they were seen by the court not to apply (Manuel, 2009), with the court failing to recognise the specific gendered impacts of colonialism, including family disruption, child removal and sexual assault.

The *Fernando principles* are a prime example where the Aboriginality of the offender is based predominantly on a set of negative characteristics. The principles, and their interpretation in later case law, establish a hierarchy of Aboriginality to the extent that the principles are seen as more appropriate in their application to Indigenous people from rural or remote areas – a familiar trope in judicial pronouncements on Aboriginality. See Cunneen (1993), Flynn (2005), Behrendt et al (2009) and Anthony (2013) for cases referring to this well-rehearsed distinction.

The *Fernando principles* also established that for an Indigenous person:

> who has little experience of European ways, a lengthy term of imprisonment may be particularly, even unduly, harsh when served in an environment which is foreign to him [*sic*] and which is dominated by inmates and prison officers of European background with little understanding of his culture and society or his own personality. (*R v Fernando* at 63)

On this point, the court was reiterating, seemingly in more humane terms, what had been a common understanding and practice since the early days of the colony – that specific forms or modalities of punishment were applicable to Indigenous offenders. Australian justice systems materialise this cultural understanding of penality today in a variety of ways, one of which is through self-conscious attempts on the part of correctional services to create 'Indigenous' prisons (Cunneen et al, 2013, pp 113-14, 146-7).

The communicative and performative aspects of *Fernando* are seen in the act of first determining the actual harms of colonialism and then deciding which Indigenous *individuals* may have suffered social, economic and psychological damage as a result. This individualising discourse has left open the subsequent reading down of these principles to the extent that they apply to fewer and fewer Aboriginal people before the courts (Manuel, 2009). The outcome is that courts perform a communicative act of recognition of colonialism as being injurious, while continually reducing in practice the group of Aboriginal people to which those injuries apply. Colonial impact is judicially recognised inconsistently along various dichotomies (such as urban/rural, on and off reservation) and social divisions (gender), while it is simultaneously made to disappear as a contemporary effect in the lives of most Aboriginal people.[1]

We noted in Chapter Three that the idea that Indigenous law was merely *customary* was essentially an imperialist concept, which negated

---

[1]   Manuel (2009, p 8) reviewed 102 cases involving Aboriginal offenders after *Fernando* and found that the principles were applied in 29 cases.

the integrity of Indigenous law and imposed the centrality of the law of the coloniser. Australian courts may take 'into account' customary law when sentencing an Indigenous person. They generally do so in two ways. The first is when the person has been, or will be, subject to traditional Indigenous punishment as recognised by the court. The second is through recognition that customary law may explain the reason for the commission of a particular offence (see New South Wales Law Reform Commission, 2000, pp 85-106 and Law Reform Commission of Western Australia, 2006, pp 178-84). In both circumstances, customary law *may* mitigate the sentence imposed by the court. However, the context in which Indigenous law is recognised in the colonial courts is highly individualised and is determined on a case-by-case basis.

Anthony (2013, p192), after a comprehensive analysis of the sentencing of Indigenous people by Australian courts, notes that:

> The sentencer's recognition of Indigeneity is a problematic premise for legal pluralism in the Australian criminal justice system. At best, the sentencer's use of discretion can instrumentally structure sentences to soften the devastating effect of incarceration on Indigenous Australians ... At worst, recognition in sentencing can produce harsher penalties to deter the practice of Indigenous cultures and customary laws. It can never foster Indigenous laws because the source of recognition presides in the dominant Anglo-Australian institutions.

Sentencing legislation introduced as part of the Northern Territory (NT) Emergency Response ('the Intervention') – see Chapter Five – is a key example of the federal government restricting the way in which the courts might consider Aboriginal law, and in particular reinforcing a view that Aboriginal culture is the cause of abuse and violence in Aboriginal communities. Federal legislation prohibits sentencing courts from taking customary law into consideration in the NT. As Goldflam (2013, p 71) notes, the effect of the legislation is like holding a sign at the court door stating, 'White Laws Only Allowed Within'.

Sentencing Indigenous people in Canada

The approach to sentencing Aboriginal people in Canada provides a contrast to Australia. Section 718.2(*e*) of the Canadian *Criminal Code* requires that all available sanctions other than imprisonment, that are reasonable in the circumstances, should be considered for all offenders, with particular attention to the circumstances of Aboriginal offenders. The Canadian Supreme Court in *R v Gladue* (1999) 1 SCR 688 confirmed, in referring to section 718.2(*e*), that the unique circumstances of Aboriginal people needed to be considered in sentencing. The Court found that:

> The provision is not simply a codification of existing jurisprudence. It is remedial in nature and is designed to ameliorate the serious problem of overrepresentation of aboriginal people in prisons, and to encourage sentencing judges to have recourse to a restorative approach to sentencing. (*R v Gladue* at 690)

The Supreme Court held that the effect of s.718.2(*e*) is to alter the method of analysis that sentencing judges must use in determining a fit sentence for Aboriginal offenders:

> In sentencing an aboriginal offender, the judge must consider: (a) the unique systemic or background factors which may have played a part in bringing the particular aboriginal offender before the courts; and (b) the types of sentencing procedures and sanctions which may be appropriate in the circumstances for the offender because of his or her particular aboriginal heritage or connection. (*R v Gladue* at 690)

A judge is required to obtain information through a report and other means (now referred to as a 'Gladue report'), including information on systemic and background factors that affect Aboriginal people generally and the offender in particular, and information on alternatives to incarceration. A Gladue report was described in a 2012 Supreme Court decision as 'an indispensable sentencing tool to be provided at a sentencing hearing for an Aboriginal offender and it is also indispensable to a judge in fulfilling his duties under s. 718.2(*e*) of the *Criminal Code*' (*R v Ipeelee* 2012 1 SCR 433 at 437).

The Supreme Court in *Gladue* went beyond the requirement to consider systemic factors that might explain and mitigate Aboriginal offending, to also require consideration of both sentencing *procedures* and *sanctions* that 'may be appropriate'. In this context, the Supreme Court noted the 'priority given in aboriginal cultures to a restorative approach in sentencing' (*R v Gladue* at 690). The Supreme Court found that section 718.2(*e*) applies to all Aboriginal people irrespective of whether they reside on or off a reservation, in city or rural areas. Furthermore, 'in defining the relevant aboriginal community ... the term "community" must be defined broadly so as to include any network of support and interaction that might be available, including one in an urban centre' (*R v Gladue* at 691). Even if an Aboriginal offender lacks any network of support, the judge should still try to find an alternative to imprisonment.

The effect of section 718.2(*e*) is not to render all Aboriginal offenders before the courts ineligible for sentences of imprisonment. The Supreme Court noted that 'generally, the more serious and violent the crime, the more likely it will be as a practical matter that the terms of imprisonment will be the same for similar offences and offenders, whether the offender is aboriginal or non-aboriginal (*R v Gladue* at 739). In *R v Ipeelee*, the Supreme Court reconfirmed the importance of the *Gladue* decision, and confirmed that it applies in all contexts, including violent and long-term offenders.

Canadian law that governs the way federal corrections are managed also makes specific provisions in relation to Aboriginal offenders (ss79–84, Corrections and Conditional Release Act 1992 (CCRA)). The legislation requires Correctional Services Canada (CSC) to 'provide programs designed particularly to address the needs of aboriginal offenders' and provides Aboriginal communities with the opportunity to be involved in the care and custody of offenders. The CSC can enter into an agreement with an Aboriginal community for the provision of correctional services to Aboriginal offenders, including payment for those services. The CSC may transfer an Aboriginal offender to the care and custody of an Aboriginal community, with the consent of the offender and the community. The participation of Aboriginal communities in the release planning process is encouraged, by requiring the CSC to consult with the community and seek their input. Section 83 of the CCRA clarifies that 'aboriginal spirituality and aboriginal spiritual leaders and elders have the same status as other religions and other religious leaders'. Since 1992 there have also been elder assisted parole hearings, based on the acknowledgement that Aboriginal prisoners were granted release on parole at lower rates than other prisoners (Turnball, 2014, p 386). There are no similar provisions to these in any of the Australian correctional legislation.

Compared to Australia, Canadian sentencing legislation is more developed in relation to Indigenous people. However, it is also important to note its limitation as an *adaptation* of existing sentencing processes to Indigenous offenders. Milward (2012, p 27) argues that: 'It would be a stretch, to say the least, to view this provision [s. 718.2(e)] as a legislative concession of substantive jurisdiction to Aboriginal communities'.

While Australia and Canada demonstrate differences in the way Indigeneity is considered, both systems remain predicated on the centrality of the non-Indigenous legal system. Such an approach can encourage 'culturalist responses to structural oppression' (Turnball, 2014, p 400). Australian and Canadian courts may attempt to ameliorate the extent of Indigenous over-representation, however they do so in a way that continues to deny the independent integrity and legitimacy of Indigenous law.

The lack of sentencing alternatives, programmes and services for Indigenous people

The limited response of the courts is compounded by the lack of non-custodial sentencing alternatives, programmes and services and their often Eurocentric nature. Indigenous people, as both offenders and victims, lack the same access as non-Indigenous people to the programmes and services offered by the criminal justice system (Cunneen, 2005b; Indian Law and Order Commission, 2013; Law Reform Commission of Western Australia, 2006; Mahoney, 2005). These include the absence or highly restricted availability of, or in some cases the unsuitability of:

- non-custodial sentencing options;
- services for Aboriginal victims (particularly of family violence and sexual abuse);
- interpreter services;
- offender programmes (for example for sex offenders, violent offenders);
- programmes and counselling for substance abuse;
- programmes for young offenders.

There are limited Aboriginal-specific programmes to reduce offending behaviour, and there is an absence of effective supervision for community corrections in rural and remote communities. For example, interviews with judicial officers in New South Wales (NSW) found that the majority of judges and magistrates were prevented from using periodic detention when sentencing Indigenous offenders because of the lack of facilities (New South Wales Law Reform Commission, 2000, p 154).

The lack of appropriate programmes may partly explain higher recidivism rates, because there are fewer opportunities for rehabilitation (Mahoney, 2005; Law Reform Commission of Western Australia, 2006, p 85). The Australian Law Reform Commission (2006, p 723) found that rehabilitation programmes were not appropriately tailored to the needs of Indigenous offenders: 'effective rehabilitation programs for [Indigenous] offenders should be adequately resourced, incorporate principles of Aboriginal healing, and provide ongoing assistance to participants to avoid ... further offending'. Similarly, the Office of Hawaiian Affairs (2010, pp 57-8) has argued that culturally inappropriate or unavailable re-entry programmes lead to higher recidivism and to probation and parole revocations among Native Hawaiians.

The absence of effective community-based sanctions for Indigenous offenders contextualises the developments in Indigenous courts and Indigenous healing to be discussed later in this chapter. As Milward (2012, p 31) has argued in relation to Canada, 'calls for greater Aboriginal control over justice are motivated in large degree by a desire for autonomy to develop community-based alternatives to incarceration'. A further driver of change has been the relative failure of indigenisation and 'culturally appropriate' programmes that were popular from the late 1980s onwards in settler colonial states (Tauri, 1998; Cunneen, 2001).

Indigenous sentencing courts

In sentencing and punishment not all understandings of Indigeneity are negative. The growth in Indigenous sentencing courts in Australia, Aotearoa New Zealand and Canada (for example, Koorie, Nunga, Murri, Gladue, circle sentencing and Rangatahi courts) over recent decades is the outcome of Indigenous activism and official accommodation (Proloux, 2005; Marchetti and Daly, 2007; Dickson, 2011; Milward, 2012; Marchetti and Downie, 2014). In the US, tribal courts (to be discussed separately later in this chapter) have different origins and a longer history.

The aims of Indigenous sentencing courts include providing better sentencing outcomes, empowering Indigenous communities, reducing recidivism, and achieving restorative justice outcomes between offenders and victims. The courts provide an opportunity for Indigenous people to be involved in the sentencing process at a relatively formal level, although on terms set by the government and the judiciary. The courts provide the space to hear the views of a particular community in relation to matters such as whether the offender should return to the community, the seriousness of the offence, the offender's character and the nature of an appropriate penalty. Punishment is understood as the outcome of decision making by judicial officers and non-judicial Indigenous members of the court. In this context, Indigenous culture is seen as a positive contributor to the reform of Indigenous offenders.

Circle sentencing is one example of an Indigenous sentencing court which developed in Canada after a decision by the Supreme Court of the Yukon in the case of *R v Moses* [1992] 3 CNLR 116. The circle is premised on three principles, said to be part of the culture of Aboriginal people in the Yukon:

> Firstly, a criminal offence represents a breach of the relationship between the offender and the victim as well as the offender and the community; secondly, the stability of the community is dependent on healing these breaches; and thirdly, the community is well positioned to address the causes of crime. (Lilles, 2001, p 162)

Circle sentencing is part of the court process and results in convictions and criminal records for offenders (Lilles, 2001, p 163). Discretion as to whether a sentencing circle is appropriate remains with the judge. The sentencing decision lies with the judge, who is free to ignore the sentencing circle recommendations and is obliged to impose a 'fit' sentence that is still subject to appellate court sentencing guidelines (Green, 1998). Not surprisingly, there may be tensions between community involvement in the circle and the power that the judge retains (Milward, 2012, p 31). While at one level there is an appeal to 'equality' within the circle, the circle itself is constrained by the wider power of the non-Indigenous criminal justice system.

Canadian case law sets out criteria for involvement in a sentencing circle. These include that:

- the accused has roots in the community and agrees to participate in the sentencing circle;
- there are elders or respected non-political community leaders willing to participate;
- the victim is willing to participate and has not been subjected to coercion or pressure to agree;
- disputed facts have been resolved in advance. (See *R v Joseyounen* (1996) 1 CNLR 182 for further criteria, and also Green (1998, p 76)).

The criteria have been widely referred to and applied across Canada (albeit with variations such as whether the victim must attend). Milward (2012, p 28) and Marchetti and Downie (2014, p 377) identify a number of circle sentencing courts in Manitoba, Alberta, the Yukon, Newfoundland and Labrador.

In Australia, circle sentencing has been operating for Indigenous offenders in NSW since 2002. Circle sentencing guidelines, procedures and criteria are established through the *Criminal Procedure Regulation 2000* [2000-435]. The objectives of the circle sentencing court are, *inter alia*, to:

- increase the participation and confidence of Aboriginal communities in the sentencing process;
- support victims;
- provide more appropriate sentencing options;
- reduce recidivism;
- provide for the greater participation of Aboriginal offenders and their victims in the sentencing process (Potas et al, 2003, p 4).

The fundamental premise underlying circle sentencing is that the community holds the key to changing attitudes and providing solutions. The court's deliberations have been typified as power-sharing arrangements: 'It is recognised that if the community does not have confidence that the power-sharing arrangements will be honoured, the prospect that circle sentencing will be successfully implemented is likely to be diminished' (Potas et al, 2003, p 4).

In addition to circle sentencing there are other types of Indigenous sentencing courts in operation. In Australia, Koori, Nunga or Murri courts typically involve an Aboriginal elder or elders, Aboriginal community justice group members or an Aboriginal justice officer sitting with a magistrate. Elders can provide advice to the magistrate on the offender and about cultural and community issues. Offenders might receive customary punishments or community service orders as an alternative to prison. The offender is required to have pleaded guilty to the offence. The court setting may be different to the traditional settings. The offender may have a relative present at the sitting, with the offender, his/her relative and the offender's lawyer sitting at the bar table. The magistrate may ask questions of the offender, the victim (if present) and members of the family and community in assisting with sentencing options (see Marchetti and Daly, 2007; Cunneen, 2005b).

One magistrate described the Queensland Murri Court[2] sessions as 'intense, emotional occasions with a greater involvement of all parties'; and another magistrate said that, 'the acknowledgment in a public forum of the Elder's authority and wisdom and their role as moral guardians of the community by the Court honours traditional respect for the role of the Elders. The Elders mean business ...' (cited in Cunneen, 2005b, pp 148-9). The conditions placed on court orders may involve meeting with elders or a community justice group on a regular basis and undertaking courses, programmes or counselling relevant to their particular needs.

In New Zealand, the Gisborne Marae Youth Court, established in 2008, has expanded to various locations and these are now known as 'Rangatahi courts'. According to Marchetti and Downie (2014, pp 378-9), the court 'adopts Māori *tikanga* (customs and traditions) ... the judge and community elders talk to an offender about their connection to the *marae*, their Māori culture and their offending behaviour'. However, there has been criticism of the 'incorporation' of Māori *tikanga* into mainstream court processes (Tauri, 1998; Quince, 2007), and Dickson (2011) has questioned the use of *marae* (Māori meeting house) as a judicial setting.

In Canada, various types of Aboriginal sentencing courts are in operation, including the Cree Court in Saskatchewan, the New Westminster First Nations Court in British Columbia, and the Teslin Tingit Council peacemaker court in the Yukon (Milward, 2012, pp 28-9; Marchetti and Downie, 2014, pp 376-7). Perhaps the most developed of the Indigenous sentencing courts in Canada is the Aboriginal Persons Court in Toronto (or '*Gladue* courts', because they were developed to give effect to the Supreme Court decision in *Gladue*). The Aboriginal Legal Services agency in Toronto assists the court by preparing reports on the offender's background and may make recommendations in relation to sentencing. There is also a diversionary programme through the community councils, comprising representatives from Toronto's Aboriginal community (Milward, 2012, pp 29-30; Marchetti and Downie, 2014, p 376).

There have been 10 evaluations of Aboriginal courts in various states of Australia. While comparisons across these evaluations are difficult, Marchetti and Downie (2014, pp 374) note that the evaluations

---

[2]   In 2012, a conservative government in Queensland abolished the Murri court. However, magistrates continue to hold similar courts by exercising their discretion to list Indigenous matters on a single day and seek input from community members.

generally show improved rates of court appearances but not a consistent impact on recidivism rates. A common theme in the evaluations is the increased participation and ownership of the programme by local Indigenous communities. For example, the evaluation by Potas et al (2003, p iv) of circle sentencing in NSW found: more relevant and meaningful sentencing options for Aboriginal offenders; reduced barriers between the courts and Aboriginal people; improvements in the level of support for Aboriginal offenders; support for victims; and the promotion of empowerment of Aboriginal people in the community. In Canada, a Department of Justice (2007) evaluation found similar results to those conducted in Australia, but in addition that there had been reductions in reoffending.

There is a strongly performative element to Aboriginal courts. The emotion described earlier, and the use of Indigenous flags, art and other cultural objects, reinforces the importance of Indigenous culture in the sentencing process. In Canada, Proloux (2005) has argued that the philosophies and practices of Aboriginal peoples are penetrating the formal Canadian criminal justice system and we need to understand the cultural creativity involved in this process, although the formal system 'still has the power to select where, when and how the cross-cultural penetration occurs' (Proloux, 2005, p 81). The question remains open as to whether the courts are 'part of an imperfect and incomplete decolonizing trend', as suggested by Proloux (2005, p 92). Perhaps the outcome is a type of postcolonial hybridity, where institutional processes are changed and the outcome is *neither* an Indigenous process nor the dominant non-Indigenous legal process – a form of cultural creativity, as Proloux suggests. However, it is also clear that Indigenous sentencing courts in Australia, Canada and New Zealand are limited in scope and are usually unable to hear the more serious offences that continue to go before the mainstream courts. Further, it is difficult to see how Indigenous sentencing courts can satisfy the broader demands by Indigenous people for greater autonomy and control over criminal justice more generally (Milward, 2012, p 31).

Despite the accommodations made towards Indigenous values in these specialist courts, the results of these initiatives have not halted the increase in the rate of Indigenous imprisonment, particularly with the move to more punitive approaches to punishment over recent decades (Cunneen et al, 2013). There are parallels here with the argument of Turnball (2014, p 398) that 'Aboriginalisation' is a 'technique of contemporary colonialism' and 'demonstrative of symbolic adaptations, rather than meaningful change or the creation of separate justice processes'.

A major reason for the failure of Aboriginal courts to impact on Indigenous imprisonment is that they are essentially peripheral to the workings of the mainstream criminal justice system, with comparatively few Indigenous people actually appearing before the specialist sentencing courts. In Australia, for example, it is difficult to estimate the numbers but given that there are few Indigenous sentencing courts operating and on an estimate of the small number of the matters they hear, we could surmise that over 95% of Indigenous people continue to appear in mainstream court settings.[3] So perhaps like the *Fernando principles* noted earlier in this chapter, there is a double communicative function fulfilled by Indigenous sentencing courts. On the one hand, Indigenous culture is shown to have an important role in the courts – and justice is served; on the other, Indigenous sentencing courts are peripheral and tokenistic. Perhaps the existence of Aboriginal courts changes the working of the non-Indigenous justice system as part of a decolonising process, but it can also be argued that Aboriginal courts are irrelevant to what happens to the majority of Indigenous offenders passing through the mainstream justice system – that in fact they divert critical attention away from the oppressive regimes of sentencing and incarceration where Indigenous peoples are so massively over-represented.

US tribal courts

Tribal courts are operating on Indian country in over 30 states in the US. Tribal courts were formed after the Indian Reorganisation Act 1934. Under this legislation, Indian tribes were 'authorised' to establish tribal constitutions and governments, and to enact laws covering internal matters including law and order. As noted in Chapter One, Indian nations exercise limited jurisdiction on Indian country, subject to the power of Congress, and drew attention to the various curtailments on Indigenous jurisdiction and the complex 'jurisdictional maze' that has resulted. Since the Tribal Law and Order Act 2010 there has been a move to provide 'greater freedom for Indian Tribes and nations to design and run their own justice systems' (Indian Law and Order Commission, 2013, p i). Among other changes, the legislation increased the sentencing powers of tribal courts to a maximum of three years' imprisonment and fines up to $15,000 (Martin, 2014, p

[3]   It was estimated that in Queensland less than 0.5% of Indigenous adult matters and 1.5% of Indigenous juvenile matters were determined in the Murri courts (Cunneen, 2005b, p 200).

244). The Violence Against Women Reauthorization Act 2013 also extended tribal courts' jurisdiction over non-Indian offenders who commit domestic violence on Indigenous country.

Tribal courts are diverse in their operation, with some resembling mainstream Western courts in their laws and court procedures, while others use traditional means of resolving disputes, including peace making, elders' councils, and sentencing circles. Some tribal courts use a combination of both Western and traditional approaches. The courts also vary significantly in their size – from servicing small tribes with few members, to servicing the Navajo nation of over 300,000 people and a Navajo judicial system that has an annual caseload of over 51,000 matters including civil, criminal and family law (Judicial Branch of the Navajo Nation, 2015, p 31).

The Navajo Nation also provides an example of the rejuvenation of Indigenous law. A revival of Navajo justice principles and processes began in the 1980s. Navajo customs, usages and traditions have come to form what is referred to as the 'Navajo common law' (Yazzie and Zion, 1996, p 159). The Navajo system is based on peace making, described as a healing process aimed at restoring good relationships among people. Navajo methods seek to educate offenders about the nature of their behaviours and how they impact on others, and to help people identify their place in the community and reintegrate into community roles. 'Peace-making is based on relationships. It uses the deep emotions of respect, solidarity, self-examination, problem-solving and ties to the community' (Yazzie and Zion, 1996, p 170).

First Nations people who are sentenced to imprisonment for offences committed on Indian country, depending on the jurisdiction of the sentencing court, may be incarcerated in tribal, state or federal facilities – reflecting the 'jurisdictional maze' noted above. In 2012 there were 79 tribal jails operating on Indian country. The Indian Law and Order Commission (2013, p 121) noted that:

> Among these, there are an increasing number of exemplary facilities that serve as anchors along a continuum of care from corrections to community re-entry and that are able to connect detainees with core rehabilitation services, such as substance abuse treatment, mental health care, cultural programming, and education.

A major benefit of the tribal jail system has been identified as keeping tribal members close to their families and culture, while 'holding them accountable to the Indian nations themselves, which can be a significant step forward for law and order in Indian country' (Luna-Firebaugh, 2003, p 57). However, overcrowding in tribal jails has been a recognised problem since the late 1990s (Luna-Firebaugh, 2003, p 58). Some tribal prisons have been forced to close because of funding deficiencies. The Indian Law and Order Commission (2013, p 123) found that in 2011 and 2012, 'one out of five Indian country jails operated at 150 per cent of their rated capacity on their most crowded day'.

While there had been curtailment of Indian tribal courts over the years, this changed somewhat with the introduction of the Tribal Law and Order Act 2010. Perhaps more important, though, is the opportunity for tribal courts to blend 'cultural values and traditions into their adjudications' (Milward, 2012, p 74). Referring to the work of Pommerscheim (1995), Milward (2012) notes that tribal courts provide interpretive communities, which can combine and synthesise outcomes that provide the possibility of the type of hybridity referred to earlier in relation to Aboriginal sentencing courts in Australia, New Zealand and Canada. Tribal courts have greater potential autonomy than the Indigenous courts in other settler colonial states. However, like those courts, they still operate within the broad legislative frameworks set by respective federal governments that determine the nature of offences and the type of offenders and victims who appear before the court.

Justice reinvestment and Indigenous nations

A different approach to reform and empowerment that seeks to move beyond the courts and to redirect attention to community development has been justice reinvestment. Over recent years, justice reinvestment has emerged as a major policy direction for reducing imprisonment levels, starting in the US in the early 2000s and developing in other countries including Australia. We contrast the Indigenous experiences in the US and Australia, because its throws light on how differing colonial histories can structure different responses to a criminal justice and penal reform agenda. In both the US and Australia, Indigenous *nation-building* is an important priority for Indigenous peoples and organisations, and this includes developing and strengthening community and organisational governance structures which reflect Indigenous control, priorities, laws and culture. However, as noted previously, there are significantly different legal and political histories to Australia and the US, which impact on how Indigenous nation-building is understood at a practical and political level, particularly in the differing recognition of Indigenous nationhood and sovereignty between the two settler colonial states.

As far as we are aware, no Indian tribal governments have received funding under the federally organised Justice Reinvestment Initiative, which allows governments to access technical assistance and potential funding for programmes and law reform to reduce imprisonment (Brown et al, 2016). In some cases, tribal governments have been incorporated into a state initiative. In South Dakota, over-representation of American Indians in state prisons is a significant issue, where they comprise 28% of male and 40% of female prison populations (South Dakota Department of Corrections, 2015). Probation and parole violations are a significant reason for imprisonment. A pilot programme on parole supervision for Indians who return to their reservations is underway. This is controversial, because it involves supervision on reservations where state authority would normally not apply. Three tribal authorities are participating in the project, while the other six tribal governments in South Dakota are not participants. The reticence of Indian tribal participation in the state-based project is a result of the potential negative effect on tribal sovereignty.

The situation in Australia for Indigenous people is considerably different where, as previously noted, there is no legal recognition of Indigenous tribal authority. What is particularly interesting with Indigenous discussions on justice reinvestment in Australia is that justice reinvestment is presented as an *opportunity to exercise authority*. Indigenous approaches to justice reinvestment transform an understanding of the process beyond simply a technocratic means of crime control and decarceration, to one that is centrally concerned with Indigenous-controlled governance. This more radical vision of justice reinvestment has important wider implications: it is conceived within broader social democratic ideals of participatory involvement and localised democratic decision making, and specifically in the Indigenous context aligns with the collective right of self-determination (Brown et al, 2016, pp 131-8).

Indigenous governance and community capacity building have been at the heart of justice reinvestment in the Australian Indigenous context. Justice reinvestment may have the potential to open the way for Indigenous communities to redirect resources from incarceration and correctional programmes and redefine the focus towards Indigenous justice, thus providing a space for the reinvigoration of Indigenous responses to social harm.

Healing

The Indigenous approach to *healing* is an integral part of Indigenous justice, and lies at the foundation of changing and reforming criminal behaviour among Indigenous people. Indigenous healing processes have developed in many of the settler colonial states and focus on a number of different areas. These include residential school survivors, members of the Stolen Generations, and people involved in family violence, child protection, alcohol and other drug addictions, and those in various stages of the criminal justice system (for a variety of specific examples, see Archibald, 2006, pp 39-48; ATSISJC, 2008, pp 167-76).

As a political process of individual and collective change, healing involves shifting the epistemological priority given to Western understandings of crime and control. It begins from a disbelief in the functionality and the legitimacy of state-centred institutional responses, where criminalisation and incarceration are seen as destructive of family, community and culture. A focus on healing relies on inter-relationality rather than individualism, and the importance of identity and culture in the process of decolonisation. As Archibald (2006, p 49) states:

> The experience of being colonised involves loss – of culture, language, land, resources, political autonomy, religious freedom, and, often personal autonomy. These losses may have a direct relationship to poor health, social and economic status of Indigenous people. Understanding the need for personal and collective healing from this perspective points to a way of healing, one that combines the socio-political work involved in decolonization with the more personal therapeutic healing journey.

Indigenous healing approaches start with the collective experience and draw strength from Indigenous culture. Inevitably, that involves an understanding of the collective harms and outcomes of colonisation, the loss of lands, the disruptions of culture, the changing of traditional roles of men and women, the collective loss and sorrow of the removal of children, and relocation of communities.

At a broader level, healing approaches cover three pillars: reclaiming history, cultural interventions and therapeutic healing (ATSISJC, 2008, p 167). Reclaiming history allows an understanding of the past and present impacts of colonialism – 'a journey that is both individual and collective in nature' (Archibald, 2006, p 26). Cultural interventions are focused on recovering and reconnecting with language, culture and ceremony. However, 'culture isn't limited to traditions and the past, it is a living breathing thing. These programs foster identity ... [By providing] a different way of understanding ... they are actively creating a new culture of pride and possibilities' (ATSISJC, 2008, p

174). The third pillar is therapeutic healing. These pillars might include individual counselling, men's and women's groups, healing circles and traditional ceremonies. They may involve traditional Indigenous counsellors, healers and medicine people, as well as modified or adapted Western approaches.

Healing is not simply about addressing offending behaviour as an individualised phenomenon. Healing is tied to Indigenous views of self-identity, which are defined by kinship (including ancestry and communal bonds), spiritual relationships and responsibilities – all of which are inseparable from each other and the land and nature (Benning, 2013, p 130). Healing is focused on addressing various types of trauma: situational trauma caused by discrete events (for example, domestic and family violence); cumulative trauma caused by pervasive distress over time (for example, the long-term effects of racism); and inter-generational trauma which is passed down from one generation to another, for example the forced relocation of communities, the denigration of Indigenous cultures (ASTISJC, 2008, pp 153-4).

In responding to offending behaviour, healing can be contrasted with the dominant risk/need paradigms in offender management (Ward and Maruna, 2007). It is evident that Indigenous developed interventions start from a different place to conventional individualised programmes like cognitive behavioural therapy (CBT). As Benning (2013, p 134) notes: 'CBT prizes the values of rationality and scientific method … CBT tends to reinforce a worldview that is Euro-American, and masculine, and tends to undervalue spiritually orientated worldviews and cooperative interactive styles.'

Indigenous programmes start with the collective Indigenous experience: individual harms and wrongs are placed within a collective context. Programmes like CBT do not understand individual change as part of a collective experience, nor the nexus between collective grief and loss and individual healing. Indigenous healing programmes start from this nexus, and focus simultaneously on both the individual and collective experience. They begin with understanding the outcomes and effects of longer-term oppression, and move from there towards the healing of individuals. They are far more expansive than a narrow 'criminogenic needs' definition of rehabilitation, which sees the individual as a discrete, autonomous being, isolated and responsible for their own decision making (Ward and Maruna, 2007, pp 76-88). Indeed, the criminal justice system is often considered as part of the problem, rather than as a solution to resolving community dysfunction and disharmony.

Indigenous healing approaches are Indigenous-controlled and are consistent with the principle of self-determination. One consequence is the tension that is created between Indigenous approaches and state-controlled offender interventions, which rely on various behavioural modification programmes determined by narrowly defined individualised 'deficits'. This is particularly so in relation to the criminogenic risk/needs paradigm. Further, as McCaslin and Breton (2008, p 518) explain, 'coloniser programming' is permeated by a view of Indigenous peoples as the problem and the colonisers as the solution. Governments favour approaches that they can closely administer, control and monitor – and these tend to be programmes reliant on expert interventions that further privilege dominant definitions of crime and disavow the voices of Indigenous peoples. They also tend to be 'off-the-shelf' programmes that are not organic to the needs and experiences of Indigenous people and communities (Cunneen, 2014b, pp 399-401).

In summary, the assertion of Indigenous law and culture is an important part of the decolonisation process – in criminal justice, as in other areas of social and political life. The concept of healing is a fundamental part of Indigenous concepts of justice, and as a theory of justice, healing underpins many of the approaches found in Indigenous courts, circle sentencing and Indigenous programmes.

Conclusion

Sentencing and punishment in settler colonial states have developed in various ways in their approach to Indigenous people. Sentencing principles may take account of Indigeneity but this is often in a negative light, seen through the ravages of alcohol, violence and substance abuse, or where Indigenous culture itself is blamed for dysfunctional behaviour. The extent to which being Indigenous is taken into account by the court is founded on an individualised, case-by-case basis. The effect is to cast both Indigenous culture and the impacts of colonialism into a space determined by the non-Indigenous legal system. The outcome has been a restrictive reading of the broader role of colonialism in undermining and negating Indigenous law and autonomy. When combined with the punitive turn in penality, emphasising deterrence, retribution and individual responsibility, it is not surprising that Indigenous incarceration rates have grown.

We outlined the important growth in various Indigenous sentencing courts in Australia, New Zealand and Canada over recent years, as well as the longer-term existence of tribal courts in the US. These have been important developments, reflecting Indigenous activism and the desire to exercise Indigenous culture and law in responding to Indigenous offending. The extent to which they can change the existing colonial relations of justice is an open question. While Indigenous sentencing courts can reflect Indigenous culture and values, they are also subject to considerable constraints in a legal and practical sense, as well as more broadly in terms of the exercise of Indigenous autonomy. Differing colonial legal histories also need to be taken into account. The recognition of limited Native American sovereignty in the US has impacted on the development of tribal courts, which contrasts with Indigenous sentencing courts in other settler colonial states. Native American sovereignty also appears to have led to a different response to justice reinvestment compared to Indigenous people in Australia.

Indigenous law and culture are fundamental to the decolonisation process. McCaslin and Breton (2008, p 512) discuss the necessity of 'reclaim[ing] frameworks that create space for deep healing by transforming the roots of harm, and to critique those frameworks that sabotage healing efforts by reinforcing colonial power'. Unless colonialism is brought 'front and centre and named as the root cause' (McCaslin and Breton 2008, p 512) of Indigenous over-representation in the criminal justice system, Indigenous peoples will continue to be oppressed. Indigenous healing processes, based on principles of Indigenous self-determination, offer an alternative vision of responding to social harm to that of Western epistemologies and theories of punishment.

SEVEN

Indigenous peoples and the globalisation of crime control

In Chapter One, we revealed our motivations for writing this book. Paramount was a desire to contribute to the development of an Indigenous criminology, and to demonstrate the 'added value' that a critical Indigenous-informed perspective can bring to analysis of significant criminological issues. Over recent decades, one of the key issues that criminologists have been exploring is the significant expansion in global markets for crime control policies and interventions (Newburn and Sparks, 2004; Tauri, 2014). While criminological attention to this phenomenon has grown, little attention has been given to its impact 'on the ground', at the micro-level, and even less so to the experiences of Indigenous peoples. For these reasons, and to enable us to fulfil the motivations discussed previously, this chapter focuses on the Indigenous experience of the contemporary globalisation of crime control. Utilising the increasing globalisation of the Family Group Conferencing (FGC) forum that was 'invented' in New Zealand in the late 1980s, we explore the impact that the increasing cross-jurisdictional transfer of crime control products is having on Indigenous peoples residing in settler colonial contexts.

The globalisation of crime control

During the period 1980 to 2000, 'globalisation' became the focus of significant research and commentary across the social sciences (Hopkins, 2002; Scholte, 2005), including the discipline of criminology (Findlay, 1999; Sparks and Newburn, 2002). The impact and sociocultural value of the increased globalisation of economic and cultural artefacts has been looked upon with both admiration and suspicion, depending on the ideological and political positions held by commentators (Robertson, 1990). For some, the significant growth in flows of capital, people and information has opened up new opportunities for social, economic and political advancement, and experiences never before known in human history (Watson, 2004). For others, globalisation represents the unfolding of tyrannical rule of peoples by a totalitarian global economic regime; one that works for the benefit of capital and those that control it (Held and McGrew, 2000). Whatever one's position on globalisation – enthusiastic or sceptical – the reality of what may be described as the increasing globalisation of contemporary life-worlds is undeniable (Lemert et al, 2010, pp 203-4). As we will demonstrate in this chapter, this is especially the case in relation to Indigenous peoples' experiences of the practice of crime control in the settler colonial context.

Colonialism and Indigenous peoples]

Sceptics of the 'special nature' of contemporary processes of globalisation alert us to the fact that global interconnectedness is nothing new. While accepting this to be the case, Scholte (2005) and Held et al (2000) argue the necessity for recognising that the *form* that globalisation takes, and the processes that drive it, may differ between historical eras. Nelken (2004, p 375) argues that '[i]n many respects, globalisation can be seen as no more than the latest stage in the expansion of capitalism and the "spread" of modernity. Little of what is ascribed to globalisation in relation to crime or anything else is totally without precedent'. As such, we cannot begin to comprehend contemporary globalisation without analysis of interconnections with previous historical formations.

As this work privileges Indigenous experiences of discrete elements of contemporary globalisation, we seek to analyse the interconnections between the contemporary form(s) of that phenomenon, and that which came before; namely, the global expansion of European financial, social and military power through the process of the purposeful colonisation of the 'New World' (Cooper, 2005). The rationale for understanding the impact of contemporary formulations of globalisation by analysing the impact of past manifestations, is captured succinctly by Fenelon and Muguia (2008, p 1657), who write that:

> In the telling of man's global project, the story of indigenous peoples has been woven into the fabric of globality, yet the leading experts on globalisation have either ignored the role of indigenous peoples or reduced their existence to prepackaged terms such as the 'fourth world' or as ethnics in 'developing nations' or even hidden in the broader 'periphery'.

For the Indigenous peoples of the 'New Worlds', the long *colonial era* of globalisation began in 1492 with what Scholte (2005, p 89) describes as 'the Columbian Exchange'. The next two centuries saw a rapid internationalisation of trade, with a significant transworld diffusion of foodstuffs such as cassava, chocolate, potatoes and tomatoes from the New World into the social context of the colonising nations, while the transatlantic transfer of 'civilisation' and major diseases such as smallpox, syphilis, typhus and measles wrought devastating consequences on the Aztec, Inca and other Indigenous peoples (Watts, 1997; Scholte, 2005). The work of Gillen and Ghosh (2007, pp 14-15) is instructive for understanding the Indigenous experience of colonisation-led globalisation, as manifested in the following extract, where they reveal that:

> The colonised are made to work for their conquerors, sometimes by threatened or actual violence, sometimes through the imposition of discriminatory labour and trade relationships. They are compelled to accept laws and political institutions of their conquerors, or to have restrictions placed on their own. Their ways of life and patterns of culture are altered, sometimes to the point where their languages and traditions are lost. Their territory is settled by immigrants from colonising states, and by people forcibly brought from elsewhere to work for the colonisers.

Franz Fanon's (1963, p 38) work on the colonial context of North Africa further reveals the immense impact of the globalisation of Western European sociopolitical authority, when he contends that:

> The colonial world is a world cut in two. The dividing line, the frontiers are shown by barracks and police stations. In the colonies it is the policeman and the soldier who are the official, instituted go-betweens, the spokesmen of the settler and his rule of oppression ... [I]n the colonial countries ... the policeman and the soldier, by their immediate presence and their frequent and direct action maintain contact with the native and advise him by means of rifle-butts and napalm not to budge. It is obvious here that the agents of government speak the language of pure force.

When Fanon eloquently states that 'the colonial world is a world cut in two', he reveals a colonial context where Indigenous peoples were excluded from European spaces not only in physical and territorial terms (hence the use of reservations in the settler colonial context), but also in relation to 'thought' and values (Hardt and Negri, 2000), as the 'Other' was deemed to have neither until the arrival of civilisation in the form of European law, religion, education, social mores and enterprise (Akbar, 1992). In the *colonialist imaginary*, the colonised subject is constructed in the metropolitan imaginary as *Other*, lacking the base social and genetic features that define 'Whiteness' (Brady and Carey, 2000). In fact, they were believed to be lacking in these fundamental features of 'the civilised' to such an extent that one could not reason with them, as they were without 'reason', and so incapable of controlling their emotions and readily resorted to violence to settle disputes that they were much in need of the firm hand of white 'law' (Tauri, 2015b). In this ideological construct, the *colonised Other* is diseased, and thus capable of contaminating the European context simply by being in close physical proximity, or by the stubborn and continued practice of their primitive culture in the midst of enlightened, rational Western society (Churchill, 1997).

As we demonstrated in Chapter Three, the imposition of a Eurocentric legal system was fundamental to the successful implementation of colonial governance in all contexts. In the eyes of many observers, most notably the German philosopher Kant (1983), this imposition, regardless of the violence that was necessary to ensure its success, was a force for peace and justice: it was essential for the future development of republicanism where once despotic institutions of 'savage societies' reigned over the unenlightened.

Employing Foucault's analysis of power, Nandy (1983) hypothesises that the eventual victory of colonialism was achieved through military and technological prowess, but just as importantly through the application of *knowledge as a technology of control* (see Foucault, 1977). Nandy writes of two initial waves of colonialism: the first he characterises as the era of 'rapacious banditry', where the initial European colonisers robbed, raped and murdered, *but without a civilising mission*, meaning the focus was primarily on the conquest of territory and space, and not for the 'souls and minds' of the Indigenous population (Armitage, 2000). In contrast, the second wave was dominated by liberals, teachers, modernists, 'scientists' and, at the forefront, the missionaries; all driven by a civilising zeal to 'progress' the natives toward a Western way of life (Bush, 2006).

The second wave of colonialists unleashed upon the colonised peoples more subtle, but arguably much more effective techniques of subjugation: the 'enduring hierarchies of subjects and knowledge including the *coloniser and colonised*, the *Occidental and the Oriental*, the *civilised and primitive*, the *scientific and superstitious*, and the *developed and the developing'* (Gandhi, 1998, p 15, emphasis added). Nandy (1983, p vii) effectively summarises these subtle technologies thus:

> This colonialism colonises minds in addition to bodies and it releases forces within colonised societies to alter their cultural priorities once and for all. In the process, it helps to generalise the concept of the modern West from a geographical and temporal entity to a psychological category. The West is now everywhere, with the West and outside, in structures and in minds.

No successful colonial enterprise could flourish after the initial phases of contact, conflict and conquest, without developing sophisticated processes designed to:

- control the influx of settlers;
- control Indigenous peoples and frame the way(s) in which they interact with settlers;
- shore up the growing power and authority of colonial government;
- enhance colonialist domination of resource extraction.

According to Bush (2006), colonial technologies of governance were designed to facilitate smooth administration of the settlers and the colonised Other with the minimum use of force or coercion, albeit that '[a]ll empires ... resorted to the "hard" power of military might if imperial power was threatened or obstructed' (Bush, 2006, p 33). The technologies were varied, from mass communications and media, to technological developments in transport and industry that enabled settler colonies to move military forces quickly and efficiently. Just as importantly, the introduction of key institutions of European custom, culture and belief were central to the subjugation of Indigenous populations, namely religion (the Christian church), education, and civil and criminal law jurisdictions (Byrd, 2011; Hinkson, 2012).

The contemporary globalisation of crime control and Indigenous peoples

According to Friman (2009, pp 1-2) 'crime has gone global' (see also Nelken, 2004, p 373). According to policy makers and researchers, the scale and scope of the globalisation of crime is unprecedented. Evidence to support this view can be found in the increasing internationalisation of the illegal trade in humans as sex workers and low paid labour for developed labour markets, drugs and military hardware (Naim, 2005). Types of crime may also become globalised as a result of specific economic policies. For example, World Bank and International Monetary Fund policies that require structural readjustment in developing economies may also bring about increasing levels of street crime and disorder as prices for basic commodities rise along with levels of unemployment. The international economic prescriptions of modernisation and development may be seen as legitimate at one level, but are also simultaneously criminogenic (Findlay, 1999).

Molina and Alberola (2005, p 5), during an analysis of the impact of policy globalisation on youth justice in Spain, argue that:

> not only has globalisation produced economical effects but also important political ones. The new frame of reference designed by globalisation has also changed the logic of criminal policy in all the different countries, as much because of what the phenomenon has meant regarding the internalisation of crime as because of the policy transfer.

Much of the focus of criminological and state policy analysis of this phenomenon focuses on: those activities defined by nation-states and international representative bodies (such as the United Nations Office on Drugs and Crime), as 'criminal'; and largely the actions of individuals and 'organised crime elites' viewed as placing the stability and values of specific nation-states and the entire world community at risk (Dobriansky, 2001; United Nations Office on Drugs and Crime, 2006, 2010). Conventional criminological analysis of the internationalisation of crime focuses on the strategies and techniques that criminals use, including technological innovations, bribery, violence, deregulation and free markets to triumph over the sovereign integrity of the state (Friman, 2009). However, critical commentators have widened the analysis to include the activities of the state and corporations, highlighting their complicity in the expansions of criminal activities on a global scale (Naim, 2005).

The globalisation of crime has also seen the rise in the practice (and importance) of cross-jurisdictional transfer of crime control theories, policies and interventions. There are a number of artefacts of globalisation that might explain this phenomenon:

• the development of highly sophisticated transport systems (increasing human movement across and between nation-states);

- IT processes and internet networks that have significantly increased financial transactions across jurisdictions;
- the development of 'super-jurisdictions' such as the European Union, which have freed up border restrictions and rationalised economic markets, and the growing importance of international bodies in regulating law, law enforcement, economic and monetary policies and regulations (Gill, 1994; Amin, 1997; Held and McGrew, 2000);
- the rise of transnational criminal organisations and the related internationalisation of criminal markets (the drug trade, illegal trade in military hardware, and so on), summarised by Nelken (2004, p 373) when he states that '... the changing nature of crime threats means that it is less and less possible to formulate the response to crime in purely national terms'.

Just as crime has gone global through the development of international markets in drugs and money laundering, so too has the response to crime (Andreas and Nadelmann 2009). For example, the increased globalisation of crime control is evident in the proliferation of new criminal laws and the push for cross-national homogenisation of such laws (most notably in the area of 'terrorism law' post-9/11), the development and implementation of sophisticated global surveillance systems and tracking technologies, efforts by various sovereign states to extend their claims to extraterritorial jurisdiction, and heightened interjurisdiction police cooperation and communication (Andreas and Nadelmann, 2009 p 21-22); the cross-jurisdictional transfer of zero tolerance policing strategies, mandatory three strikes legislation and sentencing frameworks (Schiraldi et al, 2004; Cavadino and Dignan, 2006), militaristic correctional policies and architecture (Christie, 2000); and a whole range of instruments for testing the risk profile of offenders and inmates, and even those yet to have committed 'crime' (Aas, 2007). Last but not least, the global expansion of crime control markets is evident in the cross-jurisdictional transfer of restorative justice initiatives like the FGC forum and sentencing circles (Cunneen, 2012; Tauri, 2014).

The rise of restorative justice as a globalised crime control industry

We take the case study of the spread of restorative justice in Canada as a particular example of the globalisation of crime control and its impact on Indigenous peoples. According to popular origin myths, the antecedents of contemporary restorative justice began in Canada in the late 1970s, when a parole officer from Kitchener, Ontario, introduced a process that enabled victims and offenders to meet face to face (Peachey, 1989). From there it steadily grew, with the development of community boards in San Francisco in the 1980s; the proliferation of justice boards throughout North America through the 1980s and 1990s; the FGC forum in New Zealand in the early 1990s; and sentencing circles in Canada.

All this activity has since been followed by an explosion of restorative justice related activity across North America, Western Europe and, of late, throughout parts of Asia and South America. Restorative justice is now a full-blown *industry*, playing an increasingly important, lucrative role in the globalised crime control market. Miers (2007, p 447) noted that, 'viewed globally, informed observers estimate that, by 2000, there were some 1,300 [restorative justice] programmes across 20 countries directed at young offenders'. By 2002, restorative justice was established on the United Nations agenda when the Economic and Social Council adopted the *Basic Principles on the Use of Restorative Justice Programs in Criminal Matters*. By 2010, there were at least 9,000 publications on restorative justice (Cunneen and Hoyle, 2010, p 101).

The impact on Indigenous peoples of the globalisation of restorative justice cannot be underestimated. Indigenous and critical commentators have recently revealed that the globalisation of restorative justice has been boosted by the *purposeful and significant commodification of Indigenous life-worlds* by policy workers, restorative justice advocates and justice entrepreneurs, especially in settler colonial jurisdictions (see Richards, 2007; Palys and Victor, 2007; Tauri, 2014). This in turn has facilitated the spread of restorative justice products across the increasingly globalised crime control market (Lee, 1997; Tauri, 2004; Moyle, 2013). For example, Deukmedjian (2008, pp 122-3) recounts the introduction by the Royal Canadian Mounted Police (RCMP) of restorative justice into its practices via *community justice forums* that were based heavily on the police-centred, Australian-formulated 'Wagga Wagga' model. The global trajectory of this youth justice intervention that, according to its architects was based on the so-called 'Māori' model of justice developed in New Zealand in the late 1980s, can be traced from its successful insertion into the US in 1994 in Anoka, Minnesota (McDonald et al, 1995). As Deukmedjian (2008, p 122) recounts, this successful foray into the US 'inspired McDonald and O'Connell [two of the architects of the Wagga Wagga model] to form the Transformative Justice Australian advocacy and consultancy group', members of which travelled across North America in the mid-1990s marketing their standardised FGC process to policy makers, legislators and restorative justice practitioners, and included meetings with Indigenous elders' councils in Ottawa and other Canadian cities (Rudin, 2013, personal communication).

As a result of the marketing activities of this group, a version of the Wagga Wagga model became *the* standard for restorative justice-related service delivery by the RCMP throughout Canada (Deukmedjian, 2008). Further highlighting the rapid globalisation of the FGC as part of the developing market in restorative justice products, both Chatterjee (1999) and Richards (2000) recount that RCMP officials visited New Zealand and Australia in 1996 to see at first hand the FGC model, from which the Wagga Wagga version was developed. Not long afterwards, the RCMP negotiated a cost-sharing agreement with the Department of Justice (Canada) for $3.75 million each, for a roll-out in 1997 of the revamped model known as the Community Justice Forum (Deukmedjian, 2008). Subsequently, the RCMP contracted Transformative Justice Australia to train members to run their restorative justice programme.

It is at this point – the insertion of a globalised restorative justice intervention at the provincial and federal government level in Canada – that we employ our case study, the FGC forum, to demonstrate:

- the impact of the globalisation process on discrete population groups, in this instance Indigenous peoples in Canada;
- the utility of moving from the macro-level of analysis to the micro- or community level for the purpose of criminological inquiry;
- the utility of an Indigenous-centred, critical analysis of key criminological issues, in this case with the specific analysis of the impact of the globalisation of crime control (see Tauri, 2014).

The globalisation of the FGC forum and its impact on Indigenous peoples

The appropriation of components of Indigenous life-worlds by state functionaries and criminologists for the purpose of Indigenising crime control products and culturally sensitising systems and products, is well documented (see Havemann, 1988; Tauri, 1998; Victor, 2007; Cunneen and Hoyle, 2010). Arguably, the most influential *colonising project* of this kind to arise in contemporary times, came with the passing of the Children, Young Persons, and Their Families Act 1989 (the Act) by the New Zealand Government, and with it the introduction to crime control of the Family Group Conferencing (FGC) forum.

Advocates of the FGC process make a number of claims about the relationship between the format of the process, traditional Māori justice practices, and the role the forum has played in responding to Māori concerns with the formal criminal justice system (see Jackson, 1988). Over the past two decades, the oft-made claims of the Māori/Indigenous origin of the FGC forum and its ability to culturally sensitise New Zealand (and other settler colonial) youth justice systems, has been uncritically replicated in criminological literature, especially that produced by advocates of restorative justice (for example, see Zehr, 1990; Braithwaite, 1996; McCold, 1997; Griffiths and Bazemore, 1999; Leung, 1999; Lupton and Nixon, 1999; Weitekamp, 1999; Carey, 2000; Roach, 2000; Strang, 2000; Umbreit, 2001).

Especially important to selling the FGC forum on the international crime control market has been what Daly (2002), Richards (2007) and Tauri (2004, 2014) refer to as the 'origin myths' developed around certain restorative justice products. A particularly potent myth is the often told story of the 'Māoriness' of the FGC forum. A similar myth has also been associated with the judicially focused sentencing circle forum exported out of Canada in the late 1990s (Goldbach, 2011). The origin myth of the FGC forum, especially the constant refrain to its supposed 'Māoriness', is exposed in the following statement from a well-known advocate of the restorative justice movement: 'The river [of restorative justice] is also being fed by a variety of indigenous traditions and current adaptations which draw upon those traditions: family group conferences adapted from Māori traditions in New Zealand, for example ...' (Zehr, 2002, p 62).

The constant reiteration of the origin myth and its various components within the restorative justice literature of (mostly) Western European criminologists and practitioners has resulted in it acquiring the status of a seemingly uncontestable, taken-for-granted 'truth' (see Pavlich, 2005) – one that restorative justice advocates refer to constantly in their accounts of the emergence of restorative justice practice in the contemporary moment. In response, the research and commentary of critical Indigenous and non-Indigenous scholars contest the monolithic origin myths attached to restorative processes like the FGC. Their work provides evidence of high levels of dissatisfaction among Indigenous communities with the introduction of restorative justice interventions more broadly, and of the FGC forum in particular (see Blagg, 1998; Tauri, 1998; Zellerer and Cunneen, 2001; Cunneen, 2002; Moyle, 2013). In particular, critics take advocates of restorative justice to task for making 'selective and ahistorical claims ... about indigenous social control conforming with the principles of restorative justice, while conveniently ignoring others' (Cunneen, 2002, p 43; see also Pratt, 2006).

In her ground-breaking critique of the philosophical foundations of the modern restorative justice industry, Richards (2007) exposed how the restorative justice advocates and policy workers formulate then perpetuate origin myths of forums like the FGC, in particular the well-worn claim of the 'Indigenousness' of the forum. For example, Richards demonstrated that the *Daybreak* report, authored by the Ministerial Advisory Committee for the New Zealand Department of Social Welfare (Ministerial Advisory Committee, 1988) is consistently and erroneously portrayed by restorative justice advocates and policy entrepreneurs alike as evidence of extensive Māori influence in the development of the FGC (for examples of this approach, see Braithwaite, 1996; Fulcher, 1999; and Lupton and Nixon, 1999). The exaggerated nature of such claims was made clear by one of the key architects of the legislation and the FGC forum, Mike Doolan (2005, p 1), who stated that 'those of us who were involved in the policy development process leading up to the new law had never heard of restorative justice', and that it was never the intention of the policy sector to provide Māori *whanau* (families) or 'communities of concern' with the authority to control the way the forum responded to the offending of their youth.

Despite the rise of research and commentary that contests the claims of Indigenous empowerment, it is evident that the FGC forum has become an increasingly popular commodity on the international crime control market, especially in jurisdictions experiencing significant levels of over-representation of Indigenous peoples in their criminal justice system, such as Canada, Australia and the US (Tauri, 2014). Much of the marketing, especially that produced by private, franchise-based restorative justice companies and academic entrepreneurs, uncritically promotes this particular aspect of the origin myth associated with the FGC (for example, see Morris and Maxwell, 1993; Consedine, 1995; Olsen et al, 1995; LaPrairie, 1996; Umbreit and Stacey, 1996). The 'FGC as Indigenous' component of the origin myth has also featured heavily in commentaries on the historical and geographical spread of restorative justice forums across Great Britain and Western Europe (Barnsdale and Walker, 2007), and Central and South America (Scuro, 2013).

Undoubtedly, the exportation of the FGC forum across Western jurisdictions has been heavily supported by the marketing of the forum as an 'Indigenous-inspired process', one that is grounded in Indigenous philosophies and responses to social harm. Particularly important is the fiction that the FGC product provides a forum that empowers Māori/the Indigenous Other, and signals the ability of the criminal justice system to culturally sensitise itself. A principle strategy for achieving this is Indigenisation, whereby policy makers utilise elements of Indigenous justice philosophies and practice in place of providing Indigenous peoples with jurisdictional autonomy (Havemann, 1988). The process of Indigenisation itself is supported by the *co-option* of Indigenous/Māori cultural practices, and the purposeful *utilisation* of supposed sacred and powerful cultural elements (such as 'circles') as a key tool for marketing restorative justice products in Western crime control markets, and more recently across Asia and Latin American jurisdictions (Tauri, 2014).

It is evident that many restorative justice practitioners and advocates are driven by a desire to do good, but what is also driving this process is the desire to strengthen the selling potential of products on the competitive international (and national) crime control market. But let's be clear what it is *not* about – the empowerment of the Indigenous Other. Nor is all this marketing activity intended to provide Indigenes with the 'gift' of being able to practise their traditional responses to social harm (Tauri, 2013b). Having established that the increasing globalisation of restorative justice is principally about expanding markets, and less about Indigenous empowerment, means we can now turn our attention to the question of why this issue is important, both for Indigenous peoples and critical criminological inquiry.

The Indigenous experience of the globalisation of restorative justice

The developing literature on the Indigenous experience of the cross-jurisdictional transfer of certain restorative justice 'products', like the FGC, demonstrates the value of the Indigenous analysis of the globalisation of crime control, and in particular the cross-jurisdictional transfer of policies and interventions, and of the Indigenous experience of globalisation. It also demonstrates the need for the discipline to take up Aas's (2009) instructions for its members to revisit the impact that the colonial context is having on Indigenous people's contemporary experiences of settler colonial 'justice'. For there is growing evidence, both empirical and anecdotal, that the increasing global transfer of crime control policies and interventions is impacting on Indigenous peoples in settler colonial contexts in negative as well as positive ways (see Tauri, 2005 with regard to New Zealand; and Lee, 1997 and

Victor, 2007 with regard to Canada). From a distance it appears that the globalisation of crime control, and in particular of restorative justice, is impacting on Indigenous peoples in a number of ways, including:

- containment of Indigenous critique of neo-colonial justice within state-sanctioned and dominated processes (Moyle, 2013);
- blocking Indigenous activities aimed at enhancing their jurisdictional autonomy and ability to develop their own responses to social harm, via the importation of 'culturally appropriate' crime control products (Victor, 2007).

In 1997, Gloria Lee, a member of the Cree First Nation in Canada, published an article entitled 'The Newest Old Gem: Family Group Conferencing'. Lee expressed concerns about the recently imported FGC forum being forced upon Canadian Indigenous peoples at the expense of their own justice mechanisms and practices. In particular, she argued that: 'First Nation communities are vigorously encouraged to adopt and implement the Māori process and to make alterations to fit the specific community needs, customs and traditions of people who will make use of the new process' (Lee, 1997, p 1). Lee's concerns with the nature of the importation of the FGC process into the Canadian jurisdiction, and the impact it might have on Indigenous peoples' justice aspirations in that country, have been shown to be valid.

The importation of the FGC forum into the North American context provides a timely warning on the potential impacts of the activities of policy entrepreneurs/makers, restorative justice practitioners, academics and franchise companies of the continued expansion in the globalised restorative justice market. Since the publication of Lee's article in 1997, many Canadian Indigenous peoples are still struggling to gain state support for the implementation of their own interventions and systems. The increasing utilisation of elements of Indigenous life-worlds, especially their language and justice philosophies minus their actual application, to enhance the marketability of restorative justice products, is a significant component in the neo-colonisation of Indigenous peoples. Having faced a sustained period of colonisation, during which their systems of justice were all but destroyed, Indigenes are now having to deal with a new but no less disempowering *colonising project*, namely the exportation of the Indigenised FGC forum from New Zealand and Australia to the North American continent.

We can demonstrate the potentially negative impact of this process by citing just one example: that of the Stó:lo First Nation of British

145

Columbia and their experience of the importation of the so-called 'Māori justice process, FGC' (Tauri, 2015b) by the Royal Canadian Mounted Police in the mid 1990s. Katz and Bonham (2006, p 190) relate that in 1997, the RCMP adopted a policy that gave the police the discretion to utilise restorative justice. Based on FGC processes deployed in Australia and New Zealand, as presented around Canada by 'Real Justice' advocates such as Moore and O'Connell (Rudin, private communication, 2012), the RCMP subsequently developed guidelines for community justice forums (Chatterjee and Elliott, 2003). The forum that was heavily marketed around North America at the time was based on the police-dominated 'Wagga Wagga model' developed by Terry O'Connell (see O'Connell, 1993).

Dr Wenona Victor, a criminologist from the Stó:lo Nation of the Fraser Valley in British Columbia (whose work was discussed in Chapter Two), underlines the impact that the transfer of FGCs to Canada had on Indigenous justice aspirations in that jurisdiction, thus demonstrating not only the effectiveness of the marketing process, but also the concerns that Lee expressed in the late 1990s. Wenona describes receiving training on implementing FGC within Stó:lo territory, a process that had been sold to them as 'developed by the Māori, the indigenous people of New Zealand':

> On the first day [of FGC-related training] we all eagerly awaited her [the trainer's] arrival. We were somewhat surprised to see an extremely 'White' looking lady enter the room; however, we have blonde blue-eyed, even red-headed Stó:lo among us, and so, too, we presumed, must the Māori. However, it did not take us long to come to realise this lady was not Māori and was in fact *Xwelitem* [European]. Ah, the Māori had sent a *Xwelitem*; okay, we do that too, on occasion. It is one of the many ironies of colonisation whereby *Xwelitem* often become our teachers ... [t]here are times when it is a *Xwelitem* who is recognised as the Stó:lo 'expert' and therefore, is the one talking even when there are Elders present. But by the end of the three day training course I was convinced the Māori had lost their minds! There was absolutely nothing Indigenous about this [FGC] model of justice whatsoever! (Palys and Victor, 2007, p 6)

Through the experiences of Māori, having seen their cultural context 'Indigenised', and through the Stó:lo, having experienced the importation of 'indigenous' crime control products that inhibit their own practices, we might view restorative justice products such as these in terms of Tsing's (2005) 'packages of political subjectivity', meaning that they are:

> [C]reated in a process of unmooring in which powerful carriers reformulate the stories they spread transnationally … These packages carry the inequalities of global geo-politics even as they promote the rhetoric of equality. Those who adopt and adapt them do not escape the colonial heritage, even as they explore its possibilities.

The exports in question, namely restorative justice products like FGCs, are seen by some, including Indigenous peoples, as a welcome and overdue extension of formal state justice processes beyond the Eurocentric bias of its response to social harm; of enabling 'other' ways of doing justice (Hakiaha, 1997; Māori Council of New Zealand, 1999; Quince, 2007). Yet, we must always be mindful of what Aas (2009, p 412) refers to as the 'geo-political imbalances of power between "exporters" and "importers" of penal policies and interventions'. In the context of this chapter, we need to be wary of the parasitic relationship between some exporters (government or think-tank or academics or corporation), importers (another nation state or government agency) and the 'customer'; all too often a community or an individual who has been given little choice but to receive these culturally appropriated 'gifts'. As Tsing (2005, p 76) argues, we should always keep in mind 'the particularity of globalist projects', critically analysing who constructs them, and for whose (primary) benefit they are subsequently exported and implanted on the globalised crime control market.

Conclusion

The story told in this chapter, of the Indigenous experience of the globalisation of crime control, serves to demonstrate the hollow nature of much of mainstream criminology's musings on the 'Indigenous experience'. It serves also to demonstrate what mainstream criminology will accrue from engaging with the critical Indigenous scholarship, namely data and experiences that add flesh to the bones of what has largely until now been macro-level theorising on the process(es) of contemporary globalised crime control, and its impact 'on the ground' (Aas, 2009).

But it is not the Indigenous experience alone that is essential for a fully informed criminological perspective on globalisation. Engagement with Indigenous theorising and analysis of the processes involved and their impact on Indigenous communities are essential for the discipline's ruminations to be taken seriously, for as de Sousa Santos (2006, p 395) eloquently argues:

> Apparently transparent and without complexity, the idea of globalisation masks more than it reveals of what is happening in the world. And what it masks or hides is, when viewed from a different perspective, so important that the transparency and simplicity of the idea of globalisation, far from innocent, must be considered an ideological and political move.

Thus far, a significant amount of criminological writing on the globalisation of crime control masks or simply ignores the lived experience of 'it' by our most vulnerable communities, including Indigenous peoples (Tauri, 2014). Also masked is the Indigenous response, because it is erroneous to think of Indigenous peoples as simply the passive and compliant recipients of 'white man's justice'. They are in fact, as Geyer and Bright (2000, p 62) observe, confronting:

> Western power in complex patterns of collaboration and resistance, accommodation and co-option, as they tried (often against great odds but also, we may add, with remarkable success) to reproduce and renew local worlds, using imperialists to shore up or to create positions of power, using sites of indigenous power to make deals, using the European ... positions as interlopers in order to selectively appropriate the ways of the conquerors to local ends.

The Indigenous periphery is not simply the site of unchallenged reception of imported policy goods: it can be, and is: 'a space that defies simplistic perceptions of chaos and social exclusion; it is marked by potential, innovation and creativity, organisation of new social movements and new conceptions of citizenship' (Aas, 2009, p 415). We see examples of this capability, this resistance in the Idle No More movement that flourished in Canada in 2012, and the 'South American Spring' that emerged in Brazil in late June 2013. Furthermore, we discussed in more depth in Chapter Six how Indigenous organisations in Australia have taken up the idea of justice reinvestment and moulded it in such a way as to enhance Indigenous autonomy and nation-building.

In relation to the specific issue of the globalisation of restorative justice products such as the FGC forum and other manifestations of restorative justice, resistance has been expressed in many forms – at the academic level with the recent critiques of the forum and its globalisation by Moyle (2013), Tauri (2014) and Victor (2007), and with the subversion of state-sanctioned practices wherein Indigenous peoples amend 'practice' to accommodate 'traditional' approaches to social harm (see Blagg, 2008). In more extreme cases, Indigenous peoples are rejecting state-sponsored justice processes in favour of community-centred, Indigenous-dominated initiatives, such as the *marae* (meeting house) justice process introduced in the 1990s by Aroha Terry to deal with sexual abuse cases separate from police and formal court involvement (Jantzi, 2001). Terry's motivations for introducing a 'separate' process for dealing with sexual abuse cases involving Māori women says a lot about the drivers of Māori resistance to 'Western' approaches to social harm, in particular the inability of imported processes to adequately accommodate Māori approaches to social harm in ways that empower them to find appropriate and long-lasting responses (Wickliffe, 2005; Terry et al, 2010). Policy entrepreneurs and restorative justice advocates should take note that as the mythology of the Indigenous foundations of the FGC and other restorative justice forums are further exposed, they risk the Indigenous critique turning into outright rejection.

EIGHT

Critical issues in the development of an Indigenous criminology

Why Indigenous criminology?

One of the main motivations for this book was to provide the basis for a discussion of an alternative approach to mainstream criminological theorising, explanations and commentary on Indigenous peoples' experiences of settler colonial criminal justice. The importance of an alternative, Indigenous-centred perspective on this relationship can be justified through the significant over-representation of Indigenous peoples in police contacts, stop and search, arrest, court appearances, convictions, imprisonment, and victimisation data. Apart from over-representation, the added value of an Indigenous criminology is predicated on a number of interrelated issues, two of which we will expand on here. These are:

- the need to include the process of colonisation as a key component to any theoretical and analytical framework for understanding and redefining the so-called 'Indigenous problem';
- the right of Indigenous peoples to self-determination.

Throughout this book, and particularly in Chapters Two and Three, we identified the shortcomings in the approach of many mainstream criminologists dealing with Indigenous peoples, crime control and the formation of criminological knowledge about them. We demonstrated the historical development of criminology as a key discipline of colonial control over Indigenous peoples. Whether knowingly or not, many contemporary criminologists continue to perform the role of neo-colonial intellectuals through their use of disempowering methodologies that silence Indigenous experience and knowledge of social harm.

The focus of criminological analysis on the individual antecedents of Indigenous crime and victimisation removes by default the impact of colonial and neo-colonial policies and interventions from theorising and analysis of Indigenous over-representation. In comparison, we argue that any attempt to understand the Indigenous experience that ignores the impact of coloniality, is inadequate for understanding the drivers of Indigenous over-representation, and developing effective responses. A thorough policy process must include analysis of issues such as the forced removal of children, missionary/residential schools, stolen wages and trust funds, discriminatory legislation, excessive, and often violent policing strategies, the biased application of discretionary powers by police, limitations in sentencing, and mass incarceration. Lastly, as will be discussed later in this chapter, these neo-colonial approaches work against the right of Indigenous peoples to self-determination both within criminal justice and in other spheres of social, economic and political life.

In contrast, criminological inquiry informed by Indigenous-informed research and approaches to knowledge demonstrate the significant value of an Indigenous criminology, *contra* the claims by Western scholars such as Marie (2010) and Weatherburn (2010, 2014) that Indigenous knowledge adds little to our understanding of crime and victimisation. We know, for example, the work of successive Aboriginal and Torres Strait Islander social justice commissioners in Australia have been fundamental to identifying and understanding a broad range of issues central to contemporary criminological inquiry, including violence against Indigenous women, Indigenous women's experiences of imprisonment and post release, the theoretical and practical development of Indigenous healing, the role of justice reinvestment and the importance of self-determination (ATSISJC, 1993, 2006, 2008, 2011).

Furthermore, the efficacy of Indigenous knowledge to the development of a meaningful criminological analysis can be found across all four settler colonial jurisdictions. One such example, from Aotearoa New Zealand, is Jackson's (1988) pioneering and evocative inquiry into Māori experiences of criminal justice and crime. Jackson's research demonstrated the ongoing impact on Māori communities, including contemporary high rates of offending and imprisonment, of purposeful attempts to destroy the Māori cultural context through legislation banning language, cultural transmission, and so forth. However, this substantial body of Indigenous-focused work is either dismissed or often totally ignored in mainstream criminological accounts of the 'Indigenous problem' (for example Weatherburn, 2014). What we have sought to do in this book is to demonstrate that criminology, as both an academic endeavour and as part of the state's policy apparatus, is not only poorer for ignoring Indigenous approaches, but perhaps more importantly enables crime control to continue in a neo-colonial mode that actively serves to oppress Indigenous peoples.

The importance of colonialism in explaining Indigenous over-representation

A key theme throughout this book has been the necessity of including colonialism as part of any conceptual and theoretical analysis of the Indigenous experience of the settler colonial justice. In particular, we align with the perspective voiced by McCaslin and Breton (2008, p 512), who argue:

> [T]o discuss issues around 'justice' as many Indigenous people experience them, we need both a critique of colonialism and a deeper understanding of Aboriginal culture, practices, traditions, and historical experiences. Because the existing criminal justice system is not only alien and damaging to us but also the ultimate enforcer of colonial oppression, rethinking justice from the ground up [and from the historical context within which colonialism occurred to the contemporary moment] is what Indigenous peoples – and arguably all peoples – must do.

To reiterate, we believe that building 'from the ground up' a criminology that privileges the Indigenous perspective and requires a meaningful analysis of colonialism as an explanatory factor in Indigenous peoples' experiences of settler colonial justice, is a theoretical and practical necessity. Chapter Three, in particular, focused on the interactions between colonial processes and Indigenous peoples' contact with criminal justice systems. The fundamental point from this exploration is that the impacts of colonisation on Indigenous peoples are not simply historical. The contemporary relationship between Indigenous people and crime, punishment and justice is structured by policies and political ideologies that manifest themselves today with particular effects, for example through the generational and inter-generational impacts of forced child removals and residential schools on current Indigenous contact with criminal justice and child protection systems. For this reason the ongoing effects of these processes are referred to as neo-colonial (Ross, 1998; Cunneen, 2001) or as a type of internal colonialism (Baker, 2007), particularly when contact with the criminal justice system itself *reproduces* social and economic marginalisation.

Contemporary law and order politics have also had an effect on the relationship between Indigenous peoples and criminal justice systems. Harsher criminal justice policies and ever-increasing imprisonment of Indigenes have been the hallmark of the four settler colonial jurisdictions, at least over the last two decades (see, for example, Wacquant, 2009b; Baldry et al, 2011; Cunneen et al, 2013). A result has been what some have called the 'waste management' prison, which 'promises no transformation of the prisoner ... [i]nstead, it promises to promote security in the community simply by creating a space physically separated from the community' (Simon, 2007, p 143; see also Davis, 2003). The data shows that Indigenous peoples fill these expanding prison systems at ever-increasing rates.

The colonial context of neo-liberalism

The changed political conditions around law and order in settler colonial and other Western jurisdictions reflects the growing ascendancy of neo-liberalism (Wacquant, 2009b). Given the overarching theme of this book, it is worthwhile spending some time discussing why neo-liberalism has proved hostile to the reform of criminal justice systems and, relatedly, to the recognition of Indigenous rights.

Among Western-style democracies it is those who have most strongly adopted neo-liberalism that have the highest imprisonment rates (particularly the US, Australia, Aotearoa New Zealand, the UK, South Africa and, more recently, Canada), while social democracies with coordinated market economies have the lowest (Sweden, Norway, Finland and Denmark) (Lacey, 2008). The development of the neo-liberal state has coincided with a decline in welfarism and an expansion in, and increasing privatisation of, what were historically state-focused services, such as prisons and policing (Larner, 2000; Palaez, 2014). The realignment of values and approaches primarily within Anglophone justice systems has emphasised deterrence and retribution. Individual responsibility and accountability have increasingly become the focus of the way justice systems approach offenders. The privatisation of institutions and services, widening social and economic inequality, and new or renewed insecurities around fear of crime, terrorism, 'illegal' immigrants and racial, religious and ethnic minorities have all impacted on the way criminal justice systems operate.

These changes have fuelled demands for authoritarian law and order strategies, a focus on pre-crime and risk as much as actual crime (Zedner, 2007, p 262), and a push for narrowly conceived 'what works', evidence-based responses to crime and disorder (Muncie, 2005, p 41).

The conditions of neo-liberalism have given rise to what Wacquant (2008) refers to as 'advanced marginality', much of which we can see reflected in the Indigenous social, economic, health and educational indicators and criminal justice over-representation we elaborated in Chapter One. As we have identified elsewhere, the targets of advanced marginality and hyperincarceration do not appear *de novo* (Cunneen et al, 2013). They are the colonised peoples of the Anglophone world. We argue, therefore, that the effects of neo-liberalism can only be appreciated within a contextualised understanding of colonialism.

Indigenous self-determination: where are the criminologists?

The failure of settler colonial states, and of mainstream criminology, to develop meaningful responses to Indigenous over-representation, is exposed by the lack of regard for Indigenous rights to self-determination. International recognition of the right to self-determination by Indigenous peoples can be found in the United Nations *Declaration on the Rights of Indigenous Peoples*, which has been ratified by the four countries who are the subject of this book. The *Declaration* provides a new standard-setting document, which recognises Indigenous rights to self-determination. However, at the moment there is a significant political disjuncture between the rights embedded in the *Declaration* and the operation of criminal justice systems. Indigenous people still struggle with the damaging effects of one of the leading institutions of colonial control, and struggle to change the ongoing cycles of marginalisation brought about as an outcome of criminalisation. Yet with few exceptions (Blagg, 2008; Cunneen, 2008; Cunneen and Rowe, 2015; Deckert, 2014; Tauri, 2014), most criminologists proceed with their analysis and prescriptions with little attention paid to the importance of the right of Indigenes to self-determination, or indeed of the other core principles found in the *Declaration*, including: Indigenous participation in decision making and free, prior and informed consent; non-discrimination and equality; and respect for and protection of culture, which by definition also means Indigenous knowledge.

The rights of Indigenous peoples to self-determination, whether self-proclaimed or based on national covenants (such as the Treaty of Waitangi in New Zealand) or international formulations such as the United Nations *Declaration*, are given little weight by those charged with reforming criminal justice in settler colonial jurisdictions (Cultural Survival, 2013). Furthermore, Indigenous perspectives on crime control – in particular what causes crime and over-representation, and how best to respond – have little place in the policy formulation processes of the state. One result has been the reinvigorated hegemony of administrative and authoritarian criminologies discussed in Chapter Two, which arguably has led to a retraction in some of the (slight) gains made by Indigenous peoples in the 1980s and 1990s in the development of community-centred justice initiatives (Tauri, 2005). The problem is amply identified through, for example, the experience of the Stó:lo First Nation, who were forced to train to deliver restorative justice conferencing, at the expense of the development of a wholly Stó:lo response to social harm (Palys and Victor, 2007). The impact of this reinvigoration of administrative criminology can be seen in the Australian context, where some states have begun cutting Indigenous-run programmes (Cunneen, 2011b), including the discontinuation of the Murri (Aboriginal) sentencing courts programme in 2012 by the former Queensland state government, often on the basis of cost-cutting and limited evaluations that ignore Indigenous self-determination and participation, and instead focus on narrow measures of recidivism – a measure of success that few interventions initiated by the state appear to be able to meet.

At a programmatic level, settler colonial states can – and do – point to a range of interventions to highlight their concern for, and response to, the wicked problem of Indigenous over-representation. As highlighted throughout this book, many supposed Indigenous initiatives, such as Family Group Conferencing, are best understood as state-centred processes that have been indigenised through the purposeful co-option of what state functionaries determine to be 'acceptable' customary practices. A recent example was the implementation in Aotearoa New Zealand of Rangatahi (youth) courts, which entail holding the sentencing phase of the youth court process on *marae* (meeting house). While there is no denying that Māori *tikanga* (philosophies and practices) play an essential part in this process, the sentencing framework and the judicial authority remains very much with the state (Ministry of Justice, 2010).

Enhancing Indigenous self-determination in criminal justice

As argued throughout this book, the Indigenous search for solutions to social disorder and dislocation lie in enhanced Indigenous authority through self-determination. However, significant barriers exist which problematise any moves to deal constructively with this issue. Not least is the tension between Indigenous claims to their right to self-determination in criminal justice matters, and the settler colonial states' preference for tougher law and order responses to crime.

To some extent, the policy implications and responses will be specific to particular nations because, inter alia, constitutional and other legal arrangements between federal governments and Indigenous peoples structure the possibilities for change. Contrast, for example, the US recognition of limited tribal sovereignty to the Australian context with its absence of treaties or recognition of Indigenous law-making capacity. As discussed in Chapter One, further exacerbating the situation is the need for an Indigenous criminology to deal constructively with the issue of 'difference' that exists within the Indigenous body politic, such as the issues of 'on-and-off reservation' and 'in-and-out of country' in Canada, the US and Australia, and between neo-traditionalists and urbanised identity formulations in Aotearoa New Zealand.

On a general level, our immediate research priorities in response to these issues might include analysis of effective mechanisms and outcomes for the development of cross-cultural hybrid ways of doing justice including, for example, through Aboriginal courts, community patrols, sentencing circles, healing lodges and other interventions which are, to a greater or lesser extent, built on Indigenous cultures and ways of knowing. Perhaps even more important is the need to engage with Indigenous communities across all settler colonial jurisdictions on four interrelated empirical questions:

- What type of policies and interventions do they prefer (if not those designed by state functionaries)?
- What would be the design of these initiatives (in terms of core features and practices) and their application (who would run them and how)?
- How would the policies and interventions cater for the often significant differences within Indigenous populations that manifest themselves through various dynamics? These include: living in or out of Indigenous communities; differences in how individuals, families and communities choose to 'live as Indigenous'; and the impact of colonialism on the power dynamics within Indigenous communities, especially in relation to the status of women.
- What programmes or interventions already exist that are designed and delivered by Indigenous peoples, whether known to the state or not, and, importantly, are they 'working' to deliver social justice to Indigenous communities?

The last empirical question is, in our view, important for Indigenous scholars and justice practitioners, to enable them to argue against the oft-expressed view of policy makers and administrative criminologists (such as Weatherburn, 2014), who criticise the efficacy of non-Western (Indigenous) programmatic responses to crime. Added to the belief in the lack of efficacy of Indigenous approaches, is the broader impact of the current political economy framing criminal justice in settler colonial contexts. The politics of insecurity in neo-liberal societies like Australia, Canada, the United States and Aotearoa New Zealand have led to a preoccupation with, and aversion to, risk, uncertainty and dangerousness. One reaction to the 'ontological insecurity' generated by risk aversion is a decline in tolerance and a greater insistence on the policing of moral boundaries. The state has increasingly represented itself as the guardian of internal and external security, and there is a greater emphasis on order and conformity over difference. This insecurity and risk aversion has been accentuated in the post 9/11 world. Respect for human rights and progressive reform of institutions (particularly criminal justice systems) is more difficult in an environment of paranoia and punitiveness.

Self-determination and risk

Along with the politics of insecurity and the ascendancy of neo-liberalism, developments in managerialism and risk-thinking have increasingly permeated criminal justice policy (Cunneen et al, 2013). Criminal justice classification, programme interventions, supervision and incarceration are increasingly defined through the management of risk. The assessment of risk in criminal justice involves the identification of statistically generated characteristics drawn from aggregate populations of offenders, including drug and alcohol problems, school absenteeism, rates of offending and reoffending, living in crime-prone neighbourhoods, single parent families, domestic violence, prior child abuse and neglect, high levels of unemployment, and low levels of education. These characteristics are treated as discrete 'facts' devoid of historical and social context (Cunneen, 2014b).

A core problem is the relationship between these risk factors, being Indigenous and the outcomes of colonialism. As we have noted, the contemporary socioeconomic marginalisation of Indigenous people did not just magically appear, it was created through colonial dispossession and maintained through ongoing laws and policies of exclusion. Paternalistic and authoritarian government approaches (such as we have seen in Australia and elsewhere) to, for example, school attendance, restrictions on alcohol consumption, and access to social security benefits, reproduce Indigenous people as a highly controlled and criminalised group. Furthermore, Indigenous activism in finding solutions to problems such as domestic and family violence, child abuse, and social disorder are often either unsupported or subsumed within government-managed and government-controlled programmes that further marginalise Indigenous people, and in particular Indigenous women.

Many risk indicators are associated with socioeconomic marginalisation. As Indigenous adults and young people *as a collective group* are among the most socially and economically marginalised within settler colonial states, there is the real danger that they will receive more intrusive and punitive interventions. Maurutto and Hannah-Moffat (2007, p 484) warn that few risk/need assessment tools have been examined to determine whether their criteria capture the particular situation of Indigenous people, and that risk assessment tools appear not to address the broader sociocultural context or unique issues facing Indigenous people. This view has been upheld in a Canadian federal court decision (*Ewert v. Canada*, 2015, FC 1093) that was highly critical of the use of risk assessment tools by Correctional Services Canada. The tools were found to lack scientific rigour and reliability in relation to Aboriginal offenders. Further, the tools were susceptible to cultural bias and failed to consider the special needs of Aboriginal offenders.

The increased focus on risk and risk assessment within criminal justice has at least two significant implications for Indigenous people, and in particular for their struggle for self-determination:

- One is that an understanding of crime and victimisation in Indigenous communities is removed from specific historical and political contexts. Mainstream criminology increasingly understands racial or ethnic over-representation as the result of essentially individualised factors drawn from aggregate populations (as identified previously). These factors are reproduced as individualised characteristics devoid of the social, economic and political relations of colonialism that lie at the root of Indigenous marginalisation under contemporary neo-liberalism.
- The second implication is that within the risk paradigm, any rights of Indigenous peoples (both collectively such as self-determination, and individually such as citizenship rights) are seen as secondary to the membership of a risk-defined group. In other words, the group's primary definition is centred on the type of risk characteristics they are said to possess. Within criminology these characteristics are

invariably negative and represent Indigenous people as collectively dysfunctional. Within this context it is difficult to conceive of Indigenous people as bearers of collective rights, or as having their own law and preferred solutions to social problems. Indigenous rights are considered irrelevant to solving the problem of crime, which is increasingly defined as an acceptable threat from risk-prone populations whose human rights can be 'legitimately' ignored in the interests of public safety.

Criminal justice and Indigenous empowerment

It is clear that the Indigenous domain[1] has continued not only to survive, but it has also developed and extended itself in the settler colonies of the United States, Canada, Australia and Aotearoa New Zealand. Indigenous space continues to be defended and extended. In contrast, non-Indigenous governance through the criminal justice system and the broad spectrum of government policy and programmes tends to circumscribe and delimit the struggle for Indigenous autonomy.

In many cases where Indigenous community justice initiatives have flourished, there have been successes in reducing levels of arrests and detention, as well as improvements in the maintenance of social harmony (Blagg, 2008). The success of these programmes has been acknowledged as deriving from active Aboriginal community involvement in identifying problems and developing solutions (Morley, 2015). Indigenous resistance to colonial power has been productive of new spaces for the exercise of Indigenous governance over criminal justice. Throughout settler colonial states, Indigenous communities have continued to exercise authority, and have fought to develop localised methods of dealing with problems of social disorder. Indigenous practice has provided us with the opportunity and the necessity to rethink the possibilities of a decolonised postcolonial relationship between criminal justice institutions and Indigenous communities with their demands for the exercise of authority derived from claims of sovereignty.

[1] The concept of the 'Aboriginal domain' refers to the social, political and cultural space of Aboriginal people – a space that maintains the dominant social and cultural life and the language of Indigenous people. The 'Aboriginal domain' provides a point of resistance to colonising processes and insulates Indigenous cultural, social and political space from being overtaken. This is where Indigenous knowledge, culture and governance reside (see Cunneen, 2001, 2002; Blagg, 2008).

As discussed throughout this book, the outcomes of this struggle between Indigenous governance and state policy and programmes is far from settled. The outcomes may be indicative of new hybrid justice spaces that are neither completely decolonised nor completely colonial; or it may result in the curtailment and containment of Indigenous initiatives, that is a process of *indigenisation* where justice institutions provide a façade of cultural sensitivity. A critical Indigenous criminology has great potential to work through and expose the relations of power that structure these essentially political and historic struggles over justice.

In contrast, a significant barrier to achieving greater understanding is the state of the relationship between mainstream criminology and Indigenous people. More than 25 years ago, after reviewing introductory American textbooks on criminal justice and criminology, Young (1990) lamented the fact that there was no mention of American Indians or Indigenous Alaskan. Perry (2009b, p 3) noted that: 'the paucity of research on Native Americans is more than perplexing. It is disturbing.' Martin (2014) found that in 31 introductory criminology and criminal justice textbooks, the experiences of American Indigenous peoples were poorly acknowledged. For Martin (2014, p 237) this disregard 'illustrated the ongoing effects of colonialism'.

The same cannot be said of the Australian context, where a veritable criminological industry has arisen that focuses on Aboriginal crime, with an especial concern with violent offending (see, for example, the special edition on this issue that appeared in the *Australian & New Zealand Journal of Criminology* in 2010). However, as demonstrated in Chapters Two and Six, few of the publications produced by Western criminologists in this particular jurisdiction are based on 'engaging methodologies' where the authors have deemed it necessary to gather the views and experiences of Indigenous peoples directly (Tauri, 2014).

Deckert's (2014) analysis of criminology journal publications on Indigenous peoples and issues adds empirical weight to this argument. In her study, Deckert sought to quantitatively evaluate the (de)colonised state of contemporary criminology, by reviewing research on Indigenous peoples published in elite criminology journals over the decade 2001-10. In summary, Deckert found that publication rates on Indigenous peoples and Indigenous justice issues were low when compared to the high Indigenous incarceration rates, and when compared to the quantity of academic discourse about other disproportionately incarcerated social groups. Perhaps more troubling, and indicative of mainstream criminology's response to Indigenous peoples, is Deckert's finding in relation to the prevalence of the use of 'silencing methods' (meaning methods that do not facilitate direct engagement with Indigenous peoples) to study Indigenous issues, namely that:

> On average three-quarters (80) of the studies employed one or more silencing research methods to investigate the topic 'Indigenous peoples in the criminal justice context'. A minimal upward trend in the use of non-silencing research methods can be noticed between the first and second half of the decade. (Deckert, 2015)

It is apparent from Deckert's work, from the overarching neglect of Indigenous perspectives by mainstream criminology, and from the 'denigration' of Indigenous knowledge and scholarship as 'unscientific' or adding little value to our understanding of social harm (for example Marie, 2010 and Weatherburn, 2014), that the time has come for the development of a wholly Indigenous criminology. This point should not be mistaken for an argument that *only* Indigenous peoples can undertake such an endeavour. On the contrary, we ascribe to the approach of such luminaries of Indigenous research, knowledge and scholarship as Linda Smith (1999) and Lester-Irabinna Rigney (1997) that the involvement of non-Indigenous scholars is both welcome and essential. It is neither inaccurate nor disrespectful to acknowledge the shortfall in experienced criminological researchers and scholars within Indigenous communities. Of course, it is always helpful to have on side those who can research effectively the social contexts and institutions through which Indigenous criminalisation occurs.

That non-Indigenous scholars can – and do – undertake emancipatory research based on the principles identified in Chapter Two is evident in the work of Blagg and Cunneen in relation to Australia mentioned throughout this book, Ted Palys (1993) in Canada, and Antje Deckert (2014, 2015) in New Zealand. But it is the development of a set of Indigenous scholars within and external to criminology and Indigenous-led forums, such as annual/biannual conferences and journals, that makes us confident that a critical Indigenous criminology is not only possible, but likely. In the US there is the work of American Indian scholars such as Ross (1998) and Smith (2005) focusing particularly on Indigenous women. The work of Stó:lo academic Wenona Victor (2007), on the inequities of the Canadian criminal justice and child care and protection systems, augers well for critical Indigenous scholarship in that particular jurisdiction. There has also been an increase of late in critical Māori scholarship in New Zealand, driven by the likes of University of Auckland academics Robert Webb

(2012), Khylee Quince (2007) and Tracey McIntosh (2011a), as well as Ricki Mihaere (2015). In particular, McIntosh's groundbreaking work on Māori experiences of the borstal (youth detention) system of the 1960s/1970s and imprisonment generally, is especially important given the paucity of research on this issue.

In contrast, the outlook for the Australian context appears somewhat bleak, with few Aboriginal students moving on to postgraduate studies and academic careers in criminology (although see Porter, 2014; Porter, in press). But it would be short-sighted to focus solely on criminology as the source of critical Indigenous scholarship in justice issues. One only has to engage with the critical scholarship of a range of Indigenous scholars in Australia in law, social work, social sciences and public health who are undertaking research essential to a critical Indigenous criminology. For example, we point to Kyllie Cripps' (2012, co-authored with Megan Davis) and Hannah McGlade's (2012) work on Aboriginal issues around sexual assault and child abuse, and Maggie Walter's (2013, co-authored with Chris Anderson) critique of the way in which 'Eurocentric statistics' are used to pathologise Indigenous peoples. Through this work we can see that critical Indigenous scholarship on the broad issue of social harm is not only alive, but growing, and can only benefit the development of future Indigenous criminologists.

In the past decade, another significant gap has been steadily eroded: namely, the lack of Indigenous-led journals. Until recently, researchers interested in publishing critical Indigenous criminology were forced to rely on the journals of the mainstream Western criminological academy. However, as noted above (Deckert, 2014, 2015), these 'top shelf' journals rarely publish Indigenous-centred work that privileges the experiences of Indigenous peoples. It is obvious that we are increasingly turning to an expanding range of Indigenous journals to publish our work, all of which regularly publish papers on criminological issues. These include:

- the New Zealand-based journals *MAI Review* and *AlterNative*;
- the *African Journal of Criminology and Criminal Justice Studies*, which in 2014 published a special edition on Indigenous perspectives;
- Australian-based publications such as the *International Journal of Critical Indigenous Studies* and the *Journal of Global Indigeneity*, as well as the more established journals, the *Indigenous Law Bulletin*, the *Journal of Indigenous Policy* and the *Australian Indigenous Law Review*;
- the *International Indigenous Policy Journal* and *Indigenous Policy Journal* from North America.

We see this book as a contribution towards the critical reframing of the parameters of Indigenous criminology. Such a reframing involves a necessary engagement with comparative literature on the experiences of Indigenous people across settler colonial societies. We are conscious that our attempt has been limited to the Anglophone world. However, we acknowledge that future research could do well to consider Indigenous experiences in other settler colonial states, in particular in Central and South America. In addition, the Indigenous experience in former colonies that are now independent, such as India, Malaysia and Myanmar (to name but a few), where there are substantial 'tribal' populations, has been largely ignored.

Irrespective of specific colonial histories and important legal, administrative and political differences, there are some fundamental issues that must be addressed in developing a critical Indigenous criminology. These include the long-term impacts of colonisation, the role of Indigenous activism, the primary role of Indigenous rights, the centring of Indigenous experiences, and the valorisation of Indigenous knowledges and methodologies.

References

Aas, K. (2007) *Globalisation and crime*, London: Sage Publications.

Aas, K. (2009) 'Visions of global control: Cosmopolitan aspirations in a world of friction', in M. Bosworth and C. Hoyle (eds) *What is criminology?* Oxford: Oxford University Press, pp 407–422.

Aboriginal Justice Advisory Council (2002) *Speaking out speaking strong*, Sydney: Aboriginal Justice Advisory Council.

ABS (Australian Bureau of Statistics) (2012) *Corrective Services, Australia. September 2011*, Cat. No. 4512.0, Canberra: ABS.

ABS (2013) *Estimates of Aboriginal and Torres Strait Islander Australians, June 2011*, Cat. No. 3238.0.55.001, Canberra: ABS.

ABS (2014) *Prisoners in Australia, 2014*, Cat. No. 4517.0, Canberra: ABS.

ABS (2015) *Corrective Services, Australia. June quarter 2015*, Cat. No. 4512.0, Canberra: ABS.

Agozino, B. (2003) *Counter-colonial criminology: A critique of imperialist reason*, London: Pluto Press.

Agozino, B. (2004) 'Imperialism, crime and criminology: Towards the decolonisation of criminology', *Crime, Law and Social Change*, vol 41, pp 343–58.

Agozino, B. (2010) 'What is criminology? A control freak discipline!', *African Journal of Criminology and Justice Studies*, vol 4, no 1, pp i–xx.

Akbar, A. (1992) *Postmodernism and Islam*, London: Routledge.

Alfred, T. (2005) *Wasa:se: Pathways to action and freedom*, Toronto: University of Toronto Press.

Alfred, T. and Corntassel, J. (2005) 'Being indigenous: Resurgences against contemporary colonialism', *Government and Opposition*, vol IX, pp 597–614.

Allard, T. (2010) *Understanding and preventing Indigenous offending*, Canberra: Australian Institute of Criminology.

Altman, J. (2009) 'After the NT Intervention: Violence up, malnutrition up, truancy up', *Crikey*, 9 November.

Altman, J. and Hinkson, M. (eds) (2007) *Coercive reconciliation*, Melbourne: Arena Publications.

Altman, J. and Russell, S. (2012) 'Too much "dreaming": Evaluations of the Northern Territory National Response Intervention 2007–2012', *Evidence Base*, vol 3, pp 1–24.

Alvarez, A. and Bachman, R. (1996) 'American Indians and sentencing disparity: An Arizona test', *Journal of Criminal Justice*, 24 (6), pp 549–61.

Amnesty International (n.d.) *Leonard Peltier*, www.amnestyusa.org/our-work/issues/security-and-human-rights/leonard-peltier

Amnesty International Canada (2004) *Stolen sisters: A human rights response to discrimination and violence against Indigenous women in Canada*, AMR 20/003/2004, www.amnesty.ca/sites/default/files/amr200032004enstolensisters.pdf

Amin, A. (1997) 'Placing globalisation', *Theory, Culture and Society*, 14 (2), pp 123-137.

Anaya, J. (1996) *Indigenous peoples in international law*, NY: Oxford University Press.

Andreas, P and Nadelmann, E. (2009) 'The internationalisation of crime control', in H. Friman (ed), *Crime and the global economy*, Boulder CO: Lynne Riemer, pp 21-33.

Anghie, A. (1999) 'Francisco de Vittoria and the colonial origins of international law', in P. Fitzpatrick and E. Darian-Smith (eds) *Laws of the postcolonial*, Ann Arbor: University of Michigan Press.

Anthony, T. (2012) 'The Northern Territory Intervention: The ongoing story of withheld Indigenous money', *Ngiya: Talk the Law*, vol 3, pp 2-12.

Anthony, T. (2013) *Indigenous people, crime and punishment*, Milton Park: Routledge.

Anthony, T. and Blagg, H. (2012) *Addressing the 'crime problem' of the Northern Territory Intervention: Alternate paths to regulating minor driving offences in remote Indigenous communities*, Canberra: Criminology Research Advisory Council.

Anthony, T. and Blagg, H. (2014) '"If those old women catch you, you're going to cop it": Night patrols, Indigenous women and place based sovereignty in outback Australia', *African Journal of Criminology and Justice Studies – special edition: Indigenous Perspective and Counter-Colonial Criminology*, November, pp 103-24.

Archibald, L. (2006) *Decolonization and healing: Indigenous experiences in the United States, New Zealand, Australia and Greenland*, Ottawa: Aboriginal Healing Foundation.

Armitage, D. (2000) *The ideological origins of the British Empire*, Cambridge (UK): Cambridge University Press.

ATSISJC (Aboriginal and Torres Strait Islander Social Justice Commissioner) (1993) *Social justice report 1993*, Sydney: Australian Human Rights Commission.

ATSISJC (2006) *Ending family violence and abuse in Aboriginal and Torres Strait Islander communities*, Sydney: Australian Human Rights Commission.

ATSISJC (2008) *Social justice report 2008*, Sydney: Australian Human Rights Commission.

ATSISJC (2011) *Social justice report 2011*, Sydney: Australian Human Rights Commission.

Australian Law Reform Commission (2006) *Same crime, same time: Sentencing of Federal offenders*, Report No 103, Sydney: Australian Law Reform Commission.

Baker, D. (2007) 'American Indian Executions in Historical Context', *Criminal Justice Studies: A Critical Journal of Crime, Law and Society*, vol 20, no 4, pp 315-73.

Baldry, E. and Cunneen, C. (2014) 'Imprisoned Indigenous women and the shadow of colonial patriarchy', *Australian and New Zealand Journal of Criminology*, vol 47, no 2, pp 276-98.

Baldry, E., Brown, D., Brown, M., Cunneen, C., Schwartz, M. and Steel, A. (2011) 'Imprisoning Rationalities', *Australian and New Zealand Journal of Criminology*, Special Issue on Prisons, vol 44, no 1, pp 24-40.

Balfour, G. (2008) 'Falling between the cracks of retributive and restorative justice: The victimisation and punishment of aboriginal women', *Feminist Criminology*, vol 3, pp 101-20.

Barker, M. (1998) *Policing in Indian country*, Albany: Harrow and Heston.

Barnsdale , L. and Walker, M. (2007) *Examining the use and impact of family group conferencing*, Edinburgh: Scottish Executive.

Bartels, L. (2010) *Indigenous women's offending patterns: A literature review*, Canberra: Australian Institute of Criminology.

Bartels, L. (2012) *Sentencing of Indigenous women*. Research Brief No 14, Sydney: Indigenous Justice Clearinghouse.

Behrendt, L. (2003) *Achieving social justice: Indigenous rights and Australia's future*, Leichhardt: Federation Press.

Behrendt, L., Cunneen, C. and Libesman, T. (2009) *Indigenous legal relations in Australia*, Melbourne: Oxford University Press.

Beirne, P. (1993) *Inventing criminology: Essays on the rise of 'Homo Criminalis'*, Albany: SUNY Press.

Belich, J. (1986) *The Victorian interpretation of racial conflict. The Māori, the British and the New Zealand Wars*, Montreal: McGill-Queen's University Press.

Belich, J. (2001) *Paradise reforged: A history of the New Zealander's from 1880s to the 2000's*, Honolulu: University of Hawaii Press.

Benning, T.B. (2013) 'Western and Indigenous conceptualizations of self, depression and it healing', *International Journal of Psychosocial Rehabilitation*, vol 17, no 2, pp 129-37.

Bhargava, R. (2013) 'Overcoming the epistemic injustice of colonialism', *Global Policy*, vol 4, no 4, pp 413-17.

Bielefeld, S. (2014) 'Compulsory income management and indigenous people – exploring counter-narratives amidst colonial constructions of "vulnerability"', *Sydney Law Review*, vol 36, pp 695-726.

Blagg, H. (1998) 'Restorative visions and restorative justice practices: Conferencing, ceremony and reconciliation in Australia', *Current Issues in Criminal Justice*, vol 10, no 1, pp 5-14.

Blagg, H. (2000) *Crisis intervention in Aboriginal family violence, Summary report,* Partnerships Against Domestic Violence, Canberra: Commonwealth of Australia.

Blagg, H. (2002) *Aboriginal community patrols research project*, Perth, WA: Department of Indigenous Affairs.

Blagg, H. (2008) *Crime, aboriginality and the decolonisation of justice*, Leichhardt: Hawkins Press.

Blagg, H. and Anthony, T. (2014) '"If those old women catch you, you're going to cop it": Night patrols, Indigenous women, and place-based sovereignty in outback Australia', *African Journal of Criminology and Justice Studies, Special Issue: Indigenous Perspectives and Counter Colonial Criminology*, vol 8, no 1, pp 103-24.

Bogues, A. (2005) 'Working outside criticism: Thinking beyond limits', *Boundary*, vol 2, pp 71-93.

Bond, C. and Jeffries, S. (2011) 'Indigeneity and the judicial decision to imprison', *British Journal of Criminology*, vol 51, pp 256-77.

Boulton, M. (2003) 'Monture takes advocacy for aboriginal women to national stage on Person's Day', *University of Saskatchewan on Campus News*, vol 11, no 6 (Oct 31).

Boyce, J., Cotter, A. and S. Perreault (2013) 'Police-reported crime statistics in Canada 2013', *Juristat*, vol 34, no 1, pp 1-39.

Brady, W. and Carey, M. (2000) 'Talkin' up whiteness": A black and white dialogue', in J. Docker and G. Fischer (eds) *Race, colour and identity in Australia and New Zealand*, Sydney: UNSW Press, pp 271-82.

Brennan, S., Gunn, B. and Williams, G. (2004) 'Sovereignty and its relevance to treaty-making between Indigenous peoples and Australian governments', *Sydney Law Review,* vol 26, pp 307-52.

Brooks, M. (1996) 'The incarceration of aboriginal women', in G. Bird, G. Martin and J. Neilsen (eds) *Majah: Indigenous peoples and the law*, Leichhardt: The Federation Press, pp 266-80.

Brown, D., Cunneen, C., Schwartz, M., Stubbs, J. and Young, C. (2016) *Justice reinvestment: Winding back imprisonment*, Houndmills, Basingstoke: Palgrave Macmillan.

Brown, D., Farrier, D., McNamara, L., Steel, A., Grewcock, M., Quilter, J. and Schwartz, M. (2015) *Criminal Laws*, Leichhardt: Federation Press.

Brown, M. (2005) 'That heavy machine: Reprising the colonial apparatus in 21st century social control', *Social Justice*, vol 32, no 1, pp 41-52.

Bureau of Justice Statistics (2015) *Tribal law enforcement*, Bureau of Justice Statistics, www.bjs.gov/index.cfm?ty=tp&tid=75

Burton, R. (2013) 'Neoliberalism, social harm and the financial crisis', *Internet Journal of Criminology*, online.

Bush, B. (2006) *Imperialism and postcolonialism*, Harlow (UK): Pearson Education.

Byrd, J. (2011) *The transit of empire: Indigenous critiques of colonialism*, Minneapolis: University of Minnesota.

Canadian Centre for Justice Statistics (2006) *Victimisation and offending among the aboriginal population in Canada*, Ottawa, ON: Ipsos Reid.

Canby, W. (2009) *American Indigenous law*, St Paul: Thomson Reuters.

Cardinal, H. (1999) *The unjust society*, Vancouver: Douglas and McIntyre.

Carey, M. (2000) *Restorative justice – A new approach with historical roots: Corrections retrospective 1959-1999*, St Paul: Minnesota Department of Corrections.

Castan, M. and Yarrow D. (2006) 'A charter of (some) rights... for some?', *Alternative Law Journal*, vol 31, p135.

Castells, M. (1996) *The information age: Economy, society and culture*, Oxford: Blackwell Publishers.

Castro-Gomez, S. (2002) 'The social sciences, epistemic violence, and the problem of the "invention of the other"', *Nepantla: Views from the South*, vol 3, no 2, pp 269-85.

Cavadino, M. and Dignan, J. (2006) *Penal systems*, London: Sage.

CEDAW (Committee on the Elimination of Discrimination Against Women) (2015a) *Report of the inquiry concerning Canada of the Committee on the Elimination of Discrimination Against Women*, CEDAW/C/OP.8/CAN/1, Geneva: United Nations.

CEDAW (2015b) *Observations of the government of Canada on the report of the Committee on the elimination of discrimination against women*, CEDAW/C/OP.8/CAN/2, Geneva: United Nations.

CERD (Committee on the Elimination of Racial Discrimination) (2008) *Concluding observations of the Committee on the Elimination of Racial Discrimination: United States of America*, Seventy-second Session, Geneva: United Nations.

CERD (2012) *Concluding observations of the Committee on the Elimination of Racial Discrimination: Canada*, Eighty-fifth Session, Geneva: United Nations.

CERD (2014) *Concluding observations of the Committee on the Elimination of Racial Discrimination: United States of America*, Eightieth Session, Geneva: United Nations.

Chan, C. and Cunneen, C. (2000) *Evaluation of the implementation of the New South Wales police service aboriginal strategic plan*, Sydney: Institute of Criminology.

Chesterman, J. and Galligan, B. (1997) *Citizens without rights*, Melbourne: Cambridge University Press.

Christie, N. (2000) *Crime control as industry: Towards gulags western style* (3rd edn), London: Routledge.

Chunn, D. and Menzies, R. (2006) 'So what does all this have to do with criminology? Surviving the restructuring of the discipline in the twenty-first century', *Canadian Journal of Criminology and Criminal Justice*, vol 48, no 5, pp 663-80.

Churchill, W. (1997) *A little matter of genocide: Holocaust and denial in the Americas, 1492 to the present*, San Francisco: City Lights Books.

Clark, N. (2012) 'Perseverance, determination and resistance: An Indigenous intersectional-based policy analysis of violence in the lives of Indigenous girls', *Policy Analysis Framework*, pp 133-58.

Clark, N. and Hunt, S. (2011) 'Navigating the crossroads: Exploring rural young women's experiences of health using an intersectional framework', in O. Hankivsky (ed) *Health inequities in Canada: Intersectional frameworks and practice*, Vancouver: UBC Press, pp 131-46.

Clark, S. and Cove, J. (1999) 'Canadian commissions of inquiry into Aboriginal peoples and criminal justice', in P. Havemann (ed) *Indigenous peoples in Australia, Canada and New Zealand*, Auckland: Oxford University Press, pp 302-15.

Clayworth, P. (2014) 'Prisons - Māori imprisonment', Te Ara - the Encyclopedia of New Zealand, www.TeAra.govt.nz/en/prisons

Cleland, A. and Quince, K. (2014) *Youth justice in Aotearoa New Zealand*, Wellington: Lexis Nexis.

Clement, D. (2005) 'An exercise in futility? Regionalism, state funding and ideology as obstacles to the formation of a national social movement organization in Canada', *BC Studies*, Summer, pp 63-91.

Cohen, S. (1988) *Against criminology*, New Brunswick: Transaction Books.

Colvin, M. and Pauly, J. (1983) 'A critique of criminology: Towards an integrated Structural-Marxist theory of delinquency production', *American Journal of Sociology*, vol 89, pp 513-51.

Comack, E. (2006) 'The Feminist engagement with criminology', in G. Balfour and E. Comack (eds) *Criminalising Women*, Halifax, NS: Fernwood Publishing, pp 22–55.

Commission on the Social Determinants of Health (2008) *Closing the gap in a generation: health equity through action on the social determinants of health*, Geneva: World Health Organisation.

Committee on Labour and Public Welfare, United States Senate (1969) *Indian education: A national tragedy – A national challenge,* Washington: US Government Printing Office.

Consedine, J. (1995) *Restorative justice: Healing the effects of crime*, Wellington: Ploughshare Publishing.

Cooper, F. (2005) *Colonialism in question: Theory, knowledge, history*, Berkeley: University of California Press.

Correctional Services of Canada (2012) *Aboriginal corrections: Quick facts*, www.csc-scc.gc.ca/text/pblct/qf/01-eng.pdf

Correctional Services of Canada (2014) *Aboriginal offenders research results: Quick facts*, www.csc-scc.gc.ca/publications/092/005007-3027-eng.pdf

Correctional Services Program (2015) *Adult correctional statistics in Canada, 2013/2014*, Statistics Canada, www.statcan.gc.ca/pub/85-002-x/2015001/article/14163-eng.htm?fpv=2693

Cox, D., Young, M. and Bairnsfather-Scott, A. (2009) 'No justice without healing: Australian aboriginal people and family violence', *The Australian Feminist Law Journal*, vol 30, pp 151–61.

Cox, E. (2012) 'What's data got to do with it? Reassessing the NT Intervention', *The Conversation*, 25 January.

Coyle, M. (2010) 'Notes on the study of language: Towards critical race criminology', *Western Criminological Review*, vol 11, no 1, pp 11–19.

Crenshaw, K. (1991) 'Mapping the margins: Intersectionality, identity politics, and violence against women of colour', *Stanford Law Review*, vol 43, no 6, pp 1241–1299.

Cripps, K. and Davis, M. (2012) *Communities working to reduce Indigenous family violence*, Indigenous Justice Clearing house, briefing 12.

Cultural Survival (2013) 'Over-representation of Indigenous Peoples in Incarceration is a Global Concern', in *The Stringer: Independent News*, 12 July.

Cunneen, C. (1993) 'Judicial racism', in S. McKillop (ed) *Aboriginal justice issues*, Canberra: Australian Institute of Criminology, pp 117–34.

Cunneen, C. (1997a) 'Community conferencing and the fiction of indigenous control', *Australian New Zealand Journal of Criminology*, vol 30, pp 292–311.

Cunneen, C. (1997b) *'The new stolen generations'*, paper presented at the Australian Institute of Criminology conference – Juvenile Crime and Justice: Toward 2000 and Beyond, Adelaide, 26 and 27 June.

Cunneen, C. (2001) *Conflict, politics and crime: Aboriginal communities and the police,* St Leonards: Allen and Unwin.

Cunneen, C. (2002) 'Restorative justice and the politics of decolonisation', in E. Weitekamp and H. Kerner (eds) *Restorative justice – Theoretical foundations,* Uffcome: Willan Publishing, pp 32-49.

Cunneen, C. (2005a) 'Consensus and sovereignty: Rethinking policing in the light of Indigenous self-determination', in B. Hocking (ed) *Unfinished constitutional business? Rethinking Indigenous self-determination,* Canberra: Aboriginal Studies Press, pp 47-60.

Cunneen, C. (2005b) *Evaluation of the Queensland Aboriginal and Torres Strait Islander justice agreement,* Report to the Justice Agencies CEOs, Brisbane: unpublished.

Cunneen, C. (2006) 'Racism, discrimination and the over-representation of indigenous people in the criminal justice system: Some conceptual and explanatory issues', *Current Issues in Criminal Justice,* vol 17, no 3, pp 329-46.

Cunneen, C. (2007a) 'Riot, resistance and moral panic: Demonising the colonial other' in S. Poynting and G. Morgan (eds) *Outrageous! Moral panics in Australia,* Hobart: ACYS Publishing, pp 20-9.

Cunneen, C. (2007b) 'Assimilation and the re-invention of barbarism', *Australian Indigenous Law Review,* vol 11, pp 42-45.

Cunneen, C. (2008) 'State crime, the colonial question and Indigenous peoples', in A. Smeulers and R. Haveman (eds) *Supranational criminology: towards a criminology of international crimes,* Antwerp: Intersentia Press, pp 159-79.

Cunneen, C. (2009) 'Indigenous incarceration: The violence of colonial law and justice', in P. Scraton and J. McCulloch (eds) *The violence of incarceration,* London: Routledge, pp 209-24.

Cunneen, C. (2011a) 'Postcolonial perspectives for criminology', in M. Bosworth and C. Hoyle (eds) *What is criminology?,* Oxford: Oxford University Press, pp 209-24.

Cunneen, C. (2011b) 'Indigeneity, sovereignty and the law: Challenging the processes of criminalisation', *South Atlantic Quarterly (Special Issue),* vol 110, no 2, pp 309-23.

Cunneen, C. (2011c) *State crime, the colonial question and indigenous peoples,* Sydney: University of New South Wales Faculty of Law.

Cunneen, C. (2012) 'Restorative justice, globalisation and the logic of empire', in J. McCulloch and S. Pickering, (eds) *Borders and Transnational Crime: Pre-Crime, Mobility and Serious Harm in an Age of Globalization*, London: Palgrave Macmillan, pp 99-113.

Cunneen, C. (2014a) 'Youth Justice in Australia', in M. Tonry (ed) *Criminology and criminal justice, Oxford Handbooks Online*, NY: Oxford University Press, pp 1-16.

Cunneen, C. (2014b) 'Colonial processes, Indigenous peoples, and criminal justice systems', in T. Bucerius and M. Tonry (eds) *The Oxford Handbook of Ethnicity, Crime, and Immigration*, Oxford: Oxford University Press, pp 386-407.

Cunneen, C., Allison, F. and Schwartz, M. (2014) 'Access to justice for Aboriginal people in the Northern Territory', *Australian Journal of Social Issues*, vol 49, no 2, pp 219-42.

Cunneen, C., Baldry, E., Brown, D., Brown, M., Schwartz, M. and Steel, A. (2013) *Penal culture and hyperincarceration*, Farnham: Ashgate.

Cunneen, C. and Hoyle, C. (2010) *Debating restorative justice*, Oxford and Portland: Hart Publishing.

Cunneen, C. and Kerley, K. (1995) 'Indigenous women and criminal justice: Some comments on the Australian situation', in K. Hazlehurst (eds) *Perceptions of justice: Issues in indigenous community empowerment*, Sydney: Avebury, pp 71-94.

Cunneen, C. and Rowe, S. (2014) 'Changing Narratives: Colonised Peoples, Criminology and Social Work', *International Journal for Crime, Justice and Social Democracy*, vol 3, no 2. pp49-67.

Cunneen, C. and Rowe, S. (2015) 'Decolonising Indigenous victimisation', in D. Wilson and S. Ross (eds) *Crime, victims and policy*, London: Palgrave Macmillan, pp10-32.

Cunneen, C., White, R. and Richards, K. (2015) *Juvenile justice. Youth and crime in Australia* (5th edn), Melbourne: Oxford University Press.

Curry, S. (2004) *Indigenous sovereignty and the democratic project,* Aldershot: Ashgate.

Curtis-Fawley, S. and Daly, K. (2005) 'Gendered violence and restorative justice', *Violence Against Women*, vol 11, pp 603-38.

Czyzewski, K. (2011) 'Colonialism as a broader social determinant of health', *The International Indigenous Policy Journal*, vol 2, no 1, article 5 (online).Daly, K. (2002) 'Restorative justice – The real story', *Punishment and Society*, vol 4, no 1, pp 55-79.

Davis, A. (1998) 'Racialised punishment and prison abolition', in J. James (ed) *The Angela Y Davis Reader*, Oxford: Blackwell, pp 96-107.

Davis, A. (2003) *Are prisons obsolete?* NY: Seven Stories Press.

Deckert, A. (2014) 'Neo-colonial criminology: Quantifying the silence', *African Journal of Criminology and Justice Studies*, vol 8, no 1, pp 39-60.

Deckert, A. (2015) 'Criminologists, duct tape, and Indigenous people: Quantifying the use of silencing research methods', *International Journal of Comparative and Applied Criminal Justice*, May: online.

Delgado, R. and Stefancic, J. (2007) 'Critical race theory and criminal justice', *Humanity and Society*, vol 31, no 2-3, pp 133-45.

Dell, C. and Kilty, J. (2013) 'The creation of the expected Aboriginal drug offender in Canada: Exploring relations between victimisation, punishment, and cultural identity', *International Review of Victimology*, vol 19, no 1, pp 51-68.

Department of Corrections (2013) *Prison facts and statistics – September 2013*, www.corrections.govt.nz/resources/research_and_statistics/quarterly_prison_statistics/PS_Sept_2013.html

Department of Corrections (2015) *Prison facts and statistics – December 2014*, Wellington: Department of Corrections (NZ) www.corrections.govt.nz/resources/quarterly_prison_statistics/CP_December_2014.html#ethnicity

Department of Justice, Canada (2007) *Aboriginal justice strategy summative evaluation: Final report*, Ottawa: Department of Justice, Canada.

de Sousa Santos, B. (2006) 'Globalisations', *Theory, Culture and Society*, vol 23, pp 393-9.

Deukmedjian, J. (2008) 'The rise and fall of RCMP community justice forums: Restorative justice and public safety interoperability in Canada', *Canadian Journal of Criminology and Criminal Justice*, vol 50, no 2, pp 117-151.

Deutscher, M. (1983) *Subjecting and objecting: An essay in objectivity*, Oxford: Basil *Blackwell*.

de Sousa Santos, B. (2006) 'Globalisations', *Theory, Culture and Society*, vol 23, pp 393-399.

Devi, S. (2011) 'Native American health left out in the cold', *Lancet*, vol 3771, pp 1481-2.

Dickson, M. (2011) 'The Rangatahi Court', *Waikato Law Review*, vol 19, no 2, pp 86-107.

Dobriansky, P. (2001) 'The explosive growth of organised crime', *Global Issues*, August, found at http://usinfo.state.gov.

Dodson, M. (1997a) 'Citizenship in Australia: An Indigenous perspective', *Alternative Law Journal*, vol 22, p 58.

Dodson, M. (1997b) *'Overcoming discrimination against Indigenous people: Australia's experience'*, paper presented at the Australasian Law Reform Agencies Conference, Sydney, Australia, September 16.

Doolan, M. (2005) *Restorative practices and family empowerment: Both/ and or either/or?* Available from http://www.americanhumane.org/ site/DocServer/au13 retrieved on 8 November 2013.

Douglas, M. (1966) *Purity and danger*, London: Routledge and Kegan Paul.

Doxtater, M. (2004) 'Indigenous knowledge in the decolonial era', *American Indian Quarterly*, vol 28, no 3/4, pp 618-33.

Dunbar-Ortiz, R. (2014) *An Indigenous peoples' history of the United States*, Boston: Beacon Press.

Dupont, I. (2008) 'Beyond doing no harm: A call for participatory research with marginalised populations in criminological research', *Critical Criminology*, vol 16, pp 197-207.

Dylan, A., Regehr, C. and Alaggia, R. (2008) 'And justice for all? Aboriginal victims of sexual violence', *Violence Against Women*, vol 14, no 6, pp 678-96.

Evans, J. (2005) 'Colonialism and the rule of law: the case of South Australia' in B. Godfrey and G. Dunstall (eds) Crime and empire 1840-1940: Criminal justice in local and global context, Cullompton: Willan Publishing, pp 161-76.

Fanon, F. (1963) *The wretched of the earth*, Harmondsworth (UK): Penguin Books.

Fanon, F. (1967) *Black skin, white masks*, London: Pluto Press.

Fenelon, J. and Murguia, S. (2008) 'Indigenous peoples: Globalisation, resistance, and revitalisation', *American Behavioural Scientist*, vol 51, no 12, pp 1656-1671.

Findlay, M. 1999, *The globalisation of crime. Understanding transitional relationships in context*, Cambridge: Cambridge University Press.

Findlay, M. (2008) *Governing through globalised crime*, Cullompton, UK: Willan Publishing.

Finnane, M. (1997) *Punishment in Australian society*, Melbourne: Oxford University Press.

Finnane, M. (2005) 'Crimes of violence, crimes of empire?' in B. Godfrey and G. Dunstall (eds) Crime and empire 1840-1940: Criminal justice in local and global context, Cullompton (UK): Willan Publishing, pp 43-56.

Finnane, M. and McGuire, J. (2001) 'The uses of punishment and exile: Aborigines in colonial Australia', *Punishment and Society*, vol 3, no 2, pp 279-98.

Fleras, A. and Elliott, J. (1992) *The nations within, Aboriginal - state relations in Canada, the United States and New Zealand*, Toronto: Oxford University Press.

Flynn, M. (2005) 'Not Aboriginal enough for particular consideration when sentencing', *Indigenous Law Bulletin*, vol 6, no 9, pp 15-17.

Foley, G. (1988) 'One Black Life', *Rolling Stone*, issue 426, pp 107-11.

Foucault, M. (1977) *Discipline and punish*, NY: Vantage.

Frideres, J. (2008) 'Aboriginal identity in the Canadian context', *The Canadian Journal of Native Studies*, vol 28, no 2, pp 313-42.

Friman, H. (2009) 'Crime and globalisation', in H. Friman (ed) *Crime and the global political economy*, London: Lynne Rienner Publishers, pp 11-19.Fulcher, L. (1999) 'Cultural origins of the contemporary family group conference', *Child care in practice: Northern Ireland journal of multi-disciplinary child care practice*, vol 5, no 4, pp 328-339.

Gallagher, P. and Poletti, P. (1998) *Sentencing disparity and the ethnicity of juvenile offenders*, Sydney: Judicial Commission of New South Wales.

Gandhi, L. (1998) *Postcolonial Theory – An Introduction*, New Delhi: Oxford University Press

Gardiner, G. and Takagaki, T. (2001/2002) 'Indigenous women and police in Victoria: Patterns of offending and victimisation in the 1990s', *Current Issues in Criminal Justice*, vol 13, pp 301-21.

Garland, D. (2001) *The culture of control: Crime and social order in contemporary society*, Chicago: University of Chicago Press.

George, L., Ngamu, E., Sidwell, M., Hauraki, M., Martin-Fletcher, N., Ripia, L., Davis, R. and Wihongi, H. (2014) 'Historical trauma and contemporary rebuilding for Māori women with experiences of incarceration', *MAI Journal*, vol 3, no 3, pp 183-96.

Geyer, M and Bright, C. (2000) 'World history in a global age', in D. Held and A. McGrew (eds) *The global transformations reader: An introduction to the globalisation debate*, Cambridge: Polity Press, pp. 61-67.

Gilchrist, L. (1997) 'Aboriginal communities and social science research: Voyeurism in transition', *Native Social Work Journal*, vol 1, pp 69-85.

Gill, S. (1994) 'Structural change and global economy: Globalising elites and the emerging world order', in Y. Sakamoto (ed) *Global transformation: Challenges to the state system*, New York: United Nations University Press, pp 169-199.

Gillen, P. and Ghosh, D. (2007) *Colonialism and modernity*, Sydney: University of New South Wales Press.

Glass, K. and Kaufert, J. (2007) 'Research ethics review and aboriginal community values: Can the two be reconciled?' *Journal of Empirical Research on Human Research Ethics*, vol 2, no 2, pp 25-40.

Goel, R. (2000) 'No women at the center: The use of the Canadian sentencing circle in domestic violence cases', *Wisconsin Women's Law Journal*, vol 15, pp 293-334.

Goldbach, T. (2011) 'Sentencing circles, clashing worldviews, and the case of Christopher Pauchey', *Illumine: Journal of the Centre for Studies in Religion and Society Graduate Students Association* 10(1): 53-76.

Goldflam, R. (2013) 'The [non-] role of Aboriginal customary law in sentencing in the Northern Territory', *Australian Indigenous Law Review*, vol 17, no 1, pp 71-80.

Goldinguy, S. and Mataki, T. (2014) 'Indigenous subjectivities: How young women prisoners subvert domination representations to maintain their sense of intrinsic worth', in M. Pollotta-Chiarolli and B. Pease (eds) *The politics of recognition and social justice: Transforming subjectivities and new forms of resistance*, NY: Routledge, pp 144-56.

Goodall, H. (1996) *Invasion to embassy. Land in Aboriginal politics, 1770-1972*, St Leonards: Allen and Unwin.

Grande, S. (2004) *Red pedagogy: Native American social and political thought*, Toronto: Rowman and Littlefield Publishers Inc.

Green, R. (1998) *Justice in Aboriginal communities. Sentencing alternatives*, Saskatoon: Purich Publishing.

Green, S. and Baldry, E. (2002) 'Indigenous welfare in Australia', *Journal of Societal and Social Policy*, vol 1, no 1, pp 1-14.

Griffiths, C. and Bazemore, G. (1999) 'Introduction to the special issue', *International Review of Victimology*, vol 6, no 4, pp 261-263.

Haebich, A. (1992) *For their own good: Aborigines and government in the South West of Western Australia 1900-1940*, Perth: University of Western Australia Press.

Haebich, A. (2000) *Broken circles. Fragmenting Indigenous families 1800-2000*, Freemantle: Freemantle Arts Centre Press.

Hakiaha, M. (1999) 'Resolving conflict from a Maori perspective', in H. Bowen and J. Consedine (eds) *Restorative justice: Contemporary themes and practice*, Lyttelton: Ploughshare Publishers, pp 90-94.

Hamilton, A. and Sinclair, M. (1991) *Report of the Aboriginal justice inquiry of Manitoba: The justice system and Aboriginal people*, vol 1, www.ajic.mb.ca/volumel/toc.html

Hardt, M. and Negri, A. (2000) *Empire*, Cambridge (MA): Harvard University Press.

Harris, C. (2002) *Making native space: Colonialism, resistance, and reserves in British Columbia*, Vancouver: University of British Columbia Press.

Harris, M., Carlson, B. and Poata-Smith, E. (2013) 'Indigenous identities and the politics of authenticity', in M. Harris, M. Nakata and B. Carlson (eds) *The politics of identity: Emerging indigeneity*, Sydney: University of Technology Sydney E-Press, pp 1-9.

Havemann, P. (1988) 'The indigenisation of social control in Canada', in B. Morse and G. Woodman (eds) *Indigenous law and the state*, Dordrecht: Foris Publications, pp 71-100.

Hayman, S. (2006) *Imprisoning our sisters: The new federal women's prisons in Canada*, Montreal and Kingston: McGill-Queen's University Press.

Held, D. and McGrew, A. (2000) 'The great globalisation debate: An introduction', in D. Held and A. McGrew (eds) *The global transformations reader: An introduction to the globalisation debate*, New York: Polity Press, pp 1-46.

Held, D; McGrew, A; Goldblatt, D and Perraton, J. (2000) 'Rethinking globalisation', in D. Held and A. McGrew (eds) *The global transformations reader: An introduction to the globalisation debate*, New York: Polity Press, pp 54-60.

Hickman, A., Poitras L. and Evans G. (1989) *Royal Commission on the Donald Marshall, Jr., Prosecution, digest of findings and recommendations*, Halifax: Province of Nova Scotia.

Hillyard, P., Sim, J., Tombs, S. and Whyte, D. (2004) 'Leaving a stain upon the silence: Contemporary criminology and the politics of dissent', *British Journal of Criminology*, vol 44, no 3, pp 360-90.

Hinkson, J. (2012) 'Why settler colonialism?' *Arena*, no 37-38, pp 1-15.

Hixson, L., Hepler, B. and Kim, M. (2012) *The Native Hawaiian and other Pacific Islander population: 2010*, 2010 Census Briefs, Washington: US Census Bureau.

Hocking, Hon. (1875) Western Australia Parliament Parliamentary Debates (Hansard) Legislative Council. 1875-76. Reading speech. 8 December 1975. Perth: Western Australia Parliament.

Hogeveen, B. (2005) 'Toward "safer" and "better" communities? Canada's Youth Criminal Justice Act, Aboriginal youth and the processes of exclusion', *Critical Criminology*, vol 13, pp 287–305.

Hood, R. (1992) *Race and sentencing*, Oxford: Oxford University Press.

Hopkins, A. (2002) 'Globalisation: An agenda for historians', in A. Hopkins (ed) *Globalisation in World History*. London: Pimlico, pp 1-11.

Howard-Wagner, D., Habibis, D. and Petray, T. (2012) *Theorising Indigenous sociology: Australian perspectives*, Sydney: The Australian Sociological Association.

Howard-Wagner, D. and Kelly, B. (2011) 'Containing Aboriginal mobility in the Northern Territory: From "protectionism" to "interventionism"', *Law Text Culture*, vol 15, pp 102-34.

Howe, A. (2009) 'Addressing child sexual assault in Australian aboriginal communities: The politics of white voice', *The Australian Feminist Law Journal*, vol 30, pp 41-61.

Huffington Post Politics Canada (2014) *Number of Aboriginal women behind bars spiking: Report*, www.huffingtonpost.ca

Human Rights Watch (2013) *Those who take us away. Abusive policing and failures in protection of Indigenous women and girls in Northern British Columbia, Canada*, Human Rights Watch, www.hrw.org/sites/default/files/reports/canada0213webwcover_0.pdf

Indian Law and Order Commission (2013) *A roadmap for making native America safer, Report to the President and Congress of the United States*, Indian Law and Order Commission, www.aisc.ucla.edu/iloc/report/

Insight (2014) *Unfinished business: Aboriginal women in Victorian prisons*, Melbourne: Victorian Council of Social Services.

International Indian Treaty Council (2007) *Racial discrimination against Indigenous peoples in the United States, consolidated Indigenous shadow report to the UN Committee on the Elimination of Racial Discrimination*, San Francisco: International Indian Treaty Council.

International Indian Treaty Council (2014) *Alternative report regarding racial discrimination by the United State criminal justice system against Indigenous peoples in the United States and the case of Leonard Peltier, Report to the UN Committee on the Elimination of Racial Discrimination*, San Francisco: International Indian Treaty Council.

IPCA (Independent Police Conduct Authority) (2012) *Thematic report: Deaths in custody – A ten year review*, Wellington, NZ: IPCA.

Jackson, M. (1988) *Māori and the criminal justice system: He whaipaanga hou: A new perspective*, Wellington: Department of Justice.

Jackson, M. (1992) 'The colonisation of Māori philosophy', in G. Oddie and R. Perret (eds) *Justice, ethics and New Zealand society*, Auckland: Oxford University Press, pp 1-10.

Jackson, M. (1994) 'Changing realities: Unchanging truths', *Australian Journal of Law and Society*, vol 115, no 10, pp 115-29.

Jackson, M. (1995) 'Justice and political power: Reasserting Māori legal processes', in K. Hazlehurst (ed) *Legal pluralism and the colonial legacy: Indigenous experiences of justice in Canada, Australia, and New Zealand*, Aldershot: Avebury, pp 243-63.

Jacobs, M. (2009) *White mother to a dark race: Settler colonialism, maternalism, and the removal of Indigenous children in the American west and Australia, 1880-1940*, Lincoln: University of Nebraska Press.

Jantzi, V. (2001) *Restorative justice in New Zealand: Current practice, future possibilities: Final report*, Auckland: Massey University.

Johnston, E. (1991) *Royal Commission into Aboriginal Deaths in Custody national report*, 5 vols, Canberra: Australian Government.

Jones, T. and Newburn, T. (2001) *Learning from Uncle Sam? Exploring US influence on British crime control policy*, paper presented the Political Studies Association, Manchester, April.

Judicial Branch of the Navajo Nation (2015) *Annual report. Fiscal year 2014*, Judicial Branch of the Navajo Nation, http://www.navajocourts.org/Reports2/JB-FY-2014-AnnualReport.pdf.

JustSpeak (2012) *Māori and the criminal justice system: A youth perspective*, Wellington: JustSpeak.

Kant, I. (1983) *Perpetual peace and other essays on politics, history and morals*, Cambridge MA: Hackett Publishing Co.

Katz, J. and Bonham, G. (2006) 'Restorative justice in Canada and the U.S: A comparative analysis', *Journal of the Institute of Justice Studies*, vol 6, pp 187-196.

Kercher, B. (1995) *An unruly child*, St Leonards: Allen and Unwin.

Kidd, R. (1997) *The way we civilise*, Brisbane: University of Queensland Press.

Kidd, R. (2000) *Black lives, government lies*, Sydney: University of New South Wales Press Ltd.

Kidd, R. (2006) *Trustees on Trial. Recovering the Stolen Wages*, Canberra: Aboriginal Studies Press.

Kitossa, T. (2012) 'Criminology and colonialism: Counter colonial criminology and the Canadian context', *The Journal of Pan African Studies*, vol 4, no 1, pp 204-26.

Kramer, R. and Michalowski, R. (2005) 'War, aggression and state crime', *British Journal of Criminology*, vol 45, pp 446-69.

Kukutai, T. and Walter, M. (2015) 'Recognition and indigenising official statistics: Reflections from Aotearoa New Zealand and Australia', *Statistical Journal of the IAOS*, vol 31, pp 317-26.

Koukkanen, R. (2014) Gendered violence and politics in indigenous communities, *International Feminist Journal of Politics*, pp 1-18.

Lacey, N. (2008) *The prisoners' dilemma: Political economy and punishment in contemporary democracies (The Hamlyn Lectures)*, Cambridge: Cambridge University Press.

Lannon, V. (2013) 'From the red power movement to Idle No More', *Socialist. CA*, www.socialist.ca/node/1872

LaPrairie, C. (1996) *Examining aboriginal corrections in Canada*, Ottawa: Ministry of the Solicitor General.

Larner, W. (2000) 'Neo-liberalism: policy, ideology, governmentality', *Studies in Political Economy*, vol 63, Autumn, pp 5-25.

Law Reform Commission of Western Australia (LRCWA) (2006) *Aboriginal customary laws, final report*, Perth: Law Reform Commission of Western Australia.

Lee, G. (1997) 'The newest old gem: Family group conferencing', *Justice as Healing*, vol 2, no 2, pp 1-3.

Lemert, C., Elliot, A., Chaffee, D. and Hsu, E. (2010) *Globalisation: A reader*, London: Routledge.

Leung, M. (1999) *The origins of restorative justice*, available at www.cfcj-fcjc.org/full-text/leung.htm, retrieved on 9 September 2013.

Lilles, H. (2001) 'Circle Sentencing: Part of the Restorative Justice Continuum', in A. Morris and G. Maxwell (eds) *Restorative Justice for Juveniles*, Oxford: Hart Publishing.

Linden, S. (2007) *Report of the Ipperwash inquiry*, Toronto: Ministry of the Attorney-General.

Lithopoulos, S. (2007) *International comparison of Indigenous policing models*, Ottawa: Public Safety Canada.

Lucashenko, M. (1996) 'Violence against Indigenous women: Public and private dimensions', *Violence Against Women*, vol 2, pp 378-90.

Luna-Firebaugh, E. (2003) 'Incarcerating ourselves: Tribal jails and corrections', *The Prison Journal*, vol 83, no 1, pp 51-66.

Luna-Firebaugh, E. (2007) *Tribal policing: Asserting sovereignty, seeking justice*, Tuscon: University of Arizona Press.

Lupton, C. and Nixon, P. (1999) *Empowering practice? A critical appraisal of the family group conference approach*, Bristol: The Policy Press.

Lynch, M. (2000) 'The Power of oppression: Understanding the history of criminology as a science of oppression', *Critical Criminology*, vol 9, no 1/2, pp 144-52.

Macartney, S., Bishaw, A. and Fontenot, K. (2013) *Poverty Rates for Selected Detailed Race and Hispanic Groups by State and Place: 2007-2011*, American Community Survey Briefs, Washington: US Census Bureau.

MacDonald, G. (2010) 'Colonising processes, the state and ontological violence: Historicising aboriginal Australian experience', *Anthropologica*, vol 52, no 1, pp 49-64.

Mahoney, D. (2005) *Inquiry into the management of offenders in custody and in the community*, Perth: Department of Premier and Cabinet.

Malik, K. (1996) *The meaning of race: Race, history and culture in western society*, London: Macmillan.

Manuel, J. (2009) *The Fernando Principles: The sentencing of Indigenous offenders in NSW: Paper prepared for the NSW Sentencing Council*, www.sentencingcouncil.justice.nsw.gov.au/Documents/sentencing_indigenous_offenders_nsw.pdf

Maori Council of New Zealand. (1999) 'Restorative justice: A Maori perspective', in H. Bowen and J. Consedine (eds) *Restorative justice: Contemporary themes and practice*, Lyttelton: Ploughshare Publishers, pp 25-35.

Marchetti, E. and Daly, K. (2007) 'Indigenous sentencing courts: Towards a theoretical and jurisprudential model', *Sydney Law Review*, vol 29, no 3, pp 416-43.

Marchetti, E. and Downie, R. (2014) 'Indigenous people and sentencing courts in Australia, New Zealand and Canada', in S. Bucerius and M. Tonry (eds) *The Oxford handbook of ethnicity, crime, and immigration*, Oxford: Oxford University Press, pp 360-85.

Marie, D. (2010) 'Māori and criminal offending: A critical appraisal', *The Australian and New Zealand Journal of Criminology*, vol 43, no 2, pp 283-300.

Markovich, D. (2003) 'Genocide, a crime of which no Anglo-Saxon nation could be guilty', *E-LAW, Murdoch University Electronic Journal of Law*, September, vol 10, no 3, online.

Marriot, L. and Sim, D. (2014) *Indicators of inequality for Māori and Pacific people*, Working Paper IV, Wellington: Victoria University of Wellington.

Martel, J. and Brassard, R. (2008) 'Painting the prison "red": Constructing and experiencing Aboriginal identities in prison', *British Journal of Social Work*, vol 38, pp 340-61.

Martin, F. A. (2014) 'The coverage of American Indians and Alaskan Natives in criminal justice and criminology introductory textbooks', *Critical Criminology*, no 22, pp 237-56.

Matsuda, M., Lawrence III, C., Delgado, R. and Crenshaw, K. (1993) *Words that wound*, Boulder, CO: Westview Press.

Matthiessen, P. (1992) *In the spirit of Crazy Horse*, London: Harper Collins.

Maurutto P. and Hannah-Moffat, K. (2007) 'Understanding risk in the context of the Youth Criminal Justice Act', *Canadian Journal of Criminology and Criminal Justice*, vol 49, no 4, pp 465-491.

McCarthy, R. (2004) 'The Bureau of Indian Affairs and the Federal trust obligation to American Indians', *Brigham Young Journal of Public Law*, vol 19, no 1, pp 1-160.

McCaslin, W. D. and Breton, D. C. (2008) 'Justice as healing: Going outside the colonisers' cage', in N. Denzin, Y. Lincoln and L. T. Smith (eds) *Handbook of critical and Indigenous methodologies*, London: Sage Publications, pp 511-30.

McCold, P. (1997) *Restorative justice: An annotated bibliography*, Monsey: Working Party on Restorative Justice, Alliance of NGOs on Crime Prevention and Criminal Justice.

McCorquodale, J. (1986) 'The legal classification of race in Australia', *Aboriginal History*, vol 10, no 1, pp 7-24.

McCulloch, J. and Stanley, E. (eds) (2012) *State crime and resistance*, London: Routledge.

McDonald, J., Moore, D., O'Connell, T. and Thorsborne, M. (1995) *Real justice training manual: Coordinating family group conferences*, Pipersville (PA): Piper's

McGlade, H. (2012) *Our greatest challenge: Aboriginal children and human rights*, Canberra: Aboriginal Studies Press.

McGrath, A. (1993) 'Colonialism, crime and civilisation', *Australian Cultural History*, vol 12, pp 100-14.

McGregor, R. (1997) *Imagined destinies. Aboriginal Australians and the doomed race theory, 1880-1939*, Carlton South, Victoria: Melbourne University Press.

McHugh, P. (2001) 'A history of crown sovereignty in New Zealand', in A. Sharp and P. McHugh (eds) *Histories, power and loss*, Wellington: Bridget Williams Books.

McIntosh, T. (2011a) 'Marginalisation: A case study: Confinement', in T. McIntosh and M. Mulholland (eds) *Māori and social issues* (vol 1), Wellington: Huia Publications, pp 263-83.

McIntosh, T. (2011b) *Prison as the norm: Researching the legacies of inequality*, paper presented at 10th European Sociological Association: Social Relations in Turbulent Times, University of Geneva, Geneva. 7-10 September.

Memmott, P., Stacy, R., Chambers, C. and Keys, C. (2001) *Violence in Aboriginal communities*, Canberra: Attorney-General's Department.

Menzies, C. (2001) 'Reflections on research with, for and among indigenous peoples', *Canadian Journal of Native Education*, vol 25, pp 19-36.

Meriam, L. (1928) *The problem of Indian administration*, Baltimore: The Johns Hopkins Press, www.npr.org/templates/story/story.php?storyId=16516865

Merton, R. (1938) 'Social structure and anomie', *American Sociological Review*, vol 3, pp 672-82.

Mihaere, R. (2015) *Māori cultural identity and Māori offending*, unpublished doctoral thesis, Victoria University of Wellington.

Miers, D. (2007) 'The internationalisation of restorative justice', in G. Johnstone and D. Van Ness (eds) Handbook of Restorative Justice, Devon: Willan Publishing, pp 447-467.

Milloy, J. (1999) *A national crime. The Canadian Government and the residential school system 1879 to 1986*, Winnipeg: The University of Manitoba Press.

Milward, D. (2012) *Aboriginal justice and the charter*, Vancouver: UBC Press.

Ministry of Justice (2010) *New Zealand crime and safety survey 2009, main findings report*, Wellington: Ministry of Justice.

Ministerial Advisory Committee. (1988) *Puao-Te-Ata-Tu (daybreak): The report of the Ministerial Advisory Committee on A Maori perspective for the Department of Social Welfare*, Wellington: Department of Social Welfare.

Molina, E. and Alberola C. (2005) 'Policies transfer: The case of juvenile justice in Spain', *European Journal on Criminal Policy and Research* 11(1): 51 –76.

Monture-Angus, P. (2006) 'Confronting power: Aboriginal women and justice', *Canadian Women's Studies*, vol 25, no 3/4, pp 25-33.

Moreton-Robinson, A. (2004) 'Preface', in A. Moreton-Robinson (ed) *Essays in Social and Cultural Criticism*, Canberra: Aboriginal Studies Press, pp vii-ix.

Moreton-Robinson, A. (2009) 'Imagining the good Indigenous citizen: Race war and the pathology of Patriarchal white sovereignty', *Cultural Studies Review*, vol, 15, no 2, pp 61-79.

Morley, S. (2015) *What works in effective Indigenous community-managed programs and organisations*, Melbourne: Australian Institute of Family Studies.

Morris, A. and Maxwell, G. (1993) 'Juvenile justice in New Zealand: A new paradigm', *Australian and New Zealand Journal of Criminology*, vol 26, no 1, pp 72-90.

Morrison, B. (2009) *Identifying and responding to bias in the criminal justice system: A review of international and New Zealand research*, Wellington: Ministry of Justice.

Morrison, W. (2004) 'Criminology, genocide and modernity: Remarks on the companion that criminology ignored', in C. Sumner (ed) *The Blackwell Companion to Criminology*, Oxford: Blackwell Publishing, pp 68-88.

Morrison, W. (2006) 'Criminology, civilisation and the new world order: Rethinking criminology in the global context', *London: Glasshouse Press*.

Moses, D. (2000) 'An antipodean genocide? The origins of the genocidal moment in the colonisation of Australia', *Journal of Genocide Research*, vol 2, no 1, pp 89-106.

Moses, D. (2004) 'Genocide and settler society in Australian history', in M. Dirk (ed) *Genocide and settler society. Frontier violence and stolen Indigenous children in Australian history*, NY/Oxford: Berghahn Books, pp 312-25.

Moss, I. (1991) 'The report of the national inquiry into racist violence', *Aboriginal Law Bulletin*, vol 1, no 49, pp 3-5.

Moyer, I. (2001) *Criminological theories: Traditional and non-traditional voices and themes*, Thousand Oaks (CA): Sage Publications.

Moyle, P. (2013) *From family group conferencing to whanau ora: Maori social workers talk about their experiences*, unpublished Master's thesis, Massey University

Moyle, P. and Tauri, J. (2016) 'Indigenous peoples and the mystifications of restorative justice', *Journal of Victims and Offenders, special edition: The Future of Restorative Justice*, forthcoming.

Muncie, J. (2005) 'The globalization of crime control – the case of youth and juvenile justice: Neo-liberalism, policy convergence and international conventions', *Theoretical Criminology*, 5, vol 9, no 1, pp 35-64.

Naim, M. (2005) *Illicit: How smugglers, traffickers, and copycats are hijacking the global economy*, New York: Doubleday.

Nakata, M. (2002) *Indigenous knowledge and the cultural interface: Underlying issues at the intersection of knowledge and information systems*, paper presented at IFLA, Glasgow, 18-24 August.

Nandy, A. (1983) *The intimate enemy: Loss and recovery of self under colonialism*, Delhi: Oxford University Press.

National Congress of American Indians (2014) *Violence against American Indian and Alaska Native women – United States' violations of the International Convention on the Elimination of All Forms of Racial Discrimination*, http://tbinternet.ohchr.org/Treaties/CERD/Shared%20Documents/USA/INT_CERD_NGO_USA_17549_E.pdf

National Indian Youth Council (2013) *Commentary on the periodic report of the United States of America on the elimination of racial discrimination pursuant to the International Convention*, http://tbinternet.ohchr.org/Treaties/CERD/Shared%20Documents/USA/INT_CERD_NGO_USA_17638_E.pdf

National Inquiry into Racist Violence (1991) *Racist Violence*, report of the National Inquiry into Racist Violence, Sydney: Human Rights and Equal Opportunity Commission.

Native Women's Association of Canada (2004) *Background paper: Aboriginal health Canada: Aboriginal people's roundtable, health sectoral session*, Ottawa: Author.

Nelken, D. (2004) 'Globalisation and crime', in P. Kennett (ed) *A handbook of comparative social policy*, Chettelham (UK): Edward Elgar, pp 373-387.

Newburn, T. and Sparks, R. (2004) 'Criminal justice and political cultures', in T. Newburn and R. Sparks (eds) *Criminal justice and political cultures: National and international dimensions of crime control*, Devon: Willan Publishing, pp 1-15.

New South Wales Law Reform Commission (NSWLRC) (2000) *Sentencing: Aboriginal offenders*, Report No 96, Sydney: NSWLRC.

New South Wales Office of the Ombudsman (1999) *Policing public safety*, Sydney: Office of the Ombudsman.

New Zealand Law Commission (2001) *Māori custom and values in New Zealand law*, Study Paper No 9, Wellington: New Zealand Law Commission.

Nicholson, A., Watson, N., Vivian, A., Longman, C., Priest, C., De Santolo, J., Gibson, P., Behrendt, L. and Cox, E. (2012) *Listening but not hearing: A response to the NTER futures consultations June to August 2011*, Sydney: Jumbunna Indigenous House of Learning, University of Technology, Sydney.

NISATSIC (National Inquiry into the Separation of Aboriginal and Torres Strait Islander Children from Their Families) (1997) *Bringing them home: report of the National Inquiry into the Separation of Aboriginal and Torres Strait Islander Children from their Families*, Sydney: Human Rights and Equal Opportunity Commission.

Nisga'a Final Agreement Act (2000), www.bclaws.ca/civix/document/LOC/complete/statreg/--%20N%20--/Nisga%27a%20Final%20Agreement%20Act%20%5BSBC%201999%5D%20c.%202/00_Act/99002_14.xml#ch11-1

Norris, T., Vines, P. and Hoel, E. (2012) *The American Indian and Alaska native population: 2010*, 2010 Census Briefs, Washington D.C: US Census Bureau.

O'Connell, T. (1993) 'Wagga Wagga juvenile cautioning program: It may be the way to go!' in L. Atkinson and S. Gerull (eds) *National conference on juvenile justice. Conference proceedings No. 22*, Canberra: Australian Institute of Criminology, pp 221-232.

O'Connor, I. (1994) 'The new removals: Aboriginal youth in the Queensland juvenile justice system', *International Social Work*, vol 37, pp 197-212.

Olsen, T., Maxwell, G. and Morris, A. (1995) 'Maori and youth justice in New Zealand', in K. Hazlehurst (ed) *Popular justice and community regeneration: Pathways to indigenous reform*, Westport: Praeger, pp 45-66.

O'Malley, P. (2000) 'Criminologies of catastrophe: Understanding criminal justice on the edge of the new millennium', *Australian and New Zealand Journal of Criminology*, vol 33, 153-67.

Office of Hawaiian Affairs (2010) *The disparate treatment of native Hawaiians in the criminal justice system*, Honolulu: Office of Hawaiian Affairs.

Ontario Human Rights Commission (2004) *Paying the price: The human cost of racial profiling*, Toronto: Ontario Human Rights Commission.

Palaez, V. (2014) The prison industry in the US: Big business or a new form of slavery? *Global Research*, March 31.

Palys, T. (1993) *Prospects for aboriginal justice in Canada*, unpublished position paper, www.sfu.ca/~palys/prospect.htm

Palys, T. and Victor, W. (2007) 'Getting to a better place: Qwi:qwelstóm, the Stó:lo and self-Determination' in Law Commission of Canada (ed) *Indigenous Legal Traditions*, Vancouver: UBC Press, pp 12-39.

Pavlich, G. (2005) *Governing paradoxes of restorative justice*. London: Glasshouse Press.

Payne, S. (1993) 'Aboriginal women and the law', in P. Easteak and S. McKillop (eds) *Women and the law: Proceedings of a conference held 24-26 September 1991*, Canberra: Australian Institute of Criminology.

Peachey, D. (1989) 'The Kitchener experiment', in M. Wright and B. Galaway (eds) *Mediation and criminal justice: Victims, offenders and community*, London: Sage Publications, pp 14-26.

Perreault, S. (2011) *Violent victimisation of Aboriginal people in the Canadian Provinces, 2009*, Ottawa: Statistics Canada.

Perry, B. (2008) *Silent victims: Hate crime against Native Americans*, Tucson: University of Arizona Press.

Perry, B. (2009a) 'Impacts of disparate policing in Indian Country', *Policing and Society: An International Journal of Research and Policy*, vol 19, no 3, pp 263-81.

Perry, B. (2009b) *Policing race and place in Indian country*, Lanham, MD: Lexington Books.

Perry, B. (2013) *Household incomes in New Zealand: Trends in indicators of inequality and hardship 1982-2012*, Wellington: Ministry of Social Development.

Perry, S. (2004) *American Indians and crime. A BJS statistical profile, 1992-2002*, NCJ 203097. Washington DC: US Department of Justice, Office of Justice Programs.

Piecuch, J. and Lutz, J. (2011) 'Indian ring scandal', in S. Tucker (ed) *The encyclopaedia of North American Indian wars, 1607-1890. A political, social and military history*, Santa Barbara: ABC-CLIO, p 384.

Pierpaoli, P. (2011) 'Bureau of Indian Affairs', in S. Tucker (ed) *The encyclopaedia of North American Indian wars, 1607-1890. A Political, social and military history*, Santa Barbara: ABC-CLIO, p101.

Poata-Smith, E. (1996) 'He pokekeuenuku i tuai: The evolution of contemporary Māori protest', in P. Spoonley, D. Pearson and C. Macpherson (eds) *Nga patai: Racism and ethnic relations in Aotearoa/New Zealand*, Palmerston North: The Dunmore Press, pp 97-116.

Pollack, S. (2012) 'An imprisoned gaze: Practices of gendered, racialised and epistemic violence', *International Review of Victimology*, vol 19, no 10, pp 103-14.

Pommerscheim, F. (1995) *Braid of feathers: American Indian law and contemporary tribal life*, Berkeley, University of California Press.

Porter, A. (2014) *Decolonising juvenile justice: Night patrols, safety and the policing of Indigenous communities*, unpublished PhD thesis, University of Sydney.

Porter, A. (in press) 'Decolonising Policing: Counter-policing, night patrols and safety', *Theoretical Criminology*.

Potas, I., Smart, J., Bignell, G., Lawrie, R. and Thomas, B. (2003) *Circle sentencing in New South Wales. A review and evaluation*, Sydney: New South Wales Judicial Commission and Aboriginal Justice Advisory Committee.

Powis, T. (2007) '"Doing our own work": Re-working whiteness in psychology', in the *Proceedings of the inaugural annual conference, Psychology and Indigenous Australians: Teaching, practice and theory*, Adelaide: University of South Australia, pp 58-64.

Pratt, J. (1992) *Punishment in a perfect society*, Wellington: Victoria University Press.

Pratt, J. (2000) 'Return of the wheelbarrow men? Or, the arrival of postmodern penality?', *British Journal of Criminology*, vol 40, pp 127-45.

Pratt, J. (2002) *Punishment and civilisation*, London: Sage.

Pratt, J. (2006) 'Beyond evangelical criminology: The meaning and significance of restorative justice', in I. Aevtsen; T. Daems and L. Robert (eds) *Institutionalising restorative justice*, Devon: Willan Publishing, pp 44-67.

Prison Justice Canada (2005) *Facts and statistics*, www.prisonjustice.ca/politics/facts_stats.html

Proloux, C. (2005) 'Blending justice: Interlegality and the incorporation of Aboriginal justice into the formal Canadian justice system', Journal of Legal Pluralism, vol 51, pp 79-109.

Public Safety Canada (2013) *Corrections and conditional release statistical overview. 2013 annual report*, Ottawa: Public Works and Government Services Canada, www.publicsafety.gc.ca/cnt/rsrcs/pblctns/crrctns-cndtnl-rls-2013/crrctns-cndtnl-rls-2013-eng.pdf

Quijano, A. (1999) 'Colonialidad del poder, Cultura y conocimiento en América latina', in S. Castro-Gomez, O. Guardiola-Rivera and C. Millán de Benavides (eds) *Pensar (en) Los intersticios: Teoría y práctica de la crítica poscolonial*, Bogotá: Pontificia Universidad Javeriana, pp 99-110.

Quijano A. (2007) 'Coloniality and modernity/rationality', *Cultural Studies*, vol 21, no 2-3, pp 168-78.

Quince, K. (2007) 'Māori and the criminal justice system in New Zealand', in J. Tolmie and W. Brookbanks (eds) *The New Zealand criminal justice system*, Auckland: Lexis Nexis, pp 333-58.

Razsa, M. and Kwanik, A. (2012) 'The occupy movement in Zizek's hometown: Direct democracy and a politics of becoming', *American Ethnologist*, vol 39, no 2, pp 238-58.

RCAP (Royal Commission on Aboriginal Peoples) (1996a) *Bridging the cultural divide,* Ottawa: Minister of Supply and Services Canada.

RCAP (1996b) *Report of the Royal Commission on Aboriginal Peoples,* Volume 1, Ottawa: Minister of Supply and Services Canada.

Reynolds, H. (1993) 'The unrecorded battlefields of Queensland', in H. Reynolds (ed) *Race relations in North Queensland*, Townsville: Department of History and Politics, James Cook University, pp 40-62.

Reynolds, H. (1995) *Fate of a free people*, Ringwood: Penguin.

Reynolds, H. (1996) *Aboriginal sovereignty*, St Leonards: Allen and Unwin.

Riccardi, L. (2009) 'U.S. settles Indian trust account lawsuit', *Los Angeles Times*, 9 December 2009, http://articles.latimes.com/2009/dec/09/nation/la-na-indian-settlement9-2009dec09

Richards, K. (2007) *Rewriting history': Towards a genealogy of 'restorative justice'*, unpublished PhD thesis, University of Western Sydney.

Richards, L. (2000) 'Restorative justice and the RCMP: Definitions and directions', *Royal Mounted Police Gazette*, vol 62, no 5/6, pp 8-11.

Rigney, L. (1997) 'Internationalisation of an Indigenous anti-colonial cultural critique of research methodologies. A guide to indigenist research methodology and its principles', in *HERDSA Annual International conference proceedings; Research and development in Higher Education: Advancing International Perspectives*, vol 20, pp 629-36.

Rigney, L. (2001) *A first perspective of Indigenous Australian participation in science: Framing Indigenous research towards Indigenous Australian intellectual sovereignty*, https://ncis.anu.edu.au/_lib/doc/LI_Rigney_First_perspective.pdf

Roach, K. (2000) 'Changing punishment at the turn of the century: Restorative justice on the rise', *Canadian Journal of Criminology*, vol 42, no 3, pp 249-274.

Roberts, T. (2005) *Frontier justice. A history of the Gulf Country to 1990*, St Lucia: University of Queensland Press.

Robertson, R. (1990) 'Mapping the global condition: Globalisation as the central concept', *Theory, Culture and Society*, vol 7, pp 15-30.

Rose, D. (1996) 'Land rights and deep colonising: The erasure of women', *Aboriginal Law Bulletin*, vol 3, no 85, pp 6-14.

Ross, L. (1998) *Inventing the savage: The social construction of native American criminality*, Austin: University of Texas Press.

Royal Canadian Mounted Police (RCMP) (2014) *Missing and murdered Aboriginal women. A national operational overview*, www.rcmp-grc.gc.ca/pubs/mmaw-faapd-eng.pdf

Royal Commission into Aboriginal Deaths in Custody (1991) *Royal Commission into Aboriginal Deaths in Custody national report: Overview and recommendations*, Canberra: Australian Government Publishing Service.

Royal Commission on Aboriginal Peoples (1996) *People to people, nation to nation: Highlights from the report of the Royal Commission on Aboriginal Peoples*, Ottawa: Supply and Services Canada.

Rudin, J. (2007) 'Aboriginal peoples and the criminal justice system', paper prepared for the *Ipperwash Inquiry*, www.archives.gov.on.ca/en/e_records/ipperwash/policy_part/research/pdf/Rudin.pdf

Ruggiero, V. (2000) *Crime and markets: Essays in anti-criminology*, Oxford: Oxford University Press.

Ruggiero, V. and Welch, M. (2009) 'Power crime', *Crime, Law and Social Change*, vol, 51, pp 297-301.

Ryser, R. (2012) *Indigenous nations and modern states: The political emergence of nations challenging state power*, NY: Routledge.

Said, E. (1993) *Culture and imperialism*, London: Chatto and Windus.

Said, E. (1996) *Representations of the intellectual*, NY: Vintage Books.

Sakala, L. (2014) *Breaking down mass incarceration in the 2010 Census: State-by-state incarceration rates by race/ethnicity*, Northampton: Prison Policy Initiative.

Sapers, H. (2010a) *Annual report of the Office of the Correctional Investigator 2009-2010*, www.oci-bec.gc.ca/cnt/rpt/annrpt/annrpt20092010-eng.aspx

Sapers, H. (2010b) *Backgrounder: Aboriginal inmates*, Ottawa: Office of the Correctional Investigator, Government of Canada.

Schiraldi, V., Colburn, J. and Lotke, E. (2004) *Three strikes and you're out.* Available at: www.justicepolicy.org.downloads/JPIOUTOFSTEPREPORTFNL.doc

Schmidt, H. (2009) *Conducting research with First Nations and for First Nations: A reflective study of Aboriginal empowerment within the context of participatory research*, unpublished doctoral thesis, York University.

Schneider, C. (2003) 'Integrating critical race theory and postmodernism: Implications of race, class and gender', *Critical Criminology*, vol 12, pp 87-103.

Scholte, J. (2005) *Globalisation: A critical introduction* (2nd ed.), New York: Palgrave.

Schon, D. (1973) *Beyond the stable state: Public and private learning in a changing society*, Harmondsworth: Penguin Books.

Scraton, P. (2005) *The authoritarian within: Reflections on power, knowledge and resistance,* inaugural Professorial lecture, Queen's University, Belfast, 9 June.

SCRGSP (Steering Committee for the Review of Government Service Provision) (2014) *Overcoming Indigenous Disadvantage: Key Indicators 2014*, Canberra: Productivity Commission.

Scuro, P. (2013) 'Latin America', in G. Johnstone and D. Van Ness (eds) *Handbook of restorative justice*, Cullompton: Willan Publishing, pp 500-510.

Sefa Dei, G. (2002) *Rethinking the role of Indigenous knowledge in the academy*, NALL working paper no 58, Toronto: NALL.

Sheleff, L. (1999) *The future of tradition: Customary law, common law and legal pluralism*, London: Frank Cass.

Shenhav, Y. (2012) 'Imperialism, exceptionalism and the contemporary world', in M. Svirsky and S. Bignall (eds) *Agamben and Colonialism*, Edinburgh: Edinburgh University Press, pp 17-31.

Sibley, D. (1995) *Geographies of exclusion*, London: Routledge.

Simon, J. (2007) *Governing through crime: How the war on crime transformed American democracy and created a culture of fear*, Oxford: Oxford University Press.

Simpson, S. (1989) 'Feminist theory, crime, and justice', *Criminology*, vol 27, pp 605-31.

Sisters Inside (2013) 'The over-representation of Aboriginal and Torres Strait Island women in prison', *The Stringer*, 25 April.

Smart, C. (1989) *Feminism and the power of law*, London: Routledge.

Smart, C. (1990) 'Feminist approaches to criminology, or, post-modern women meets atavistic man', in A. Morris and L. Gelsthorpe (eds) *Feminist perspectives in criminology*, Milton Keynes: Open University Press, pp 70-84.

Smith, A. (2004) 'Boarding school abuses, human rights, and reparations', *Social Justice*, vol 31, no 4, pp 89-102.

Smith, A. (2005) *Sexual violence and American Indian genocide*, Brooklyn: South End Press.

Smith, A. (2007) *Soul wound: The legacy of Native American schools*, Amnesty International, www.amnestyusa.org/node/87342

Smith, L. (1999) *Decolonising methodologies: Research and Indigenous peoples*, Dunedin: University of Otago Press.

Smith, L. (2005) 'On tricky ground: Researching the native in the age of uncertainty', in N. Denzin and Y. Lincoln (eds) *The Sage handbook of qualitative research* (3rd edn), Thousand Oaks (CA): Sage, pp 85-107.

South Dakota Department of Corrections (2015) *Inmates by race/ethnicity, May 1, 2015*, http://doc.sd.gov/documents/about/stats/adult/InmatesbyRaceMay12015.pdf

Spitzer, S. (1974) 'Towards a Marxist theory of deviance', *Social Problems*, vol 22, pp 638-51.

Spivak, G. (1985) 'Subaltern studies: Deconstructing historiography', in R. Guha (ed) *Subaltern studies IV: Writings on South Asian history and society*, New Delhi: Oxford University Press, pp 330-63.

Standing Committee (Senate Standing Committee on Legal and Constitutional Affairs) (2006) *Unfinished Business: Indigenous Stolen Wages*, Canberra: Commonwealth of Australia.

Stannard, D. (1992) *American holocaust*, NY: Oxford University Press.

Statistics Canada (2006) *Aboriginal population profile*, Ottawa: Statistics Canada.

Statistics Canada (2011) *Aboriginal peoples in Canada: First nations people, Metis and Inuit*, National Household Survey 2011, Cat No 99-011-X2011001, Ottawa: Statistics Canada.

Statistics Canada (2013) *The education attainment of Aboriginal peoples in Canada*, Ottawa: Statistics Canada.

Statistics New Zealand (2013) *2013 Census: Quick stats about Māori*, Wellington: Statistics New Zealand.

Steffensmeier, D. and Demuth, S. (2000) 'Ethnicity and sentencing outcomes in US Federal Courts: Who is punished more harshly?', *American Sociological Review*, vol 65, pp 705-29.

Stenson, K. (1999) 'Crime control, governmentality and sovereignty', in R. Smandych (ed) *Governable places: Readings on governmentality and crime control*, Aldershot: Ashgate.

Strang, H. (2000) 'The future of restorative justice', in D. Chappell and P. Wilson (eds) *Crime and the criminal justice system in Australia: 2000 and beyond*, Sydney: Butterworths, pp 22-33.

Stubbs, J. (2011) 'Indigenous women in Australian criminal justice: Over-represented but rarely acknowledged', *Australian Indigenous Law Review*, vol 15, no 1, pp 47-63.

Sumner, C. (ed) (1982) *Crime, justice and underdevelopment*, London: Heinemann.

Sumner, C. (1994) *The sociology of deviance: An obituary*, Buckingham: Open University Press.

Sutherland, E. (1949) *White collar crime*, NY: Holt Rinehart and Winston.

Tauri, J. (1998) 'Family group conferencing: A case study of the indigenisation of New Zealand's justice system', *Current Issues in Criminal Justice*, vol 10, no 2, pp 168-82.

Tauri, J. (2004) *Conferencing, indigenisation and orientalism: A critical commentary on recent state responses to indigenous offending* (key note address), paper presented at Qwi: Qwelstom Gathering: 'Bringing Justice Back to the People', Mission, BC, 22-24 March.

Tauri, J. (2005) Indigenous perspectives, in R. Walters and T. Bradley (eds) *Introduction to criminological thought*, Auckland: Pearson Longman, pp 129-45.

Tauri J. (2009a) 'An indigenous commentary on the standardisation of restorative justice', *Indigenous Policy Journal* (December - online).

Tauri, J. (2009b) 'The Māori social science academy and evidence-based policy', *MAI Review* (June – online).

Tauri, J. (2011) *Criminology and the disempowerment of First Nations in settler societies*, paper presented at Crime, Justice and Social Democracy: An International Conference, Queensland University of Technology, Brisbane, 25-28 September.

Tauri, J. (2012) 'Indigenous critique of authoritarian criminology', in K. Carrington, M. Ball, E. O'Brien and J. Tauri (eds) *Crime, justice and social democracy: International perspectives*, London: Palgrave Macmillan, pp 217-33.

Tauri, J. (2013a) 'Criminological research and institutional ethics protocols: Empowering the indigenous other or the academy?', *Proceedings for the crime, justice and social democracy 2nd international conference*, Brisbane: Queensland University of Technology, pp 202-10.

Tauri, J. (2013b) *Globalisation of crime control: Restorative justice and indigenous justice*, 10 September, http://juantauri.blogspot.co.uk/search

Tauri, J. (2014) 'Settler colonialism, criminal justice and Indigenous peoples', *African Journal of Criminology and Justice Studies*, vol 8, no 1, pp 20-37.

Tauri, J. (2015a) 'A comment on the epistemic violence of white academic privilege – part 2', *The Indigenous Criminologist* (blog), juantauri.blogspot.au

Tauri, J. (2015b) 'Breaking the criminal justice-criminology nexus, empowering Indigenous communities', *The Indigenous Criminologist* (blog), available via juantauri.blogsspot.au

Tauri, J. and Webb, R. (2012) 'A critical appraisal of responses to Māori offending', *The International Indigenous Policy Journal*, vol 3, no 4, online.

Te Puni Kokiri (2002) *Update briefing on the criminal justice system*, Wellington: Te Puni Kokiri.

Te Puni Kokiri (2007) *Report on engagement with Māori providers, practitioners and offenders to inform the development of a programme of action for Māori*, Wellington: Te Puni Kokiri.

Terry, A., Jackson, M., Hikaka, G. and Brown, M. (2010) *Marae justice system*, Radio New Zealand, 30 May.

The Treasury, New Zealand (2009) *Challenges and choices: New Zealand's long-term fiscal statement*, www.treasury.govt.nz/government/longterm/fiscalposition/2009/15.htm

The Treasury, New Zealand (2013) *Affording our future: Statement on New Zealand's long-term fiscal position*, Wellington: The Treasury, New Zealand.

Thomas, N. (1994) *Colonialism's culture: Anthropology, travel and government*, Melbourne: Melbourne University Press.

TRCC (Truth and Reconciliation Commission of Canada) (2012a) *Interim report*, Winnipeg: TRCC.

TRCC (2012b) *Backgrounder*, Winnipeg: Truth and Reconciliation Commission of Canada.

Trudgeon, R. (2000) *Why warriors lie down and die*, Darwin: Aboriginal Resource and Development Services.

Tsawwassen First Nation Final Agreement (2007), https://www.aadnc-aandc.gc.ca/DAM/DAM-INTER-BC/STAGING/texte-text/tfnfa_1100100022707_eng.pdf

Tsing, A. (2005) *Friction: An ethnography of global connection*, Princeton: Princeton University Press.

Turnball, S. (2014) 'Aboriginalising the parole process: "Culturally appropriate" adaptations and the Canadian federal parole system', *Punishment and Society*, vol 16, no 4, pp 385-405.

Turner, K., Giacopassi, D. and Vandiver, M. (2006) 'Ignoring the past: Coverage of slavery and slave patrols in criminal justice texts', *Journal of Criminal Justice Education*, vol 17, no 1, pp 181-95.

Umbreit, M. (2001) *The handbook of victim offender mediation: An essential guide to practice and research*, San Francisco: Jossey-Bass Inc.

Umbreit, M. and Stacey, S. (1996) 'Family group conferencing comes to the U.S: A comparison with victim offender mediation', *Juvenile and Family Court Journal*, vol 47, no 2, pp 29-38.

United Nations Office on Drugs and Crime. (2006) *Handbook on restorative justice programmes*. Vienna: United Nations Office on Drugs and Crime.

United Nations Office on Drugs and Crime (2010) *The globalisation of crime: A transnational organised crime threat assessment*. Vienna: United Nations Office on Drugs and Crime.

United States Sentencing Commission (2013) *Native Americans in the Federal offender population*, Washington DC: United States Sentencing Commission, www.ussc.gov/sites/default/files/pdf/research-and-publications/quick-facts/Quick_Facts_Native_American_Offenders.pdf

Victor, W. (2007) *Indigenous justice: Clearing space and place for Indigenous epistemologies*, research paper for the National Centre for Indigenous Peoples Governance.

Victorian Equal Opportunity and Human Rights Commission (2013) *Unfinished business: Aboriginal women and prison in Victoria*, Melbourne: Victoria Equal Opportunities and Human Rights Commission.

Vincent, K. and Eveline, J. (2008) 'The invisibility of gendered power relations in domestic violence policy', *Journal of Family Studies*, vol 14, pp 322-33.

Wacquant, L. (2008) *Urban outcasts: A comparative sociology of advanced marginality*, Cambridge: Polity Press.

Wacquant, L. (2009a) *Prisons of poverty*, Minneapolis: University of Minneapolis Press.

Wacquant, L. (2009b) *Punishing the poor: The neoliberal government of social insecurity*, Durham and London: Duke University Press.

Wacquant, L. (2010) 'Class, race and hyperincarceration in revanchist America', *Daedalus*, vol 139, no 3, pp 74–90.

Waitangi Tribunal (2014) Whaiate mana motuhake / In pursuit of mana motuhake: Report on the Māori community development act claim, Wellington: Waitangi Tribunal.

Wakeling, S., Jorgensen, M., Michaelson, S and Begay, M. (2001) *Policing on American Indian reservations*, Washington DC: National Institute of Justice.Walker, R. (1990) *Ka whawhai tonu matou: Struggle without end*, Penguin Books, Auckland.

Walter, M. and Andersen, C. (2013) *Indigenous statistics: A quantitative methodology*, Los Angeles: Left Coast Press.

Wane, N. (2013) '[Re]claiming Indigenous knowledge: Challenges, resistance and opportunities', *Decolonisation, Indigeneity, Education and Society*, vol 2, no 1, pp 93-107.

Ward, T. and Maruna, S. (2007) *Rehabilitation*, Milton Park: Routledge.

Watson, G. (2004) 'Liberalism and globalisation', *Asia Europe Journal*, vol 2, pp 167-173.

Watson, I. (2000) 'There is no possibility of rights without law: So until then, Don't thumb print or sign anything!', *Indigenous Law Bulletin*, vol 5, no 1, pp 4-7.

Watson, I. (2009) 'Aboriginality and the violence of colonialism', *Borderlands E-Journal*, vol 8, no 1, pp 1-8.

Watts, S. (1997) *Epidemics and history: Disease, power and imperialism*, New Haven: Yale University Press.

Weatherburn, D. (2010) 'Guest editorial: Indigenous violence', *Australian and New Zealand Journal of Criminology*, vol 3, no 2, pp 197-8.

Weatherburn, D. (2014) *Arresting incarceration: Pathways out of Indigenous imprisonment*, Canberra: Aboriginal Studies Press.

Webb, R. (2012) 'Culture and crime control in New Zealand', *Crime, justice and social democracy conference proceedings* (2nd edn), Brisbane: School of Justice, Queensland University of Technology, pp 73-88.

Weitkamp, E. (1999) 'The history of restorative justice', in G. Bazemore and L. Walgrave (eds) *Restorative juvenile justice: Repairing the harm of youth crime*, New York: Criminal Justice Press, pp 75-102.

Wesley, M. (2012) *Marginalised: The Aboriginal women's experience in federal corrections*, Ottawa (ON): Public Safety Canada.

Wickliffe, C. (2005) 'Te Timatanga: Maori Women's access to justice', in A Mikaere (ed) *Yearbook of New Zealand jurisprudence, special edition: Te Purenga*, Hamilton: University of Waikato, pp 217-263.

Wild, R. and Anderson, P. (2007) *Ampe akelyernemane meke mekarle – Little children are sacred*, Darwin: Northern Territory Government.

Williams, R. (1989) *The American Indian in western legal thought. The discourses of conquest*, NY: Oxford University Press.

Wolfe, P. (2010) 'Race and racialisation: Some thoughts', *Postcolonial Studies*, vol 5, no 1, pp 51-62.

Wolfe, P. (2014) 'Settler colonialism and the elimination of the native', *Journal of Genocide Research*, vol 8, no 4, pp 387-409.

Wolpert, C. (1999) 'Considering race and crime: Distilling non-partisan policy from opposing theories', *The American Criminal Law Review*, vol 36, no 2, pp 265-89.

Woolford, A. (2013) 'The next generation: Criminology, genocide studies and settler colonialism', *Revista Critica Penal y Poder*, vol 5, pp 163-85.

Wootten, H. (1991) *Royal Commission into Aboriginal Deaths in Custody, regional report of inquiry in New South Wales, Victoria and Tasmania*, Canberra: Australian Government Publishing Service.

Workman, K. and McIntosh, T. (2013) 'Crime, punishment and poverty', in M. Rashbrooke (ed) *Inequality: A New Zealand crisis*, Wellington: Bridget Williams Books, pp 120-131.

Wright, D. (2004) *Report of the Commission of Inquiry into Matters Relating to the Death of Neil Stonechild*, Regina: Ministry of Justice.

Yazzie, R. and Zion J. (1996) 'Navajo restorative justice: The law of equality and justice', in B. Galaway and J. Hudson (eds) *Restorative justice: International perspectives*, Monsey: Criminal Justice Press, pp 157-73.

Young, J. (2003) 'Merton with energy, Katz with structure: The sociology of vindictiveness and the criminology of transgression', *Theoretical Criminology*, vol 7, pp 388-414.

Young, J. (2011) *The criminological imagination*, Cambridge: Polity Press,

Young, T. (1990) 'Native American crime and criminal justice require criminologists' attention', *Journal of Criminal Justice Education*, vol 1, pp 111–16.

Zavala, M. (2013) 'What do we mean by decolonising research strategies? Lessons from decolonising, Indigenous research projects in New Zealand and Latin America', *Decolonisation: Indigeneity, Education and Society*, vol 2, no 1, pp 55-71.

Zedner, L. (2007) 'Pre-crime and post-criminology?', *Theoretical Criminology*, vol 11, no 2, pp 261-81.

Zehr, H. (1990) *Changing lenses: A new focus for crime and justice*, Scottsdale: Herald Press.

Zehr, H. (2002) *The little book of restorative justice*, Scottsdale (PA): Good Books

Zellerer, E. and Cunneen, C. (2001) 'Restorative justice, indigenous justice, and human rights', in G. Bazemore and M. Schiff (eds) *Restorative community justice*, Cincinnati: Anderson Publishing, pp 245-263.

Zion, J. (1988) 'Searching for Indian common law', in B. Morse and G. Woodman (eds) *Indigenous law and the state*, Dordrecht: Foris Publications, pp 121-50.

Index

Index

justice systems 126–7
study on revival of *Qwi:qwelstom* justice
system 31–4
see also Canadian indigenous peoples
fraud and corruption (against Indigenous
peoples) 60–2
Frideres, J. 2
funding for Indigenous institutions 83,
84–5, 127, 128

G

gender
incarceration rates 90–1
and race intersectionality 99–103
victimisation rates 8
gender-based violence, lack of protection
measures 80–1
genocides 49–50
George, L. 92, 94
Geyer, M. 148
Ghosh, D. 11, 135
Gillen, P. 11, 135
'give back' principles 34–5
Gladue courts (Canada) 123
Gladue report 117–18
globalisation of crime control 133–49
background history under colonialism
134–7
contemporary measures 137–47
rise of restorative justice 139–41,
141–4, 144–7
impact on Indigenous peoples 144–7
globalisation and sovereignty 18
governance *see* Indigenous governance
government fraud 60–2
guardianship duties, breaches of 60–2

H

Harper, Prime Minister Stephen 58
Havemann, P. 9, 141, 144
Hawaiians
lack of non-custodial programmes 120
lack of tribal policing 84
healing 128–31
key interventions 129
health outcomes, by country 5
Huffington Post 95

I

identity-building 129–30
Idle No More movement 148
'immiseration' 5, 57, 62
imprisonment rates 6–7, 90–1
post-2007 intervention (Australia) 105–6
Indian Act (1876) (Canada) 53
Indian Act (1951) (Canada) 62
Indian Civil Rights Act (1968) (US) 14,
62
Indian Law and Order Commission 3, 14,
84–5, 119, 125–7
Indian reserves, used as confinement
places 53–5

Indigeneity and court sentencing 111–13
in Australia 113–16
in Canada 116–19
and colonial impact 115
Indigenes *see* Indigenous peoples
'Indigenisation' 9, 65, 144, 161
and co-option of cultural practices 144
failures of 120
Indigenous criminological research 10,
29–30, 151–64
barriers 161–4
critical issues for 151–64
governance and empowerment 160–4
pathways for 30
political nature of 34–40
principles 10, 30–42
committed objectivity 31–4
'real' and authentic voices 31, 41–2
'speaking truth to power' 31, 34–40
publication difficulties 163
silencing methods for 161–2
Indigenous 'customs' 50–2
Indigenous empowerment 41, 160–4
Indigenous governance 87, 160–1, 160–4
and empowerment 160–4
lack of recognition 113, 128
and 'risk' 158–60
and self-determination 155–8, 158–60
Indigenous justice
key concepts 47
as 'customary law' 50–1, 115–16
denigration of 50–2
and 'healing' 128–31
and justice reinvestment initiatives
127–8
over non-Indian offenders 126
restoring Indigenous self-determination
156–8
separate community-centred initiatives
37, 40, 149, 155–6, 160–4
vs. colonial concepts 47, 50–2
vs. restorative justice initiatives 139–49
see also Indigenous criminological
research; Indigenous law enforcement;
Indigenous sentencing courts
Indigenous knowledges and
methodologies 9–10, 33–4, 152–3,
155
'othering' of 23–6, 136
Indigenous law enforcement
community policing 82–3
night patrols 85
US tribal police 84–5
Indigenous peoples
criminalisation rates 6–7, 8–9
definitions 2
demographics and socioeconomic
profiles 2–4
educational attainments 5
health outcomes 5

Index

R

R v Bugmy (2013) 113
R v Fernando (1992) 114–16
R v Gladue (1999) 117–18
R v Ipeelee (2012) 118
R v Lowe [1827] 16
R v Moses [1992] 121
R v Murrell [1836] 16
'race'
 conflated with criminality 68
 and court sentencing 111–12
 as legitimising discourse 47–52
racial discrimination legislation 113
racial profiling 71
racism
 amongst colonial settlers 47–9
  continuing legacies 68–70
 amongst law enforcement officers 70–6
 use of force and violence 76–8
 institutionalised 70
Rangatahi courts (New Zealand) 123
rape of Indigenous women 48
RCADIC (Royal Commission on
 Aboriginal Deaths in Custody) 67–70,
 74, 77, 95
RCAP (Canadian Royal Commission on
 Aboriginal Peoples) 14, 45, 48, 52–4,
 59, 62, 67–70, 78, 82, 86
RCMP (Royal Canadian Mounted
 Police) 140–1
'real' and authentic voices in research 31,
 41–2
reclaiming history 129–30
Red Paper policy statement (Canada) 63–4
Redfern riot 78
regulation of daily life 53–5
religious practices
 recognition by the courts 118
 see also Christianity; Indigenous spiritual
 practices
research *with* Indigenes *see* Indigenous
 criminological research
reserves, used as confinement places 53–5
residential schools for Indigenous children
 58–60
 long-term outcomes 59–60
resistance to occupations 49–50
restorative justice
 globalisation of 139–47
 'origin myths' 142–3
 youth conferencing 74
 see also justice reinvestment approaches
Richards, K. 140, 142–3, 147
rights *see* civil rights; Indigenous rights
Rigney, L. 37, 162
risk
 profiling 139
 and self-determination 158–60
 and self-governance 158–60
Ross, Luana 8, 48, 65–6, 153, 162
Rowe, Simone 9, 24, 28, 90, 96–7, 102,
 104–5, 155

Rudin, J. 73, 76–7, 79, 141, 146
Ruggiero, V. 25–6, 29

S

Said, Edward 34–5
Sakala, L. 7
Samoans, demographics 3
Sapers, H. 90–1
'Saskatoon freezing deaths' (Canada) 77–8
Schmidt, H. 41
Schneider, C. 9, 24, 35–7
Scholte, J. 133–5
self-determination
 and decolonisation processes 68
 lack of regard for 155–6
 rights to 13–17, 64–5, 155
 as UN convention 19
sentencing of Indigenous peoples 113–19
 and discrimination 111–12
 and gender 114
 Indigeneity and social disadvantage
  114–16
 in Australia 113–16
 in Canada 116–19
'separatist' justice movements 39–40
'settler colonialism' 46–7
 see also colonialism
sexual abuse
 community-centred justice 149
 residential schools 59
'silencing methods'
 in criminology 161–2
 and women 95–9
Smith, A. 34, 48, 58–60, 162
Smith, Linda 10, 23, 29–30, 34, 37–8, 41,
 48, 95, 162
social disadvantage, and court sentencing
 114–16
socioeconomic marginalisation 4–6, 60–2
 as outcome of colonialism 5–6, 114–16
socioeconomic profiles 3–4
South American Spring 148
sovereignty 13, 17–18
 definitions and meanings 178
 in Australia 16
 in Canada 15
 in New Zealand 15–16, 64
'speaking truth to power' principle 31,
 34–40
spirituality, recognition by the courts 118
Stannard, D. 45, 47–8, 50
state funding for Indigenous institutions
 83, 84–5, 127, 128
Stó:lo justice *see* Qwi:qwelstóom (First
 Nation justice system)
Stolen Generations 58–60, 106–7, 129
Stonechild, Neil 78
'stop and search' powers 71–2
summons 74–5
surveillance measures 105

205

T

Tauri, Juan 9–10, 24–9, 37–41, 57, 65,
  95–9, 101, 104, 120, 123, 133, 136,
  139–46, 148–9, 155–6, 161
'terrorism law' 139
Terry, Aroha 149
therapeutic healing 130
'three strikes' legislation 139
Tikanga programmes 92
Torres Strait Islanders
  demographics 4
  see also Aboriginal and Torres Strait
    Islanders
Transformative Justice Australian advocacy
  and consultancy group 140–1
Trask, Haunani-Kay 51
trauma healing 129–30
treaty rights (Canada) 15
Treaty of Waitangi (1840) 15, 64
tribal jails 126–7
Truth and Reconciliation Commission
  (Canada) 60
Tsawwassen First Nation Final Agreement
  (2007) 15
Turnball, S. 118–19, 124

U

United Nations (UN), and globalised
  crime control 138
UN Committee on the Elimination of
  Racial Discrimination (CERD) 79–81
UN Convention on the Rights of the
  Child, arrest measures 75
UN conventions on Indigenous rights
  19, 155
US Bill of Rights 14
US indigenous peoples
  civil rights movements 63
  criminalisation of 7, 59–62
  demographics 3
  forced removal of children 58–60
  genocides of 49–50
  rights to self-determination 13–14
  socioeconomic marginalisation 5
  tribal law enforcement agencies 84–5
US settler legislation 52, 60–1, 62–3
US Tribal Courts 125–7
  jurisdiction over non-Indian offenders
    126
US Tribal Law and Order Act (2010) 125
US Tribal police 84–5
US Violence Against Women
  Reauthorization Act (2013) 126

V

victimisation rates 8, 93–4
Victoria Equal Opportunity and Human
  Rights Commission (2013) 92–3
Victor, Wenona 31–4, 36, 41–2, 96,
  140–1, 145, 146, 149, 156, 162
violence against Indigenous peoples
  colonial settlers 49–50

reproduced in contemporary policing
  78
female victims 8, 80–1, 93–4
police use of force 76–8, 80–1
see also child removals; penal sanctions
voting rights 62–3

W

Wacquant, L. 26, 94, 154–5
wage withholding practices 61–2
'Wagga Wagga' restorative justice model
  140–1
Waitangi Tribunal (1975) 15–16, 83
Walker v New South Wales [1994] 16,
  113
Walter, Maggie 10, 163
warfare and active resistance 49–50
Watson, I. 51, 100, 133
Weatherburn, D. 23, 42, 57, 152–3, 158,
  162
Webb, Robert 24, 28, 162–3
women from Indigenous populations
  colonial portrayals of 12–13
  colonial racial discourses on 48
  disappearances of 80–1
  engagement with colonial crime control
    90–1
  experiences of imprisonment 91–3
  genocides against 50
  incarceration rates 90–1
  state silencing of 95–9
    challenges to 99–103
    Northern Territory Intervention
      103–7
  undertaking night patrols 85–6
  as victims of harm 8, 93–4
    homicides and disappearances 80–1
    under-policing problems and violence
      78–81
  victimisation rates 8
Worcester v. Georgia [1832] 13
Workman, K. 7, 91
Wounded Knee massacre (1890) 50

Y

young people
  non-custodial sentencing options
    119–20
  over-use of arrest and detention 74–6
  use of custodial sentences 75
  use of stop and search 71–2
Young, Jock xiii, 24 27, 29, 96
Young, T. 161
youth sentencing, lack of diversion
  options 74

Z

Zedner, L. 154
zero tolerance policies 139